About the author

Suzanne Ruthven has spent many years investigating the world of contemporary occultism. These investigations resulted in the publishing of ***Malleus Satani - The Hammer of Satan*** (1995), a frank, and at times, startling examination of modern Witchcraft and Satanism. By discarding standard textbook references and viewing the Craft from inside the Circle, she has produced the definitive work for those serious students fascinated by all the socio-political-religious aspects of present-day occult Traditions.

Ruthven grew up in the ***Whittlewood*** in Northamptonshire and her first novel (1997) of that name was based on personal research and attempts to transpose genuine occult lore into highly readable fiction in the teaching tradition of Dion Fortune.

What You Call Time is a sequel to the *Malleus* and continues to draw on the tabloid myths and mis-information surrounding the practice of Witchcraft and Ritual Magic. Her reputation has ensured that even more people have been willing to discuss, in some depth, the dangers both real and imagined, of occultism.

In addition to bringing her professional judgement to co-editing the esoteric newsletter, *The Broom Cupboard*, she is also a founder-member of the *Comhairli Cairde*, a Pagan publishing and information network and editor of *Comhairle*, the quarterly journal of the organisation. She has two more esoteric reference works in the pipeline, including a second novel scheduled for 1999.

What reviewers said about
Malleus Satani - The Hammer of Satan:

"Ruthven proves her journalistic expertise with her clear objectivity, her obvious discernment for the truth, and her insistence upon interviewing those at the core of movements themselves."

Lesley Wilkinson
Editor - *Ocular Magazine*

"This a thought provoking account which well illustrates the dangers inherent in any religion or social institution which maintains that its way is the only true one and all others are therefore to be condemned."

Editor - *Bulletin of the Welsh Academy*

"It's an objective, well-researched and well-written book - really smashing a lot of the misconceptions about Satanism from all sides."

Blanche Barton - Church of Satan
Author of *The Secret Life of a Satanist*

"A very interesting book written without the usual diatribe of what we must believe or must do because this is what the media says of us ... It makes a pleasant change to have the subject treated as a serious religion rather than a melodramatic method of selling newspapers."

Dr Meriem Clay-Egerton
Editor - *Phoenix Magazine*

"It was very refreshing to read - for once! - a sympathetic study of the subject, and one which was, not only very well researched, but also managed to avoid ever being dull or academic."

Dr Terry Hale
University of East Anglia

"As well as being very interesting, it was so easy to read. When once I'd started it, I had to finish the book before putting it down. I shall certainly pass the word around that here is a book worth reading ..."

Evan John Jones
Author of *Witchcraft - A Tradition Renewed*

"The purpose of the book is to show that the occult bears little resemblance to its image in literature and the media, and Ruthven succeeds in this admirably, and entertainingly."

Carole Baldock - *Singled Out Magazine*

"The author has researched her subject enthusiastically, she is full of information, and gives sharp, incisive judgements wherever necessary to move the story along. For these descriptions alone the book deserves a place in all theological colleges and should be read by every social scientist ... Having thoroughly enjoyed her factual account, there is every likelihood I will be riveted by her fiction."

Trevor Lockwood
Author-Publisher Enterprise

Dedicated to the Memory of
Alastair (Bob) Clay-Egerton

"Paganism is the ancestral religion of the whole of humanity. This ancient religious outlook remains active throughout much of the world today, both in complex civilisations such as Japan and India, and in less complex tribal societies world-wide. It was the outlook of the European religions of classical antiquity - Persia, Egypt, Greece and Rome - as well as of their 'barbarian' neighbours on the northern fringes ... Magic, the deliberate production of results in this world by Otherworld means, is generally accepted as a feasible activity in Pagan societies, since the two worlds are thought to be in constant communication."

Prudence Jones

WHAT YOU CALL TIME

A Practical Guide to Modern Witchcraft & Western Ritual Magic

Suzanne Ruthven

First published in Great Britain by ignotus press
BCM-Writer, London WClN 3XX

British Library Cataloguing in Publication Data
ISBN: 0-9522689-3-0

Cover Illustrations by Shona McDonald.
Printed by A2 Reprographics, Carmarthen

Printed in Great Britain by Antony Rowe Limited.
Set in New Baskerville 11pt

Index:

A recommended reading list and glossary have been added at the end of the book. These will enable the reader to understand some of the more esoteric terms and to go on to a clearly defined reference work covering the subject of each chapter in more depth.

Author's Note:

From Me Flows What You Call Time* is the title of an evocative piece of contemporary music by the late Japanese composer Toru Takemitsu, and aptly describes the floating, magical world which has no tangible 'time'. Takemitsu blends classical orchestral techniques and the use of modern electronics; adding the inimitable touch of Zen in the titles of his compositions and by using traditional Japanese music to create hauntingly beautiful sounds. ***What You Call Time*** is an exploration of the old, the new and the mystical world of magic put under the scrutiny of Buddhist scepticism.

My previous book, *Malleus Satani - The Hammer of Satan* explained why a 'black' magician or a 'white' witch is a misconception. Magic is morally neutral; on a lower level than the world of intellect and imagination, or the vital creative forces of Nature. Magic *per se* is neither black nor white, good nor evil and it is almost impossible to define what is meant by magic, because the word has different concepts for different people.

To some it merely refers to the cabaret act of card tricks and illusion; others think of it in terms of ignorant superstition; many connect it with a fictional world of wicked witches and wizards of fairy tale. To many more, the definition falls between a sinister connection with black masses and evil on one hand, and love potions and healing on the other. And to add to the confusion, it is remarkably difficult for the average person to obtain a comprehensible textbook on the subject of magic that is not tinged with bias or inaccuracy.

[*The secondary chapter titles printed in italics are also taken from Toru Takemitsu's compositions]

As with my previous research, all the contributors are Adepts of magic - several choosing to use their magical names. This reason is threefold. One, because they can be more relaxed and forthright, using their magical persona which is often separate from the 'real' world of daily living. Secondly, anonymity preserves their identity from fellow occultists and crafters who would accuse them of betraying sacred oaths. Thirdly, it offers protection from outside attack, i.e. identification by the media and religious fundamentalists.

'Learn about a pine tree from a pine tree, and about a bamboo plant from a bamboo' (Basho) is still my personal philosophy for research and those who genuinely seek to follow the Old Ways will do well to take heed of it. There may be a modicum of surprise that reference to Aleister Crowley's work crops up so frequently but this should not be the case. Crowley's sensible and erudite (although often obtuse) approach to magic is often more sympathetic, liberal and free-thinking than many of those within modern Wicca who revile his name.

Here is the truth about magic from those who practice it - and, once again, I hope that I have discharged my debt to them honourably.

Suzanne Ruthven
London - 1998

IGNOTUS PER IGNOTIUS
(To reach the unknown through the still more unknown.)

Chapter 1
Forty Shades of Grey - *Twill By Twilight*

The Devil, it is said, has all the best tunes and some of the best definitions in the dictionary. His disciples include many flamboyant and notorious figures in history; his cohorts, the motley assortment of demons that have plagued mankind since the dawning of the post-Christian era. The Witches, Necromancers, Sorcerers and Magi who make up his congregation all practice Black Magic and Masses in his diabolical name ... Or do they?

Anyone seriously exploring the realms of occultism will soon discover they are hard pressed to find a comprehensive textbook on the subject. Those volumes readily available cannot offer an accessible explanation without degenerating into fundamental bias that merely adds to the confusion. Like smoke from the Abyss, curling tendrils of mis-information cloud the issue until the seeker chokes on the sulphurous fumes of their own research. Infernal demons hound and harry the unwary along a series of blind alleyways with conflicting directions and deliberately misleading instructions. Following the darkened maze, through endless sloping corridors to a distorted hall of mirrors, the seeker emerges into the light no wiser than when they began their quest.

The First Step:

Whenever questions arise concerning magical or occult subjects, there is little point in referring to books written by non-occultists for the answers. The occult historian can pontificate from now until doomsday on Inquisitorial and trial documentation concerning European Witchcraft and Heresy. Unless he has set foot inside the circle, however, his writing carries little credence about the *true* beliefs and workings of a coven or magician's temple. Just how many so-called 'demonologists' have actually conjured up and confronted one of the inhabitants of hell's kitchen? Neither can the researcher rely on material with any form of Western religious or moral bias because everything will have been viewed with an unshakable belief in the Devil and a literal acceptance of biblical writ.

When carrying out the initial research for *Malleus Satani,* it was difficult to obtain introductions to genuine Adepts because few were willing to discuss any in-depth magical involvement with a journalist. This reluctance stemmed from a firmly entrenched belief that whatever was said during the interview would be sensationalised out of all proportion and misquoted.

The piles of press cuttings making up a large proportion of the research material testify that those fears were not ill founded - the media has rarely dealt kindly with occultism. As a result, certain journalistic 'buzz-words' such as devil worship, satanic ritual, occult obsession, black mass, etc. will always equal sexual deviancy and blasphemy in the public mind.

To illustrate the point, a recent case reported in *The Daily Telegraph* referred to a 14-year old boy who had desecrated graves because of 'his morbid fascination with the occult'. This short report, less than 250 words long, managed to include three references to the child's interest in occultism. The implication behind the words suggests that occult involvement *per se* encourages its followers to go out and excavate the local graveyard for a) ritualistic reasons best known to themselves, b) a mindless act of blasphemous vandalism or c) a perverted sense of humour. In reality, true Adepts of magic have no interest in the contents of Christian burial grounds but this is not what the public, the press or the clergy *want* to believe.

'Occult', of course, merely means 'hidden' or 'concealed' - it is not a euphemism for blood sacrifices, desecrated churches or devil worship. And while we're on the subject the word 'apocrypha' used in connection with Christian esoteric writing also means 'hidden'. The Greek word *apocryphos* being originally used to describe the contents of books which were kept hidden or secret because they "embodied the special teaching of religious or philosophical sects; it was only the members of these sects who were initiated into the secrets of this teaching" (*Encyclopaedia Britannica*).

Occult knowledge then, is that which must be sought and can apply just as accurately to a Tibetan lama, Wiccan priestess or Christian mystic, since all religious paths lead to occult understanding, i.e. the Will/Word of Deity made manifest. With this point in mind, the use of the term 'occultist' or 'Adept' in this text refers to those who follow the magical/ mystical workings of the Old Ways.

Despite the fact that there are many Paths the Old Ways can follow, *none* of them lead to the Devil's door. The Devil or Satan is of Christian origin and plays no part in the religious belief of Witch or Magus. For these reasons, any reference to the Devil in relation to occult or magical working will be conspicuous by its absence. Contrary to popular belief, the majority of those on the esoteric Paths are ordinary, everyday people, with jobs or businesses to run, families to keep and mortgages to pay. The Devil and his minions have no place in their religion or their lives.

So, before attempting to *seriously* explore the mystical realms of occultism, the reader must banish all pre-conceived ideas about devil worship, curses, conjuring tricks and excessive sexual practice. Out, too, must go ignorance, superstition, prejudice, religious bias and vulgar curiosity. Neither will the seeker find his/her answers in Dennis Wheatley, Rollo Ahmed, Montague Summers, the Hammer House of Horror or (least of all) questionable investigative journalism. The only way for the sincere seeker to discover true enlightenment is by following a Path tracing its history back to the beginning of recorded time.

What exactly is magic?

In ancient times, magic was usually the province of the priesthood. It didn't matter whether it was the pure shamanistic qualities of the Native American Indian (whose culture goes back some 25,000 years before the white man arrived on his Plains), or the more sophisticated rituals of the pre-dynastic Egyptians. Magical practises and religious belief went hand in hand until the induction of monotheism upon Western civilisation. Even then there were the 'fringe' practitioners who were consulted by the populace over matters of healing, fortune-telling and divination. Magic was a *natural* part of daily living and everyone had access to it.

Today's Adept see little change. For the seriously intentioned Witch or Magus, their magical routine is a way of life, a natural extension of their personal attributes and daily living. In *The Dagger & The Plough* the author explains that the 'witchiness' of an individual is not dependant upon which deity or pantheon is invoked but existing, or potential abilities, beyond what most people would call normal or natural. These abilities enable the occultist to 'see' the unseen, 'know' the unknowable, or change circumstances according to their desires; they are inherent in the individual, not dependent on the existence, presence or intervention of a deity.

According to magical theory, the vital forces of nature are manifest in earth, air, fire, water and spirit, as symbolised by the five points of the pentagram. All magic, whether high or low, is concerned with the acquisition of knowledge, wisdom and understanding (rather than personal power, riches and sexual magnetism) and takes many years of hard study to acquire. There will, of course, always be those who wish to use their hastily garnered 'knowledge' unwisely and to the detriment of others, but their rush of power rarely lasts for long. This particular brand of egotist is unwilling to remain a student and usually disappears in a flurry of swirling black cape and ostentatious jewellery to confound the gullible with his audacious public performances of bogus ceremonial magic.

As Eliphas Levi wrote in *Transcendental Magic*: "It is in like manner with all the miracles of magic; a law exists which is ignored by the vulgar and made use of by the initiate ... Magic is the traditional science of the secrets of Nature which has been transmitted to us from the Magi. By means of this science the adept becomes invested with a species of relative omnipotence and can operate superhumanly - that is, after a manner which transcends the normal possibilities of men."

Richard Cavendish commenting on this extract in *Man, Myth and Magic* added wryly: "Omnipotence, unqualified, supreme power over all things, is the ultimate goal of magic - though it is expected that it may take many reincarnations and lifetimes to achieve it."

As far back as the 16th century, Cornelius Agrippa defended magic as the supreme path to the understanding of the world and God and defined the Master Magus as one 'who has cohabited with the elements, vanquished Nature, mounted higher than the heavens, elevating himself to the archetype itself with whom he then becomes co-operator and can do all things'. Centuries later, Aleister Crowley put forward his own definition that 'God' was the 'Ideal Identity of a man's inmost nature' and the often quoted but least understood goal of magic - the Great Work - as 'raising of the whole man in perfect balance to the power of Infinity'.

These highfaluting and grandiose platitudes also cunningly drop a curtain over the equally simplistic side to magic. To read the works of the great magicians of the past, the would-be student could be forgiven for thinking that he needs a degree in Latin, physics, chemistry, higher mathematics, philosophy and theology before he embarks on a dubious career in magic. This is, by all traditional accounts, a closed shop to the ordinary man or woman in the street.

By pleasant contrast, however, you only have to read the chatty and down-to-earth introduction to the Raven newsletter which offers an open invitation for all to join. "Anyone has the potential to work Magic, because we all have our unique magic within. To consciously awaken and use that magic is one of the greatest adventures this world holds. You stand at the threshold of your own adventure, the world of magic lies open before you!"

Reputable and long-established magical suppliers such as Raven and The Sorcerer's Apprentice offer a wide range of teaching materials and courses to ensure that those genuinely interested in pursuing a magical way of life can be given factual, detailed information on Witchcraft and Magic. By exploring the stock lists it shows that magic, even at its grass roots level, encompasses a fascinating kaleidoscope of crystal healing, herbalism, scrying, dowsing, divination, tarot, astral travel, runic magic, geomancy, numerology, candle magic, aromatherapy, planetary magic, and so on.

Who are these magical practitioners?

Why do they do it and what do they use it for? Are they poseurs and crackpots, or simply those following an alternative religious Path? Can magic really benefit the human race or is it restricted to the elect? Does magic really exist or is it merely in the minds of the practitioners? Do they become Witches and magicians just to cultivate an interesting persona? Or is it something else?

Mélusine is a journalist with a penchant for designer clothes and expensive jewellery who, through necessity, keeps her work and magical life separate. "If these ever overlap, the most frequent comment is: 'You're not at all like we imagined a witch to be!' I'd best describe myself as following the primitive Egyptian Tradition based on the teachings of Aleister Crowley but without any of the group labels normally attached to his workings. The flamboyant style appeals to my personality, I guess. I also love the unique style of language and often use his poetry as part of my rituals."

Those having little experience of occult working may possibly surprised that women practice magic of the kind made notorious by the likes of Crowley and Austin Spare. But since the Hermetic Order of the Golden Dawn era things are different and today many of the esoteric orders include women among their ranks. In addition, the fictional works of Dion Fortune, written from her own standpoint as a *female* magician and member of the Golden Dawn, are still valuable today to those seeking an introduction to the Mystery Paths.

All of which invalidates another common misconception about occult practice: Magicians are male and Witches are female. Mélusine does not refer to herself as a Witch because she does not practice Witchcraft. "This is a title others foist on me because *they* feel more comfortable with it and understand what *they* mean by it. I would appear pretentious using that lovely old fashioned term 'sorceress' but it is probably a much more accurate description. There isn't another word for a female magician largely because historically it was always a male preserve. Classical texts, however, always refer to the likes of Circe and Medea by the term 'sorceress'."

Life, of course, is never that simple and like an over-laundered rugby-shirt, the colours eventually run into each other over repeated washing. "Witchdom has undergone dramatic changes," says Aeron Medbh-Mara. "No longer (in the eyes of the public at least) can we be allowed to simply charm away a wart, call up the wind for dinghy racers, or foretell the sex of a child. Neither can we be content with one or two finely honed abilities or skills; nor mutter conversationally to a deity whilst sitting in the bath."

Aeron Medbh-Mara is a High Priestess in the primitive Tradition of Witchcraft and Lady to a Clan based in the Midlands. She is author of *Life-Rites* and *The Dagger & the Plough,* and states quite categorically that today's Witches are, by implication or inference, demanded to be sorcerers. She is a highly respected figure in Craft circles and, until recently, operated her own teaching coven.

"We must be adept in every form of circle work (both solitary and group); work 'magic' from astral travel through candle and spell magic to the said wart charming. Ideally we should hold a university degree in archaeology, psychology and be familiar with every branch of Pagan theology; have a working knowledge of most of the world's myths; possess a copy of the poetry of both Crowley and Valiente, plus be fluent in all forms of divination and 'magical' alphabet. All this and be both willing and able to organise a pathworking or handfasting at a moment's notice. Not to mention a twitching of the nose to get the housework done!"

Chris, a former graphic designer, and Graham, a research chemist, are partners in a magical mail-order business and also give instruction in the Craft. "We are Witches of long standing and between us have a combined total of over fifty years research into the Mysteries - including Ritual Magic, Wicca and Shamanism. Our teaching programmes reflect this experience because we realise, when dealing with a novice's spiritual awakening, we have to make things as safe as possible."

Patrick is a chiropodist, founder of P.A.N, the Pagan Anti-Defamation Network and author of *The Torch & the Spear.* He and his wife practice Witchcraft and Shamanism on a daily basis from their modest suburban home in Southport. "Real Paganism is all about nature and the power behind the earth, air, fire, water and the spirit - how they affect our day-to-day lives. We do practice rituals; we actually practice them quite a lot, but we don't walk down the street with our robes on, shouting about it. That's just for show-offs, we're very private people really."

All this is a far cry from the popular media/Christian fundamentalist propaganda which claims that covens only exist to lure gullible teenagers towards mental, physical and religious degeneracy. Needless to say, when challenged by intelligent, articulate Witches, the propaganda-ists back peddle and respond with: "We're not talking about Witches and Pagans, we mean Satanists."

Frater Asmodeus, a member of the *Templi Satanas Luciferi* was quick to respond. "Yes, Satanists want power and wealth - not material wealth but a wealth of knowledge and a power of understanding. There is a balance between spirit and material but a real Satanist would never go around chopping up animals. Tales of maidens sacrificed during black magic rituals are a long way from our practises - we sacrifice nothing because our God and His counterpart do not need such sacrifices. We believe that there is a creative force which is all things. It comprises everything: material, non-material and neutral with no special care for man."

With such a broad spectrum of magical colour ranging from Thelema to Paganism at our disposal, it is obviously necessary to define exactly what is meant by magic by those who work with it on a regular basis. Again, research for *Malleus Satani* had revealed a startlingly high level of ignorance and idiocy on the part of some senior-ranking people in the Craft about the fundamentals of their own belief system. Understanding the basic principles of magical workings does, however, prevent the genuine seeker from wasting time with those who claim knowledge and titles to which they are not entitled.

For example, it was reported back to the publisher that certain Pagans were ignoring *Malleus Satani - the Hammer of Satan,* because it contained the dreaded 'S' word in the title. 'Malleus' means a small crushing instrument - hammer or mallet. Hence *Malleus Malificarum - the Hammer of Witches,* first published in 1486, was the Inquisitorial instrument (i.e. guide or text book) for crushing/destroying Witchcraft. *Malleus Satani* was intended as an instrument for destroying the Christianised-satanic concept people have of Witchcraft but it hasn't stopped today's Pagans from publicly destroying their own credibility in the eyes of the better informed.

A great number of Witches, especially those having access to media reporting, insist on referring to themselves as 'white' Witches. No doubt they feel that this appellation allays any suspicion of wrong-doing but this mis-representation has a serious backlash. By claiming a 'white' label for themselves in their practice of herbalism and crystal healing, they unwittingly (or wittingly) set up the guidelines for accusations of evil against anyone who they feel might be slightly 'greyer' than themselves. The seeker must judge whether they want a fluffy bunnies and carpet slippers approach to religion, or something that reflects the true face of Nature - often red in tooth and claw.

As Richard Cavendish explained in *Man, Myth & Magic*: "Both the theory of magic and its practice vitiate the customary moral distinction between black (evil) magic and white (good) magic. In magical theory good and evil ultimately do not exist at all ... And in magical practice all methods and all experiences tend to be grist to the magician's mill, for if the supreme goal is to become and master everything, then the magician must experience and reconcile every aspect of 'the All' in himself - evil as well as good, hate as well as love, cruelty as well as affection, tears as well as laughter."

In more down to earth terms, Chris added: "In this world there is no such thing as truly white or truly black magic. If I work a ritual to help someone to get a particular job I am, by definition, stopping anyone else from getting that appointment."

Experience has shown that when confronted with a self-confessed 'black' or 'white' practitioner, the best thing that anyone can do is smile politely and head for the door. In this instance whiteness is not a virtue, and as far as the 'black' brother is concerned, he's probably on day release from the local mental institution. When folk begin by having to justify their belief, or bragging about their power, there is little to be learned from either source and the seeker would be ill-advised to hang around.

Which, of course, brings us conveniently to those ill-used terms so beloved by advertisers in the Pagan press for 'right-hand' only group members. From earliest dynastic Egypt, the left-hand path has been used to denote the feminine-lunar aspect of the Goddess, whilst the right-hand path represents the solar-masculine aspect of the God. The terms were brought into incorrect usage following Madame Blavatsky's visit to India where she encountered the Varma Marg and identified it as deviant sexual practice.

Dr Meriem Clay-Egerton had taken up this point in an article for *The Lamp of Thoth:* "She (Madame Blavatsky) equated the Varma Marg, the left-hand path, with evil at its worst and said so, loudly and clearly, verbally and in print, all over Europe - with the result that to this day the ill-informed think that left-hand path equals evil. And if they mean to equate the right-hand path with so-called 'white' Witchcraft, what are they doing assuming titles like 'High Priestess'?"

In effect, the occult knowledge of such advertisers merely demonstrates a total lack of magical experience that results in their left-hand not understanding what their right-hand is doing. It is not unusual to find advertisements for female-only groups seeking right-hand path members "Who do they venerate if they claim to worship a right-hand path Goddess?" concluded Dr Clay-Egerton. "A transvestite?"

This imbalance can also be carried over into all-male or all-female groups when sexual polarity is undermined by the exclusion of either the male or female principle. All magic requires the balance of opposites - i.e. light/dark, lunar/solar, male/female, etc., - and by negating the vital energy force created by contrapositive harmony, the effectiveness of the magical working is diminished. Witches worship a God *and* Goddess because they believe the Universe is given expression through the unification of male and female principles, or through their interaction. Deliberate sexual alienation in magic goes against the natural laws of the cosmos.

Having high-lighted some of the initial problems posed for the genuine seeker, it is also necessary to understand why there is so much mis-information in the public domain on the subject of occultism. The counter-argument can, of course, be raised that if Witches and magicians aren't afraid of public scrutiny, why don't they publish authentic accounts of their activities? The answer to this problem is eightfold:

1. Anti-occult hype provides more interesting reading than serious esoteric writing, particularly if the protagonists have a religious bias. The 'satanic child abuse' scare, which lasted

for five years, was formulated and fuelled purely on deliberately inaccurate scaremongering of Christian fundamentalists and over-zealous social workers. Following an intensive investigation, the Government commissioned report by Professor J. S. La Fontaine (*The Extent & Nature of Organised and Ritual Abuse* - HMSO) confirmed that there was no foundation for any of the allegations but the media continues to hype 'ritual abuse' while therapists and fundamentalists are still producing 'satanic survivors' to support their claims.

2. The media prefers sex-scandal and lurid murder to accurate reporting. Editors will always find room for unsubstantiated tales of child-sex, occult related suicide, sacrificial virgins and animals because it sells newspapers or boosts viewing figures. National magazines will not accept serious feature articles showing occultism in a positive, or favourable light, because they fear censor from the readership or, more realistically, from the advertisers.

3. Consulting the wrong 'experts' also clouds the issue. A recent article in one of the more serious newspapers stated that the magician Eliphas Levi was acknowledged to be a fraud by an 'expert' occult historian. Since Aleister Crowley considered himself to be a reincarnation of Levi, the world's most famous magician would hardly pick someone who was 'acknowledged to be a fraud'. When challenged to give the credentials of their 'expert', the religious affairs correspondent for the newspaper declined to oblige.

4. The majority of established titles written on the subject of occultism and published by main-stream publishing houses are written by outsiders, i.e. those who have no practical working knowledge of Witchcraft or magic. Some of the most famous reference books are written by historians not magicians or Witches so even consulting standard textbooks can be completely misleading.

5. Many recognised occult publishers are now steering clear of what they consider to be 'heavy' occultism (Witchcraft, ritual magic, sex magic, etc.) and prefer middle of the road subjects such as alternative healing, herbalism, crystal magic, personal enlightenment, etc. Most authentic material comes from specialist or small press publishers and can often only be located through occult shops and mail order catalogues.

6. Much of the false information given in interviews is that offered by publicity seekers who claim occult status to which they have no right. They rarely come up with factual information but by then the damage is done. Unfortunately, occultism has always been a safe haven for charlatans - because genuine Adepts prefer to keep well out of the limelight and not be associated with the strange individuals who claim to represent the views of all.

7. The television programme *Desperately Seeking* series and particularly its producer Peter McCarthy, however, earned the praise of the more sensible members of the Pagan community for his ability to keep a straight face against impossible odds when confronted by some of the most famous names in the occult Traditions. "No wonder the media has such a low opinion of us - so had I after watching this programme," wrote one High Priestess. "*Why* do our 'Big Names' continue to leap willingly into the humiliation trap? Or is it true - we are all barking? Couldn't someone go on TV looking sharp, smart and intelligent just for a change?"

8. There are also a large number of Pagans who claim for themselves the titles of High Priest and High Priestess without a thorough grounding in Craft studies. They are loose cannon who have a need to be important and interesting but without the knowledge that occult teaching requires. There are hundreds of covens run by the unenlightened and as a result, their students flounder around, basking in the same eternal darkness without hope of advancement.

"I did not encounter the terms or titles, at least in the Craft, of High Priestess or High Priest, until after the advent of Dr. Gerald Gardner in the 1950s," explained Bob Clay-Egerton who has a life-time's experience as a magical practitioner. "At least one northern coven appears, from two independent sources, to have been God oriented, controlled and administered by males. I have also encountered one, and heard of others, who were Goddess oriented and female controlled. One thing I found in the three Covens of my acquaintance - there was no bitchcraft as there is today. Perhaps it was too dangerous."

But what is the point of studying magic in the late 20th century? What does it entail and what are the benefits of raking over the neolithic bones of ancient ancestors in an age of computer technology? Are there really advantages to be gained or are those practising it merely indulging in a need to be different?

As founder of P.A.N, Patrick is used to answering such questions. "Working magic and casting spells are deeply rewarding, whether it be Earth, cord, candle magic, etc. The spell provides a central focus that co-joins us with the gods. With patience and correct timing I find that most spells do come to successful fruition. However, even if I get things wrong there is always a sense of increased awareness and heightened spirituality following a rite, so positive magical growth does stem from rituals even those that may not seem to immediately hit the mark. We don't create magical energy (it's already there to start with) we heighten or raise it, then redirect it to its given target. Sometimes we miss our goal but with skill (and foresight) we often as not score a bull's-eye and achieve a desired effect."

Mélusine used a quote from Crowley's book, *Magick in Theory & Practice* to explain her approach. "'The question of magic is a question of discovering and employing hitherto unknown forces in Nature'- which sounds very much like an over simplification but does, in fact, explain everything.

"There is nothing unnatural in Nature and the Adept quickly learns that any lack of respect for the power of natural forces can rebound in a very unpleasant way. More important than anything else, magical training teaches you to know yourself - come to terms with your faults and recognise your strengths - there's no room for self-delusion."

"True magic is not a Paul Daniel's trick!" musician Brighdhe, author of *Witchcraft For the Non-Witch*, was quick to explain. "It is the art of getting results in a manner that seems to be unnatural or unexplained, but actually is using the natural forces around us. In as much as we know that *déjà vu* exists, but not why or how it works, then we know that magic works - but not exactly why or how. We believe that everyone has the innate capacity to work what is sometimes known as magic, but they need to be taught the technique."

Both Chris and Graham from Raven are also anxious to dispel any illusions that magic is unnatural or harmful. They see it as an extremely positive character-building attribute. "In magical practice, the cultivation of your magical Will includes the strengthening of your own belief; faith in your own abilities and in the success of any magic you set out to perform. In other words, when you set out on any magical operation you must believe *(with no room for doubt)* that you are a magically potent individual and that the outcome of your magical operation will be exactly what you aim for."

"True knowledge is not the mere recitation of lists of correspondences but the understanding necessary to convert the bare bones of magical teaching into magic itself," Graham added. "Neither is it enough to immerse yourself in books and learn rituals and spells by rote. This is, of course, the starting point - and a point at which many students are content to stick. The true magician, however, is able to transcend set ritual and create his own specific magical environment, in which anything and everything is possible. Once you have found that your magic does work, you will find that you no longer need to have faith in your magic, because this has been replaced by the stronger child of knowledge - certainty."

Of course, all this smacks of the 1990s cliché of Positive Mental Attitude but you cannot progress very far on the subject of Magic or Witchcraft without a direct referral to the God/dess. Despite the fact that our contributors speak of harnessing natural forces, there is no escaping the highly potent religious thread that runs through the conversation.

Who or what do Witches and Magicians worship?

Bob Clay-Egerton's view was very cut and dried: "My own and one other of the Covens I knew, held that the ultimate 'GOD' was literally everything - too abstract an idea for man to fully understand. As a result the active-solar-masculine aspects are seen by man to be attributes of 'the Lord', or God(s); while the passive-lunar-feminine attributes are those of 'the Lady', or Goddess(es). The two being equal in balance."

According to Mélusine the concept of a god or goddess is, in reality, an embodiment of the One, depending on the type of ritual she is about to work. "Each sphere of power has certain correspondences which channel the focus of that particular deity or power source. My instinctive choice are the deities of archaic Egypt; more primitive forms than those usually associated with the later Osirian/Isis pantheon."

Patrick went on to elaborate that the god-forms used in magical rituals are dependent on the psychological make-up of the individual Witch or magician concerned. Many practitioners seem to need the security of what they see as an 'established' structure with maybe a Celtic or Norse pantheon of deities. Others prefer to go more exotic with Voodoo, Japanese or Oceanic gods which matters not one iota so long as one is comfortable working with a given class of deities.

"I work with the Roman gods simply because I find that their blend of complex classical imagery and incorporated native sense of belonging suits my personality very well. After all, much of this country's culture owes its spiritual heritage to the Roman-Pagan inroads. They cross-pollinated their gods with Celtic deities and improved upon them. The

Romans anthropomorphised ideal/perfect human concepts, i.e. love, maternity, courage, joy, etc., in the form of images of the gods. This ensured that every individual could see the image being sought.

"Such personification of divinity marked a radical change in native British culture - to see images of the gods was to know them, enabling the adherent to reach greater levels of awareness and perception. The Romans had gods/goddesses for absolutely everything and that suits me, too. Not just for the sky, war or water, like Celtic deities but also for things like peace, doors, gardens, good faith, stimulation, etc. Everything and its action in creation was allocated its own presiding deity (which incidentally compliments present day magical theory that everything vibrates and has its own different aura) by the Romans. This fact alone I find immensely attractive as it lets me explore spirituality in every day life in every place I go."

Aeron's over-view is more complex when it comes to modern British Craft belief. "Many followers of what today is referred to as 'Wicca', mix their group manifestation of a Pagan religion with a selection of power raising/magical/divinatory skills in varying quantities. The religion usually quoted is a synthesis of Graeco-Romano philosophy and symbolism. The magic may be more than a little influenced by Qabalistic understanding, bastardised Christian beliefs, post-Crusade imports and mediaeval inventions. My personal viewpoint is that the actual pre-Christian/indigenous religions of England, Scotland, Ireland and Wales have their basis in the pre-Celt, with 'acknowledgement' to the modified Celt and subsequent 'invading' cultures, such as the pre-Christian Danes, Angles, Saxons and Jutes, as each overlaid the former, according to the area and political circumstances."

Brighdhe works in the Celtic Tradition and recognises a Supreme Creative Being as symbolised and manifested in the unity of the Great Goddess and Her consort the Horned God. "We accept the validity of all genuine religions as being but different paths to the same goal - oneness with the Godhead.

All Gods are but One God, whatever you perceive it to be - and by whatever name - there can only be One Creator. The Horned God and the Great Goddess are the symbols of the male and female aspects of the Godhead since they are understandable forms of the masculine and feminine principles contained in all things."

Britomartis, however, threw a spanner in the works by reminding everyone that ... "most of Western Ritual Magic is based on grimoires written by the Christian clergy and Hebrew translations. More often than not, the Magus would be calling for assistance from the archangels Gabriel, Raphael, Michael and other members of the Heavenly Host. Demons were summoned and ordered about to do the magician's bidding - they were never a focus of worship."

Regardless of the different Traditions or Paths, however, the solar-masculine-god is the personification of bringing fertility to the land, animals, humans and the goddess. He is usually the bringer of death and often depicted as the hunter as well as the hunted. The lunar-feminine-goddess is the giver of life, fruitfulness and rebirth. She ***is*** the land - the Great Mother of all things. Working together in natural harmony of existence, the god and goddess keep the cycle of life-birth, death and rebirth to everything in creation. From simple Craft working to ceremonial/ritual Magic, the principle is the same: equal balance of solar-lunar principles, the law of opposites.

How do you get started?

"You cannot be a magical Adept unless you practice magic," Chris was quick to stress. "This may seem like a self-evident truth but it is very easy to get stuck, or sidetracked, into studying books and magical and psychic exercises but never actually getting around to performing any magical operations. People give all sorts of reasons why they do not actually get down to doing any practical magic, even when they might be quite knowledgeable about the theoretical side.

"Having said that, the thought of actually trying a real magic ritual can be very off-putting. Accept that the first time you actually do try a ritual it can be very nerve-wracking. You may be excessively aware of any mistakes you make in any parts of your magical procedure and may well feel the urge to give up half way through the ritual. Take courage and continue, the first ritual is always the worst."

There really does come a time when book-learning takes a student as far as s/he can go because no amount of study can really prepare anyone for the mental and physical changes that occur when they begin to practice magic seriously. Crowley related a story concerning two fellow students at Cambridge who, having failed to conjure up various spirit-forms, concluded that all magic was rubbish. This assumption was made when one of them extended his little finger outside the circle and was not blasted to eternity by some angry demon. Since neither had the capacity for magic neither spirit nor lightning bolt deigned to appear. "If one does not understand anything about electricity, one cannot construct a dynamo; and having so failed, one cannot get oneself electrocuted," observed Crowley wryly.

"From the moment you make that first dedication you are different." Mélusine is adamant. "I hadn't got a clue where it would lead but I just knew it was something I needed to do. NOW! Using my copy of *Magick* as a guide, I cobbled together a simple ceremony. Even though I'm a writer, I still find it extremely difficult to create convincing prayers and rituals so I recited Crowley's 'One Star In Sight' and hoped that sincerity of intent would get the message across. It did and almost immediately I became aware of subtle changes in everything around me. Attitude, perception, vision - everything became clearer, more sharply defined."

Although Graham has little empathy with the purple prose and elaborate ritualistic writings of Britain's most famous Magus, his own shamanistic approach to magic is curiously similar. "When we start to explore what might be called a magical perspective of the world, we can soon find hidden depths of meaning in even the simplest things. Real magic for me is all about gradually and increasingly becoming more aware of the 'hidden' dimensions all around us.

"Learning to accept that there is a 'spirit world' which is far richer and more complex than this plane of existence, learning to communicate with its inhabitants - a path which starts in this world, often through a shamanistic approach. It really doesn't matter whether the stone you are talking to is 'alive' in the scientific sense because it can behave as if it is. A stone, like an animal or plant, is hardly likely to use human language, nor is it going to view the world as you and I do, nor think like us.

"And therein lies the magic, being able to see the world through another's eyes, to view the world as a stone 'sees' it, or as a bird or great tree. Such experiences can expand your perception enormously. Books of magical spells are all very interesting (some of them are hysterically funny, too), and spells of different kinds are often essential to the Witch and magician alike. But in no way can they match a truly magical awareness of the world, something which we are all (very) slowly attaining, over many lifetimes."

Writing in what is perhaps the finest encyclopaedia on the occult, *Man, Myth & Magic*, Richard Cavendish explained that 'all drives and forces which are powerful in man will also be powerful in the universe at large, hence the magical importance of sex' (see Chapter 7). And since the human race is influenced by signs and symbolism, all manner of colours, gemstones, animals, herbs, etc. have been allocated esoteric identities, known as 'correspondences' which can be used to control those universal driving forces.

According to Chris at Raven, one of the prime ways of working magic is through the use of the idea that if you have an object that looks like, or resembles another, then there is a sort of magical connection between the two. "For example, in herbalism this idea is sometimes called the 'doctrine of signatures' and means that a plant with heart-shaped leaves would be thought to affect the bodily heart organ. The links are not always as obvious as that, and are often symbols or even ideas which are associated with these interpretations. Many of the associations have a long history of usage, some going back many thousands of years; others are far more recent."

These ideas are part of the basic beliefs underlying Western ritual magic although Aleister Crowley went one stage further by incorporating Eastern elements when he compiled *Liber 777* - his own vast collection of correspondences. In order to give an idea of how correspondences work, here are some of the associations with the seven classical planets (see Appendix III) which are used for general magical workings. Magicians with Qabalistic leanings relate their correspondences not only to the planets but to the ten sephiroth (aspects/parts of the divine being) on the Tree of Life and the twenty-two paths represented by the major trumps of the Tarot.

As an introduction, play around with the two main planetary influences - the sun and the moon - which govern nearly all aspects of magical working. Anyone who excels at crossword puzzles will find it easy to come to terms with correspondences because the system is based very loosely on word or thought association. As a guide, a complete listing can be found in Appendix III - but beware of coming up against conflicting correspondences when Traditions from opposing hemispheres collide.

For example, magic relating to health, confidence, prosperity; the ritual should be worked on a Sunday in conjunction with the Sun, ideally three hours after sunset or during the hour of sunrise. Remember, however, that other Traditions (i.e. Egyptian) demand their rituals to be carried out during daylight hours - at dawn, midday or sunset and there are strict rules governing magical working as can be confirmed by the Pyramid Texts. This illustrates why it is important to fully understand the tools-of-the-trade for each Tradition before trying to mix them, or your magic could either backfire or be rendered sterile.

The deities normally associated with the Sun are Apollo, Re, Re-Herakhte, Lugh or Mithras - all males representing solar energy, raw power, creative ability, vitality and ambition , or right hand path energies. It was the Sun that earliest man recognised as being "beneficient and yet thoroughly dangerous; the giver of life and yet the most potent of destructive forces." Therefore the Sun was the most obvious as being the focus for divine worship although (as with all things mystical) nothing was that simple on a global level.

As *Man, Myth & Magic* explains, the mythology of Sun worship depends greatly on the geographical location The High Indian God Varuna and the Sun God Mitra were the guardians of order; the Inca on the other side of the world, queried why the Sun was forced to daily tread the same path and concluded that there must be a deity greater than he. Around the equator and tropics where the seasons are not clearly defined as in the northern hemisphere, particular importance is placed on the rising and setting of the Sun. In colder lands the seasonal cycle has a far more important emphasis. The greatest of all solar beliefs is that of the ancient Nile Valley but such a form of religious worship would have been "virtually impossible in northern Europe, where the sun emerged in the spring only after a bitter struggle with dark powers."

By using corresponding colours (gold, orange or yellow), gemstones (amber, diamonds or citrine), metal (gold) and herbs (ash, broom, frankincense, ginger) the right atmosphere is created within your sacred area. For those flirting with ritual magic, this planetary sign also corresponds to Tiphareth (sephiroth) on the Tree of Life, Leo (zodiac) and The Sun (tarot).

The Moon on the other hand offers completely opposing correspondences and relates to the left-hand, or female Path. For magical working affecting psychic powers, divination and astral travel the ritual should be worked on a Monday, ideally three hours after sunset or during the hour of sunrise. The deities invoked are Isis, Hecate, Cerridwen and Artemis although in much more ancient Traditions, including the

Egyptian, the moon god was male. The Moon is the ruler of occult power and to "rule over growth and the hidden processes of Nature, the hollow spaces of the earth, and the movements of all the fluidic elements within and upon the earth's surface."

Moon magic is extremely potent and by using corresponding colours (silver, white or midnight blue), gemstones (crystal, pearl or moonstone), metal (silver) and herbs (eucalyptus, gardenia, jasmine or vanilla) the correct working channels can be opened. This planetary sign also corresponds to Yesod (sephiroth) on the Tree of Life, Cancer (Zodiac) and The Moon, the Empress or the High Priestess (tarot).

Each day of the week is governed by one of the planets and a study of the correspondences leads into the fascinating realms of mythology and history - in which a study of the stars and constellations also play a part. The student of magic eventually become 'tuned-in' to every influence in the natural universe; not just on this earth but beyond.

These correspondences only give a brief example of the many symbols which relate to any particular area of correspondence. Taking the most popular magical request as being that of the love spell - let's take the magical working a stage further. Our hypothetical Witch or magician is intent on drawing the attentions of a lover; we know that the spell should be cast on a Friday by calling on the intervention of Aphrodite so what else do we need to know?

Firstly consult a magical year planner and work out the hourly planetary sequences for the time of year - three hours after sunset can be around seven o' clock in the winter and sometime near midnight in summer. Next take note of the moon's phases and always work attraction magic on the Waxing Moon and banishing magic on the Waning Moon whenever possible. Many people believe this means you can only work positive magic between the New and Full Moon but this is not necessarily the case. If your lover is proving to be uncooperative, you work your attraction magic as the Moon's light increases in power and brightness - and so will your spell.

After the full Moon you work to banish inhibitions and break down obstacles - you are merely viewing the same problem from a different angle.

Having set a day and time for your magical operation, you then choose corresponding accoutrements to enhance the working. Since we are working for love, the altar or magical area should be decked out with green and/or pink which should include candles and flowers. Select a suitable incense (i.e. sandalwood or jasmine) and a matching or complimentary oil for anointing yourself and the candles.

Corresponding gemstones can be used to enhance any magical operation: an emerald can be used in any love spell because of its affinity with Aphrodite/Isis/Ishtar. To give the whole operation a little added zest, you may blend incense and oil to represent your lover's and your own birth signs. To really make things move along, burn a snippet of his/her hair, photograph or sample of handwriting.

This is, of course, an over simplification of a magical working but it serves to illustrate what must be taken into account before a ritual can go ahead and what is involved in the planning of such an operation. Successful magic is not a pastime for the dilettante; some magical workings can take weeks, months, even years to come to fruition, so the need for patience as well as faith is a pre-requisite of the would-be Witch or Magus.

Divination also plays an important part in most magical routines and is considered to be gift from the gods. Usually it predicts the future or reveals hidden knowledge by a 'great variety of means, signs and occult techniques'. Basil Ivan Rakoczi (*Man, Myth & Magic*) wrote that the most remarkable thing about divination was its recorded success, despite some methods proving to be more effective than others or some diviners having a greater power of visionary insight than others. "But even from the most materialist point of view, judged by its age-old popularity and bearing in mind that divination has had to survive ecclesiastical condemnation and the gibes of rationalists and sceptics, the art was, and is, an overwhelming success."

Mélusine believes in the 'belt and braces' approach and will use several methods before she is satisfied with the results. "I will use the pendulum for general chitchat but for wider reaching readings I'll use the *Atus of Tahuti* - the Egyptian Tarot," she explained. "When there were some really important changes about to happen in my life I even went so far as to consult the pendulum, tarot, astrological charts and trance meditation before I was satisfied about the direction I was being told to take. And I always get someone to check my tarot reading because it's all too easy to read into the cards what you want to see. I never take anything on face value and although it's necessary to have faith in what you're doing, it's not a blind faith."

Aeron also uses a variety of methods including scrying for a vague overview but if she requires something more positive, will use runic stones or ogham sticks - the casting of yew wands inscribed with mystic symbols in Ogham, the earlier form of Irish writing. "I only use the tarot if I'm doing a reading for someone else. Most 'seekers' prefer something they can look at and the picture cards offer a better visual participation. I use the *Tarot of the Cat People* because if there is something nasty or unexpected to be discovered in the woodshed, the cat pictures 'soften' the impact."

Both the pendulum and tarot are popular forms of divination and often the most frequently used. Chris, however, urges a wider grasp of what is being asked of *any* method of future-divining. "Despite what some books and authorities may tell you, there is no such thing as a definitive meaning of any system and no two books will agree on the exact use or interpretation.

"Remember the future is not fixed, it is a series of probabilities and it can be changed to bring it into line with your desires. This is the purpose of divination, not merely to gain a glimpse of the future, but to ensure that your future is what you want it to be. Divination merely gives indications of the likely outcome of situations as they now stand. If you do a reading and don't like the predicted outcome, now is the time to change matters in the present, to bring about the future you do want. A further reading should be done asking simply: what should I do now to alter my future?"

The tarot is an old system of divination although the earliest examples available only date from the 14th century. Most folk regard the tarot as 'a system of fortune-telling using a special pack of fancy cards' (*Man, Myth & Magic*) but to the Adept it is a method of stimulating submerged awareness. According to classic occult writers the tarot awakens in our consciousness the memory of that which we have suppressed by subconsciously recognising associations which we have already formed in the past.

"The study of the tarot can be a life-time's work, and there are some very intellectual discourses on this method," continued Chris. "Indeed some, like a lot of occult material, seem to have been written almost to show-off the author's great wisdom and learned authority rather than educate the reader. Whatever system of divination you may use, the symbols involved are there simply to show you something that your deep mind already knows, and is trying to communicate to you. If you rely too much on intellect, you will certainly make the task far more complicated, and may miss the point all together."

The pendulum is basically a dowsing instrument, consisting of a weight on the end of a cord; the weight is simply there to help the cord swing in an easily recognisable manner. Unlike the tarot it can only answer a question with 'yes' or 'no' which limits the line of enquiry to a very basic level.

"On the other hand it can be used as a way of making contact with your own subconscious," added Graham, "and also to talk to your Spirit Guardian(s). If you wish to attempt communication at this level, on the first few occasions you will find it easier at times such as dawn or sunset - the times of change over between light and darkness are what have been referred to as 'the crack between the worlds'."

Scrying, of course, was one of the methods favoured by Dr. John Dee and his smoky quartz 'shew-stone' can still be viewed in the British Museum. Today's scryers favour all manner of objects from crystal balls, transparent rock crystals, mirrors and black bowls filled with water for active or passive scrying. In the Corvus Magical World publication on *Divination,* active is defined as setting out to gain information about a specific situation and passive is simply allowing yourself to receive impressions without any attempt at control.

By beginning with passive scrying, the images that you receive may be difficult to interpret as Chris explained. "If you see a snake in the glass, it could refer to a trip to the zoo or, if you are into Jungian psychology, it could refer to a sexual problem you are having, whereas in magical symbolism the serpent is a symbol of wisdom and intuition, and the awakening of magical power. Eventually as your sensitivity develops, you will come to recognise exactly what a symbol means to you, personally, and you will also be able to distinguish between the various levels of consciousness and know whether the object you see is a physical object or a representation of something else."

There are now many methods of reading the runes, some involving the use of a special rune board or cloth with symbolic patterns, or by simply by drawing a particular number of rune stones from a bag. According to the Roman Tacitus in his *Germanica*, the ancient Germanic tribes relied heavily on divination by the 'casting of lots'.

Their method was to cut a branch from a fruit-bearing tree which was cut into strips and then marked with runic symbols. These were cast onto a white cloth and the seer foretold the future by picking up three strips at a time and reading the meaning according to the runes scratched on them. Needless to say that as this is an extremely ancient method of divination, there is no standard reading for the 'exact uses and qualities of the runes' and like the tarot, it seems to be a question of personal empathy rather than a prescribed method of interpretation.

Long before the Inquisition declared open season on Witches and Heretics, healing and herbalism was a service that wise women provided for the community. The often quoted biblical passage which decrees "Thou shalt not suffer a witch to live" had a different connotation prior to the King James I edition, as Brighdhe points out. "The phrase was 'Thou shalt not suffer a *poisoner* to live'. The word was changed either by accident by the scribe when translating, or by design." Either way it illustrates the extensive herbal knowledge accredited to Witches of the times if the two words were synonymous.

Witch-lore also makes frequent reference to the use of the 'flying-ointment' used to *journey* to the Sabbats. It has been suggested by writers such as Dion Fortune that the preparation was used by those unable to attend a Sabbat. Having rubbed themselves with the ointment, they could lay down and concentrate on a rural, moor or forest location and transport themselves there in a dream or vision. "The broomstick flying of the medieval witches was first cousin to the temple sleep, or incubation of the Greeks, in which the worshipper, sleeping in the temple, was blessed with a vision of the god." All methods are, therefore, one and the same method with experienced Adepts using modern preparations to achieve the same results.

Although some medical practitioners can be rather 'sniffy' and supercilious when it comes to herbal treatment it is a fact that the vast majority of drugs prescribed by doctors actually derive from natural substances, i.e. plants, herbs, trees, roots, even minerals and salts. Many herbal remedies can be obtained from health food shops and even your local supermarket, but do bear in mind that certain herbs can cause allergic reactions, especially if taken in conjunction with other prescribed medicines.

Many magical practitioners channel their knowledge into psychic healing although this is another area where charlatanism abounds. A good healer is not interested in a personal power trip - the recovery of the patient is paramount and this is why they will advise a patient to explore all avenues of healing, including conventional medicine and surgery.

Psychic and magical healing should only be used as a compliment to conventional treatment, not as a substitute for it.

Healing is a holistic practice and not simply the alleviation of symptoms. It is an attempt to redress an imbalance in the body/mind/spirit; all being inter-linked and interdependent. More people are beginning to understand that holistic healing means treating the whole body, mind and psyche when an imbalance manifests itself in an illness. For those who have this natural 'gift of the gods', it can be a doubly rewarding experience to be able to develop a power that is beneficial to others.

Neither is aromatherapy a new fad although it has become labelled as 'alternative' in today's search for the purer forms of healing. The 'essential oil' used in aromatherapy is the pure, undiluted oil extracted from the plant it is named after. In various forms it can be used as an inhalant, bath, gargle/ mouthwash, or during massage; these oils are very strong and should be handled with care since it is inadvisable to use undiluted substances on broken skin, or internally, except under medical advice. Further Education courses now cater for those interested this particular form of healing - Witches still tend to brew their own, or purchase from a trusted supplier (who is usually a member of the Craft), as they prefer to work with pure, magically prepared ingredients.

The Unquiet Journey

In contrast with these more earthly pursuits, it is astral travel that causes more mirth amongst magical practitioners than any other form of psychic ability. And one which prompts Adepts to tell stories against themselves. Mélusine remembers her first experience. "I suddenly found my other self hovering above my body and came back to earth with such a jolt that I felt sick. The fear didn't come from the fact that I'd managed to achieve the separation, it was realising that it could be done with such *ease*. Now it doesn't worry me but it was a quite while before I had the courage to try again."

"In the early days I found it quite easy to leave my body," Chris confessed, "but one night I found a huge white shape hovering beside me and the shock sent me back into my physical form in a hurry. I realised afterwards that it was one of those large white paper lampshades we all had in those days. I'd obviously been floating near the ceiling and thought I was being visited by one of the guardians out of *The Prisoner*!"

Ancient cultures accepted the reality of allowing a spirit to leave the physical body to travel to different planes of consciousness. Today some still believe it to be the prerogative of an elite few, selected by birth, training or accident. Others accept everyone has the ability and that astral journeying is what happens to the soul during sleep; because of a lack of training or awareness we only recall the images as garbled remnants of dreams.

"I can only liken the sensation to that of going up, or down, in a very fast lift," said Mélusine. "You are aware of what is happening to you on the astral, but you are also very consciously aware of your physical body. On one occasion I went straight up through the roof to such a height that I could see the complete horizon in a full circle, with the hills on the skyline glowing with a blue fire. Another time I found myself in the Grand Gallery in the Great Pyramid, following a guide some distance ahead, who was carrying a flaming torch. Don't ask me how I knew where I was, I just did, but I wasn't afraid of being in that dark, narrow confined space. Astral experiences like this give you the ability to face up to what others may consider to be their worst nightmare."

As knowledgeable as she is, Chris experienced difficulties in getting out of the room once she'd left her body. "In the finish, I had my astral form bouncing up and down on the bed like a trampolinist until I was catapulted up through the roof. I remember looking down and seeing a light on at the back of the house and thought 'Oh, Graham's left the light on, I'd better go and tell him.' I lost my concentration and back I went."

Aeron uses the astral as a means of keeping tabs on the mental and spiritual welfare of her clan. "Sometimes it isn't always easy to discover if one of them has a problem that needs your undivided attention. With so many others there on coven-night, you might not always have the time to spend and miss the warning signs. On the astral things are clearer and the lines of contact are always open. You can pick up the troubled vibrations. Then it's just a matter of picking up the 'phone and saying: 'Okay, what's wrong?'"

Doesn't she feel like a snooper? "With such a large group of people, I need to know if anyone is hurt, angry or upset so it isn't allowed to interfere with the harmony of Clan working. When they join, they become my responsibility and I'm duty-bound to give help and comfort when, and wherever, it's required.

"You can lock-in to anything on the astral and I can often raise a blush by commenting, 'You were enjoying yourself last night!' If they are otherwise engaged, I don't hang around, it would be impolite but they'd love to know how I always know what they've been up to. It's all part of the fun."

Like all serious undertakings, discipline is the keyword to true magical working. There are those who earn themselves the label of 'Thursday-night witches' because they only bring their faith into the circle on a regular weekly basis. The sincere Adept works magic at any time, in any place, as and when necessary. The religious aspect becomes the essence of life's fabric and not a day goes by without some simple act of religious observance. All the posing and posturing in the world cannot compensate for a lack of discipline when it comes to the successful outcome of a ritual.

Israel Regardie (*The Eye In The Triangle*) records that discipline is not welcome as a rule by occult students, which is why Aleister Crowley insisted so emphatically upon its necessity, and why he tended to be rude and contemptuous when students sought the highest goals without proper preparation. It was Regardie's opinion that many of them are neurotic escapists who cannot tolerate themselves and their emotional difficulties. "Discipline and training, the traditional requirements in magic as well as elsewhere, are the only factors that can bring the student through. There is no other way."

"Many occultists will admit that they have to be 'in the mood' to practice magic," Chris added by way of explanation. "In other words, that in order to perform any spell or magical operation they have to 'feel' that the time is right and that they are in a spontaneous frame of mind which will give them access to their 'other' magical consciousness.

"There is nothing wrong with this kind of working, of course, except that it can be a bit hit and miss. There are times when it is imperative that certain magical spells must be performed NOW! If you have to wait for your own spontaneous magical consciousness to make up its own mind, you may well miss the moment."

Mélusine has no difficulty in accepting the disciplines imposed by a strict magical routine. "It's amazing just how quickly magic (in its broadest sense) becomes part of daily living. This doesn't mean spending hours on your knees in prayer or closeted in a temple burning incense like a suburban barbecue. I carry a piece of magical equipment with me at all times in the form of personal jewellery, a protective key ring or a small amethyst for healing. This means I'm on my contacts within seconds and can perform a working at any given time. Or offer up a quick request for guidance if a snap decision needs to be made. Without imposing a rigid discipline on myself during the early learning stages, I wouldn't be able to achieve this quite so effectively."

This sense of discipline also teaches the Adept to accept that he is subject to divine will and if plans are being 'blocked' there might be a good reason for it. The secret is being able to differentiate between self-inflicted procrastination and true divine prevention. Both Crowley and Dion Fortune recognised this as a reality and accepted that even the most experienced of magicians were powerless to fight against it.

"Throughout my life I have repeatedly found that destiny is an absolutely definite and inexorable ruler," wrote Crowley in *Confessions*. "Physical ability and moral determination count for nothing. It is impossible to perform the simplest act when the gods say 'No'. I have no idea how they bring pressure to bear on such occasions; I only know that it is irresistible. One may be whole-heartedly eager to do something which is as easy as falling off a log; and yet it is impossible."

Dion Fortune expressed similar sentiments in her novel *Moon Magic*: "I could not understand why my work should be held up thus when everything was ready on the physical plane ... When I tried to put my resolution into practice, there was a most curious subconscious blocking and resistance within myself, so I abandoned it. There was more in the situation than I realised, I saw that; but there was nothing I could do save wait for it to clarify ... The inspiration would not come; so knowing that it is useless to force these things, I set it aside and waited."

Strict learning patterns at the beginning of a magical career can lessen the chances of making mistakes through ignorance when something more ambitious is required. To some, perhaps, the prospect of admitting their mistakes could be daunting and Bob Clay-Egerton has often found himself criticised for his own inimitable method of teaching.

"I am admonished by certain occultists for 'teaching' by describing some of the mistakes which I have made in the past - and their results. The admonition is because the complaining occultists think that by admitting that I can, and do, make mistakes, and do foolish things, I lower the esteem in which Magic and/or Witchcraft may be held by newcomers to the occult. It may lower the esteem in which I am personally held, but if so, so mote it be! I am not a deity or laity, nor am I a Pope. I am by no means infallible.

"Not only do I regret many of my mistakes, though some have given rise to much merriment. I accept them. It is my hope that I have learned from them. Further I hope that by recounting them, three things may occur. One, that those who hear of my mistakes may be prevented from following the same path. Two, that the realisation that I can make mistakes, usually because of insufficient consideration of the possibilities connected with the actions or words, will have a deterrent effect.

"It may also deter the newcomer from accepting blindly 'the truth' in everything I say. Based on the false assumption that nearly five decades of occult study and the acquisition on the way of ego-boosting titles, grades and ranks in occult groups, must make it true. Experience does not always bring knowledge. Study does not always bring understanding. Age and 'High Office' do not necessarily bring wisdom.

"Thirdly, the newcomer to the occult may realise that it is necessary to continue despite mistakes and regret, even feelings of guilt. The God and Goddess chastise for our own good as well as bless; and their chastisement in itself, eventually, to be seen as a blessing. To keep silent when by speaking you might prevent distress may be wrong. However, it is sometimes best to remain silent after your initial words have been rebuffed. The decision regarding the keeping of silence is and must always be, a personal one, irrespective of Tradition, rules and regulations."

But what of the infamous 'Witches' curse'? Like all other aspects of magic, this is something else that needs to be put into perspective because 'ill-wishing' can be used just as effectively, intentionally or unintentionally, by non-witches without any form of magical training. We are all human and subject to bouts of anger or wanting to return an eye for an eye for wrongs done to us - a prolonged and concentrated effort of ill-wishing can bring about some form of retribution but this is usually considered to be just deserts if the sender is of Christian persuasion, or *karma* if practising Buddhist.

To the Adept, magical powers are as normal as using electricity, the sort of power that anyone can use whether they realise it or not. Random ill-wishing can be fuelled by the jealous thoughts of a neighbour towards a luscious garden, a falling out with a colleague at work, or any of the minor daily harassments we all experience. To Adepts these verbal or mental barbs are expressed in the form of psychic or magical darts.

The magician merely has the ability to redress the balance in a magically prescribed way. The outcome is the same but unlike the Christian, the Witch or magician cannot wash his hands of the affair because all practice is governed by Law of Threefold Return:

'The good that ye do shall be returned to thee three times over
And the evil also shall be returned to thee, three times over.'

The basic tenet of modern Witchcraft is 'An it harm none, do what you will' which means, of course, that if you attack someone for selfish, spiteful or petty reasons then you can expect the spell to rebound. The more powerful the curse or spell, the more unpleasant it will be when the return of service is a volley three times stronger. Most magicians would argue, however, that if one is subject to an attack of this nature, then one is duty-bound to retaliate on defensive grounds.

As Graham says: "A powerful curse efficiently rebounded to the sender is very much the magical equivalent of shooting oneself in the foot."

According to the Corvus Magical World publication on *Magical Defence*, although genuine magical attacks are rare, ill-wishing is much more common. Everyone, at some stage in their lives, suffers from unwanted psychic or mental intrusions which can unsettle or unbalance us psychically, mentally or even physically. "Such 'vibrations' need not be directed consciously at you," continued Graham, "but the magician learns how to protect him or herself against such random assaults, as well as against more consciously directed forces."

All experienced occultists live within a protective 'bubble' and anyone who launches a magical attack against them is in far greater danger than the intended victim because the defences are (or should be) strong enough to deflect most magical assaults. Most attacks, Graham finds, come from novices, or from an enthusiastic acolyte who has been talked into it by an Adept (who avoids any return to him/herself), or a person/group feels the needs to revenge themselves on you for some reason.

Mélusine was a victim of psychic attack in her early days and found it to be a most unpleasant experience. "I'd unwittingly offended one of the Elders and began to experience some alarming physical illnesses which were identified by my new tutor as having a psychic origin. Being a beginner I hadn't developed the superior magical strength to deflect the attack so I appealed to a Higher Law and asked that if there was a case to answer, the symptoms be returned threefold to the one who had sent them.

"Within two days, the offender had been struck by the same symptoms that had plagued me for weeks. I didn't feel badly about it. I took the attitude that if a senior occultist could attack a beginner out of pure malice, then they deserved whatever the gods wanted to hand back."

Magic then is not a simple game of dancing in a circle at full moon, administering a few chopped up herbs in a potion, an excuse for sexual gymnastics, or a plot for global domination. It is based on a sincere and deeply held religious belief that the Creator can manifest its beauty in any form in the eye of the beholder. And much of that manifestation comes in the form of laughter - because put a group of occultists together and the conversation soon degenerates into a general swapping of stories about the pranks and tricks played upon one another.

Whatever else might be written about them, it is obvious that these people enjoy their religion and the fun it brings into their lives. Which is not what one would expect to find at the type of coven meeting portrayed by the media. Most will tell a good story against themselves as Mélusine demonstrated when she related the story about her first solo ritual.

"I'd made all the correct arrangements, acquired the right incense, etc. and settled myself down in the circle to see what would happen. Clouds of white smoke billowed out from the burner, changing into weird and wonderful figures similar to the *Night On A Bare Mountain* sequence in Disney's *Fantasia*! I could not accept that this was not an hallucination and closed down the circle to destroy the contacts but the figures still writhed about in the smoke. I left the room, made a coffee, came back and peeped around the door to catch it unawares but the images were still billowing out of the smoke."

It wasn't until much later she discovered that the particular type of incense she was using does produce this effect and is in common use amongst experienced practitioners for creating 'lurkers'.

"I suspect my teacher used it to demonstrate that you should always be prepared for the unexpected, although she wouldn't have played the trick on me if she hadn't thought I could handle it."

Aeron is also familiar with this particular blend of incense. "I've had neophyte's eyes go wide with fright and then try to push the images back into burner," she added with apparent amused relish.

Brigdhe recalls the message left at a hotel reception while she was attending a summer camp. "The message *should* have read 'Don't forget the incense burner' - the receptionist had taken it down as 'Don't forget the infant burner!'. You could tell from her face that she believed it but joking apart, it does serve to illustrate what the public at large believes about us."

To the witch and magician alike, magic is morally neutral; on a lower level than the world of intellect and imagination, or the vital creative forces of Nature. It is an act of faith which is observed with religious overtones in a specially created holy place. It has no mystical or practical need to desecrate graveyards, sacrifice animals (or virgins), or control the minds of its adherents. It is psychologically and spiritually uplifting. It is neither black nor white - more a case of forty shades of grey.

Chapter 2
The Passage of Time - *Far Calls, Coming, Far!*

The initial difficulty for any would-be occultist is finding the right Path and having decided upon it, finding someone in whom they can trust to steer them in the right direction. There are as many different 'denominations' within Magic as there are in the Christian ethic and the choice is not always an easy one especially when confronted by Traditional, Hereditary, neo-Pagan, Gardnerian, Alexandrian, Wiccan, Hedge-witch, Western Ritual Magic, Northern Tradition, Solitary, Dianic, Faerie, Celtic, Shamanic or Earth Mysteries - to name but a few.

Decision Time!

So just how does one begin a serious study of magic? Firstly, by NOT answering advertisements in occult magazines or joining a group without any prior personal introductions by a member of that coven or temple. This is the area where acolytes often come to grief because impetuosity fails to check the headlong enthusiasm for their new-found religious belief. Embarking on any mystery Path involves breaking with old religious commitments in order to undertake new ones and is not something which should be considered lightly.

Joining an established group also means the novice must agree to abide by the rules and disciplines imposed by the elders, and this can often mean stifling individual 'natural' psychic talents if the coven leaders aren't capable of handling the influx of unexpected raw energy. It may also be restricting with regard to personal expression when it comes to regalia, dress and independent exploration because many insecure leaders insist that *theirs* is the only one true way. It may also mean that the beginner is not comfortable with some of the working methods of the coven, i.e. working naked (or 'sky-clad) or ritual scourging.

It has been suggested that Gerald Gardner introduced 'skyclad' working to the Craft because of his personal interest in Naturism. "I did not know it under this term but it was certainly practised by some Covens; one, to my knowledge, on all ritual occasions and another at specific times," added Bob Clay-Egerton. "The scourge appears to have been used in some Covens but not in others, either symbolically or with force." If a beginner is unhappy with the ritual then there is little point in taking part, because of the negative energy this reluctance will bring into the magical working environment.

The principle difficulty in authenticating modern claims as to the traditional aspects of any brand of Witchcraft, lies in the fact that there are no genuine historical documents, written by Witches of the time. All documentation, from medieval times onwards, which forms the basis of 'historical' Witchcraft, has its roots in Inquisitional material. Hardly an unbiased or objective source - and most sensible folk would not expect to consult a timber merchant on the intricacies of porcine genetics!

Contemporary traditions all stem from the fragmented remains surviving under the guise of folklore. W. G. Gray's valid observation that since Witchcraft saw less persecution in Britain than on the continent, the probability is that it survived in these islands in a somewhat better state of preservation than elsewhere, deserves more than a casual thought. Oral traditions can be amazingly tenuous if subjected to local variations, and in this fashion considerable fragments of the Old Religion descended to the present time. Robert Cochrane believed that during the persecutions the adherents of the Mystery (i.e. magical/mystical) system went underground and joined forces with the aboriginal beliefs of the mass, and so became part of traditional Witchcraft. In the centuries that passed, the meaning behind much of the ritual was forgotten, or relegated to a superstitious observance of elemental Nature worship.

Aeron Medbh-Mara, however, is still highly sceptical of those who want to become coven members. "After hundreds of years of persecution, misinformation and denial, it seems strange to me that as we enter the 21st century, people in the so-called 'First World' want to claim the label 'witch'."

Chris even goes a step further in supporting Aeron's scepticism. "Being a Witch is not something I would recommend to anyone. It is hard work and inevitably means you are laying yourself open to prejudice, bigotry, envy and even, sometimes, fear from practically the whole of 'normal society'. You either have to be mentally deranged to want to take this on, or extremely dedicated and strong minded. You certainly have to be aware that if your beliefs are revealed to the general population, there is the risk of both 'exposure' in the press and even physical attack."

Nevertheless, Bob Clay-Egerton has witnessed a lot of changes since he became a Witch in pre-Gardnerian times. "Beliefs change over the years and so do practises. There *must* be constant change and growth for progression, or decay sets in - although some changes do not flourish and die out. Others flourish, but change gradually, perchance out of all recognition.

"From my knowledge of my own Cheshire Coven and those I visited in Shropshire and North Wales, plus what I have ascertained from subsequent contact with people in their late 70's, their 80's and a couple in their 90's who claim old membership of the Craft, there were differences in practice between Covens. Indeed some Northern Covens seem to have called their groups, not Covens but *Cuveens* or *Courveens*. Practises then in South of England Covens may well have differed considerably from those in the Midlands and the North."

In an article published in *The Bridge* (1994) he observed that what he knew of contemporary Witchcraft came from three sources. His own experience dating from 1941; what he had been told of Coven history; and what he had learned from old Witches who contacted him over the years in response to his writings in occult magazines.

"When I became associated with Witchcraft it was still illegal in Britain. It was a further decade before the Witchcraft Act was repealed. How then did people become involved in the Craft? Certainly it did not seem to be a matter of being passed over from one member of a family to another in the case of the Coven I joined. Or those to which I was later introduced in Shropshire and North Wales. My introduction was probably unique and at an earlier age than most. My membership subsequently cost me dear and certainly changed the course of my life."

Born into an upper-middle class background in 1930, the young man was intrigued by the furtive antics of a house-maid, whilst staying at a weekend retreat in a Cheshire beauty spot. Following her through the woods he expected her to meet with her lover but instead she merely joined a small group of people. After a while he lost interest and crept away. The following month he again followed the maid but this time he was caught watching them.

"Consternation reigned! The Craft was illegal, there was a war in progress, meetings of a clandestine nature were suspect and Father presumably had access to restricted information. It was decided that I be allowed to attend meetings but I was sworn to secrecy on the word of a gentleman - which in those days was worth something. In the spring of my 13th year I was initiated into the Coven. I had quickly become aware that some of the Witches were also members of a Magical Order which met locally. I was initiated into the Order in the summer of 1943."

Unfortunately, in 1947 his occult connections were discovered and he was threatened with disinheritance unless he gave up occult study; was confirmed into the Church of England; and gave names, addresses, dates and times of both Witches and Magicians. Having refused, the threat was carried out and his younger brother became the heir to the estate, although after the repeal of the Witchcraft Act there was some reconciliation with the family.

"It may well be that the majority of Witches centuries ago were peasants or of yeoman stock, although this seems to have changed later," he concluded. "My own Coven, I was informed, had received an influx of members in the 1800's. The copper deposits in this part of Cheshire were to be exploited again and Welsh miners were imported from the Powys Mine in Anglesey. Many were Witches and joined with our Coven. In North Wales some Coven members were quarrymen. I have since heard of a pre-Gardnerian Coven whose male members were all flag-stone miners, and it was said before them, there had been a Coven there of lead miners."

Mélusine's natural abilities developed into serious occult study in the early 70's but it took a long time before she managed to find what was the right direction for her. It wasn't lack of opportunity or adverse publicity that affected her decision, it was the blatant ignorance of the High Priesthood she encountered along the way.

"Even in those days I was very well read, sometimes better than those who set themselves up as teachers and, with hindsight, I seemed to have an unswerving instinct for the truth. I didn't know what it was I wanted but I knew it wasn't the watered down, skipping around in a fairy-ring, limp-wristed type of Wicca that was then on offer. I couldn't believe that so-called High Priestesses were so paranoid and ignorant when it came down to answering what I considered to be simple, straight forward questions.

"I've since learned, of course, that they didn't know the answers and their only defence was to screech 'blasphemy'. I'd heard enough garbage from alleged high-ranking Wiccans to sink Cleopatra's barge not to mention the utter destruction of any credibility I might have held for either Craft or Ritual Magic but luckily I kept the faith. It took twenty years to find the right Path but it was worth it. It's no wonder that I have little time for these amateur luvvies - although I can, and do enjoy working with certain Traditional Craft members when called upon for a specific purpose."

Graham was another 'natural'. "From an early age, certainly by the time I was nine, I was interested in magical things. Dragons were the first magical images to fascinate me. I knew they had a magic of their own and I often sought to draw on it for my own ends, quite unaware that I was casting my first spells.

"I quickly moved on to studying anything and everything in the local library which had an element of magic in it. Witchcraft appealed to me greatly but I read widely, covering such topics as Buddhism, Yoga, folklore, all sorts of oriental philosophy, Taoism, Zen, etc. By the time I'd finished college, I'd come to understand that Zen led to exactly the same 'place' as Wicca."

In her own inimitable style of taking things to extremes, Chris felt compelled to explore all avenues of faith before becoming a witch. "I had felt drawn to the magical side of life from an early age - to be honest, for as long as I can remember. When other kids spoke of becoming doctors, or teachers, the only thing I wanted to be when I grew up was a Witch. I didn't really understand what that meant, except that I knew that it was nothing like the wicked creatures in the storybooks.

"At the age of seven I wrote my first magical Grimoire. I copied spells from books found in the library, which I wrote on individual sheets of paper and used red ink. The pages were then hand-sewn together. I don't remember being told, but I knew that it was part of the act of magic actually making the book."

Although brought up in a Christian household (her father's family were Roman Catholic), magic was a normal part of the daily routine. Each morning the family would ask one another 'What did you dream last night?' and consult 'the *Dream Book*' - a book on fortune-telling, for which her mother had collected coupons from a newspaper in the 1930s. "We would look up anything we thought was of special significance to see if there was good luck coming, or 'news from afar'. My mother also told fortunes from tea leaves pointing with a teaspoon at the symbols, because pointing with her finger would negate the reading."

Chris attended church regularly - she thought everyone read tea-leaves and discussed dreams - enjoying the singing, even the difficult psalms, and often used to read the lessons from the Bible. She went to Sunday school, helped in cleaning and decorating the church and handing out prayer and hymn books. By the age of 14 she had been confirmed but still retained a strong interest in magic and Witchcraft.

"I persuaded my parents to buy me the weekly magazine *Man, Myth & Magic* - I only ended up getting to 'J' because my dad said it was too expensive. Also around this time I was spending my pocket money buying any books I could find on any magically related or spiritual topics.

"My best find was a little paperback book, I could not believe it, entitled *Mastering Witchcraft* by Paul Huson. This really was a practical guide to Witchcraft, how to make your magical tools, how to use them, with spells and magical workings for all eventualities. Now I started gathering bits and bobs, and began doing 'proper' magic."

When she left school, Chris went to work as a clerk in a local factory. Her interests were still very wide and she found she needed both magic and spirituality in her life, and so read everything she could on Witchcraft, Buddhism, Qabalah, high and low magic - and still attended church regularly. She felt drawn to the Craft but by then understood that from the church's point of view, Witchcraft was not seen as a compatible with a Christian way of life.

"I believed then, as I do now, that all religions are merely expressions of the same striving for understanding and contact with the ultimate source of universal being. Having been brought up as a Christian I felt that before I could 'reject' Christianity as being the right spiritual path for me, I had to give it the best possible chance. I had to immerse myself in it, study it and live the Christian life. And the best way for me to do this was to test my vocation in a convent - so I became a nun!

"*That didn't last long* - I soon found that the contradictions I found mildly annoying as an ordinary churchgoer, became huge sticking points, massive obstacles which I was forced to beat my head and my 'faith' against. I was soon home again but I'd done my best by Christianity and felt free to move away from it and pursue my desire to become a fully-fledged Witch."

Angela had also immersed herself in Christianity before becoming a Witch. "From childhood I always believed in some invisible 'force' far greater than myself and learned that the 'label' for this supernatural power was God. By my early teens I began to search this God out and attended the churches of several different denominations; at the same time I began to collect the magazine, *Man, Myth & Magic.* My interest was thwarted when my frantic mother banned the magazines as 'unhealthy' and also my church attendances as she feared I was becoming a religious maniac."

After her grandmother's death, when Angela was in her late twenties, she began her search again as she was desperate to find some form of faith that felt 'true' to her. She began Bible study which subsequently led to her becoming a Jehovah's Witness - such was her zeal that she underwent heart-bypass surgery without blood or any blood products! Even so, the more she learned, the more she questioned. She had also begun to be increasingly aware of an energy flow around herself which gave her a wonderful feeling of 'oneness' with the universe and, believing it to be the product of God's holy spirit, began excitedly sharing her experience.

"To my confusion, others of my faith were puzzled and clueless ... they obviously had never shared this experience. I also noticed that by 'tuning in' to this energy whilst in prayer, I was answered in the most unbelievable ways. My husband at this time (now my ex-), was increasingly furious at his loss of 'control' over me as I now had different views on life and so he declared all-out war upon me, using physical and mental violence. He also used scare tactics by performing a type of exorcism on the living room carpet - anything to kill my joy of life. Eventually I fled ..."

While staying with friends in Holland Angela's experiences led her to reconsider Witchcraft. "I was happy to discover a Goddess rather than just the unbalanced view of a Godhead. Witchcraft is for me a celebration of life - balanced and harmonious with Nature ... I embrace the Horned God, the fertilising spirit of Nature which is much more innocent than a God who represses his subjects with feelings of guilt concerning natural bodily functions. I believe in reincarnation and I suppose Witchcraft has been with me since well before my birth in this life ... but it has taken 37 years to re-awaken."

"As a child I often experienced *deja-vu*," said Patrick, "something told me that I had been to certain 'unknown' places before. I didn't just believe this, I actually knew it to be true in my heart. I also had magnificent experiences on flights over rooftops and fields, which I later found out to be occurrences of astral projection.

"I found that in order to grow spiritually, first I had to eradicate the monotheistic mind-control systems that had been drummed into me from childhood. A thorough study of Pagan (particularly Roman) mythology was the tonic to counter my past 'brainwashed' up-bringing, as I quickly discovered that all Christian feast days were based on older Pagan festivals. I also realised that magical energy was just waiting to be explored; it was there all around me in the trees, hills and fields, so why shut it out in some stuffy old man-made church?

"Recently I found out from my mother, that my grandmother and great grandmother were very popular in their day with friends and neighbours when the subject of divination cropped up. They often read the cards, tea leaves and crystal ball, so maybe occult interest has been instinctively passed down to me from my ancestors - romantic notion or not, I like to think it's true."

The safest way to explore the various mystical Paths is to make contact with those organisations who offer some form of tuition and/or safety net and who impose no restriction to one particular Path or Tradition (i.e. Raven, the Sorcerer's

Apprentice, P.A.N., *The Broom Cupboard, Comhairle Cairde*) and become a solitary practitioner. This is not as difficult or alarming as it sounds, it merely means that the seeker must be totally reliant on raising his own energy/power rather than relying on a combined group effort.

To make it easier to channel this energy, it is advisable to chose a focus which best suits the seeker's personality and puts him (or her) in tune with his own psychic forces. "We're not talking about regressive memory, or anything like that," Mélusine explains. "I'd been a member of the Egypt Exploration Society for years so I was more familiar with Egyptian deities than those of the northern hemisphere. I didn't have to think about it since it was second nature. After all, you couldn't miss my lot in the car park, could you!"

Aeron works in both Celtic and Northern Traditions because these are the Paths indigenous to Yorkshire where she was born. "There really wasn't a choice since there wasn't anything else and the land is steeped in Celtic and Norse folklore."

The Mystic Calendar

What's more, there is a natural, universal calendar for the novice to follow with thirteen phases of the moon, equinoxes and solstices - plus the Greater and Lesser Sabbats. Regardless of the intended Path (which may *not* necessarily be indigenous to Britain) this is a good starting point. There are numerous calendars belonging to various different Traditions but the example in Appendix IV is based on the lunar and tree cycle taken from an east Mercian (fenland) Tradition.

This calendar consists of 13 lunar months of 29 days (rather than the later 12-moon calendars), including the 'day which is not a day' at 31st October, the Samhain festival and the old New Year. Although there are thirteen moon cycles within each year, there are times when, due to natural progression, there are only 12 full moons within the calendar year - this thirteenth moon is referred to as the Ice Moon and only occurs once every three years.

Calendars are of immense important to any Path since they impose a rigid discipline on present day adherants with many tracing their tenuous lineage back thousands of years. Despite these lofty claims, however, not one of these calendars can hold claim to total authenticity - no matter what the High Priesthood will tell you. On our own doorstep, Stonehenge has been described as a prehistoric computer for making highly intricate predictions of equinoctical sunrises and sunsets, moonrises and moonsets, and eclipses. Others, including the Druids, consider it to be a sun-temple and use the holy site to welcome the sun at Summer Solstice.

With the rare exception, true ancient calendars are few and far between although the Egyptian Tradition can boast two fairly well preserved papyri to draw from. *Papyrus Sallier IV* (British Museum) and the *Cairo Calendar* (Cairo Museum) the latter listing the 'lucky' and 'unlucky' dates to chart the important public festivals from around XIXth Dynasty (1293-1185BC) The calendar begins at the New Year (July) and moves on a daily basis through the three seasons - inundation, spring and harvest - consisting of 12 months of 30 days each.

Because of the length of time since the first recording of Egyptian calendars and heavenly bodies, precession has taken its toll. To illustrate just how far we have travelled during that time, consider that the pole star was Thuban in the constellation of Draco when the pyramids were built. Today, Polaris in the constellation of Ursa Minor is within one degree of the pole. When the Great Pyramid was built, the Egyptian New Year coincided with the rising of Sirius and the inundation - by Dynasty XIX the New Year fell in July. This is why, even with precise Egyptian calendars available for study, no one can lay down the law when it comes to exact dating.

The Egyptians weren't the only people to introduce an ancient method of reckoning time; the Chinese, Hebrew, Babylonian, Assyrian, Maya and Hindu all have early calendaric systems. The Greek calendar according to *Britannica* "even in its most developed forms, differed from all modern European systems in being solar-lunar, i.e. in theory, every year began when the sun was in a certain position (solstice or equinox) and every month began with a new moon.

Nearer to home, the Roman Republican calendar was of the Greek type which *Britannica* refers to as "rude and primitive, dating probably from the times of the Etruscan dynasty, but showing traces of a still earlier period". The Roman calendar was packed with festivals dedicated to their gods and is probably the most familiar of all the ancient methods of time-keeping since these gods travelled to Britain with the Roman legions.

The calendar was in a state of hopeless confusion by the end of the Republic and it was Julius Caesar who undertook the reformation by introducing the Julian calendar which lasted in Europe until the reform of 1582. Pope Gregory XIII abolished the use of the ancient calendar and substituted the Gregorian system which has been used in most Christian countries since that time.

As far as Craft working is concerned the natural Solar Year begins at the midwinter Solstice, (near the Yule festival), when the Sun is reborn. Remember that there were *no* calendars within traditional Witchcraft and the passage of time was calculated by the phases of the moon. The following should only be used as a guideline since different groups have their own calendars from which they work - some even following the old Julian system of calculating the festivals which can be 10-14 days after the days given below.

Imbolc (2nd February) is one of the major festivals, or Great Sabbats of the Craft and represents the quickening of new life in the womb of the Earth Goddess and traditionally the start of the Celtic lambing season and the feast day of the versatile Celtic goddess Bride.

Spring Equinox (21st March) is a minor festival (sabbat) which marks the move towards summer as the nights begin to get shorter. The spring equinox does not appear to be a Celtic festival although pre-Celtic megalith builders, including those who constructed Stonehenge, certainly knew about the equinoxes as various stones and other features around the monument can be used to predict sunrise on those days. The Easter festival - the only moveable feast in the Christian calendar which is sited according to the pagan Lunar cycle.

Beltane (30th April) is another Great Sabbat, second only to Samhain in importance. Held on May Eve or the 1st May - May Day, it is the feast day of the fire god Bel and the start of the Celtic summer.

Summer Solstice (21st June) is the longest day of the Solar year. The ancient name, Litha, may well also mean 'the Festival of the Stones' because many ancient stone circles, or single standing stones were used as places of worship, particularly on the day of the summer solstice.

Lughnasad (1st August) is literally the festival of the god Lugh and the fourth great Celtic Sabbat. The celebration is linked to the harvest - especially in former times when the festival dated by the Julian calendar was approximately a fortnight later in the year.

Autumn Equinox (23rd September) known in Celtic as Modron which marks the start of the Dark Half of the year. This festival represents the closing down of the Earth's fertility, growth is slowing and the leaves are beginning to change.

Samhain (31st October) is for many, the most important festival of the year. It is a time when spirits of the living and the dead can mingle freely as the veil between the worlds is at its thinnest.

Winter Solstice/Yule (21st December) represented the 'wheel' or the turning of the year and the shortest day of the Solar year, i.e. the re-birth of the Sun.

The observance of a calendar system enables the beginner to focus on set dates or times for performing magical workings. For this reason it is a good idea to keep a 'magical diary' right from the start. By pre-planning the important days it makes things much simpler when planning around your domestic or personal life. Some rituals may need to be performed throughout a complete moon-cycle and the magical diary becomes invaluable for recording the results, especially if you are experimenting with a new approach. The diary helps you to remember the sequence of events, colours and correspondences, tarot readings ... which, over the years, can evolve into a valuable record of magical/mystical progress. If, at some future date, you begin to teach others, the records of your own experience and experimentation will provide an irreplaceable data-base since memory can be notoriously vague when it comes to *exact* details of time and method.

The magical diary also functions as your yearly *Book of Shadows*. Obviously you will not be performing a ritual on every day of the year so there will be plenty of blank pages for recording spells, new incenses, poems, quotations - in fact, *anything* that is relevant to your new magical persona.

From a practical point of view, the ideal choice is a simple day-per-page A5 size diary that will fit quite comfortably in your desk, bookcase or briefcase. Simple coding using coloured dots offers a more discreet system if there is a danger of the diary being read by other members of the family or colleagues.

The magical calendar mapped out in your magical diary will record the phases of the moon (usually the new and full moons), the summer/winter solstices and the spring /autumn equinoxes, since these have been relevant to all religious and magical Traditions since history began and are compatible with all other Paths. Depending on the Tradition, the important days are the feast days pertinent to your own chosen god(s).

Using this simple method, it is much easier to fit domestic and family arrangements around your own belief. Taking Yule, as an example of the most compatible of holidays, most Pagans managed to celebrate their own feast days (i.e. Yule, winter solstice and Saturnalia) without compromising the family observance of Christmas. The modern feast of Christmas is a mixture of relics from various Pagan traditions, including Norse, Saxon, Celtic and Roman - and not incorporated into the Christian calendar until the former pagan, the Roman

Emperor Constantine changed the celebration of the unconquered sun (Mithra) into a birthday of the 'son of righteousness' (Jesus).

Summer evening parties will compliment the Beltane, summer solstice, Lughnasad or even autumn equinox, without guests even realising they are helping to celebrate a Pagan Tradition. Outdoor torches or bonfires are just as much fun in the summer months - but remember to set aside a small offering for the gods before the revels commence. Not all Pagan festivals demanded religious observance or ritual; the ancients loved to party in honour of their particular deities. It was the priesthood who had the responsibility of interceeding with the gods on behalf of the people - the people concentrated on enjoying themselves but it was still a religious ceremony.

By using any traditional Witches' calendar, the solitary practitioner has something tangible on which to build. Studying the folk-lore and myths of any chosen tradition, one or several deities will come to the fore to become a principle focus for magical working. Accept that it may not be right the first time around and that it really doesn't matter if there is a shift of allegiance at a later stage - all god/desses are ONE. What any novice will have to accept is the need to keep silence about these new beliefs.

Occultism might not be illegal but the clergy and media will go to any lengths to perpetuate damaging and totally inaccurate reports about any anti-social activities they can label 'satanic practises'. Following the tragic suicide of a young man who was convinced he was being pursued by demons, the local clergy and journalists had a field-day with inaccurate statements and damaging buzz-words. The article covering the story in a tabloid newspaper made no less than thirteen unsubstantiated claims that only led to cloud the issue over why the poor soul had taken his life. And just for good measure, Aleister Crowley's name was dragged in to add a further bit of spice. Considering that the magus died in 1947, it is highly unlikely that he could be linked to the boy's death but the press weren't interested in minor details.

Not only were 'occultists' blamed for the boy's death, unconnected church desecration, animal sacrifice and ritual burning were included as part of an alleged occult scenario within the area. In a further article written nearly a year later, the reputable name of the Sorcerer's Apprentice was dragged into the accusations when the deceased's bank statements showed two payments had been made to the business after £2,500 was found to be missing from the account. The SA's meticulous record keeping showed that the boy had bought four books to the value of £36.37 including postage and packing!

As Chris Bray pointed out in his letter to the editor of the newspaper: "In twenty-four years trading we have materially assisted the lives of tens of thousands of good people with an interest in the New Age and the supernatural. Throughout literally millions of transactions not one of our clients has died 'mysteriously' and as batting averages go, that is proof of the *stability* of our clientele not some Satanic indicator." Beginners do not have the knowledge to publicly challenge the tabloid press, so leave well alone.

"It isn't just the tabloid press you need to worry about," added Graham. "In the village next to ours, another Witch (who was not very discreet about her practises) fell foul of one of her neighbours, although she never discovered which one. Anonymous letters using cut-out pieces of newsprint were sent to everyone in the street saying things like 'The Witch Lives at Number ...' or 'You'll never sell your house with a Witch living in your street' and so on."

God or Goddess?

Because we live in a monotheistic society, God is still looked upon as being masculine although the Gaia image of Earth Mother is acceptable to the majority of the population, even non-Pagans, since political correctness renders this identification acceptable. Magic has no need for these politically correct platitudes for equality between male and female has always been thus. Polarity between opposites is essential for successful magical/mystical working.

As the Raven *Basic Wiccan Course* teaches, the Horned God and the Moon Goddess are deities who have been worshipped in many different civilisations for thousands of years, and they are still worshipped today by Witches. Craft and Magic encompasses a greater part of human experience, understanding and expression; the religion, craft and daily living are all interdependent, although different individuals will put varying emphasis on each particular part. It often becomes a way of living simply because the use of psychic powers becomes something Adepts do, almost without thinking about it.

These psychic powers are often awakened and/or strengthened by focusing magical attention on the Solar-male or Lunar-female aspects of the chosen deity. The god-forms have many faces. The Lunar-form is often referred to as the Triple Goddess symbolised as maiden (new moon), mother (full moon) and crone (last quarter) - older Traditions acknowledge the fourth or hidden aspect of the dark of the moon.

Maiden: Athene; Diana/Artemis; Persephone/Koré; Aphrodite/Venus.

Mother: Isis; Ceres/Demeter; Dana; Cerridwen; Cybele.

Crone: Juno; Hera; Hestia; Cailleach; Morrigan.

Hidden: Hecate; Kali; Erishkagel; Black Annis; Tiamat.

The Solar-form is that of the Dual God symbolised as the hunter/ warrior and Lord of the Otherworld. In other words, the two aspects of the God are Death and Life. This 'other-world' is not the hell of biblical writ, it is the spirit world which psychic power renders accessible. "Horned deities and the horns themselves, originally represented in masculine terms, qualities such as virility, speed and strength," explained Patrick. "Horns are hollow, like the womb, so naturally they also have associations with the feminine aspects of divinity, such as fertility, intuition, generosity and the grave. The age-old term for male sexual prowess 'horny' probably originates from references to the Horned God's lusty nature."

Hunter/Warrior: Wotan; Pan; Faunus; Herne; Cernunnos; Mars/Ares.

Otherworld: Pluto/Hades; Bile; Anubis; the Dagda.

Which ever deity is chosen, the choice will be influenced by the seeker's dual personality and made manifest as the god-form in whom s/he can identify. As Israel Regardie wrote in *The Eye In The Triangle*: "Magic does require faith in some religious hierarchy. These concepts may be modified or extended as you begin to obtain results, but at the beginning faith may be required. It is difficult to intone and vibrate invocations or prayers when you know you are a thoroughgoing hypocrite to address these invocations to someone or something whose very being you deny."

But what happens if all the would-be Witch or Magus has experienced are a few flashes of insight, or an unexplained gut-reaction that draws them inexplicably towards mysticism? This is not a problem and even Crowley himself admitted that it was very strange that he should have had no inkling of any tendency to mysticism and magick by means of any definite experience. "It is true that, from the beginning, I held the transcendental view of the universe," he recorded in *Confessions,* "but there was nothing to back it up in the way of experience ... When I eventually learnt how to use my astral eyes and ears, there was no confusion; the other world had certain correspondences with our own, but it was perfectly distinct."

Seeking a Teacher

Finding a teacher is an extremely chancy business although there is a firmly held belief within all occult circles that the teacher comes along when the student is ready. Crowley sent out a magical SOS call for a Master some time earlier, and eventually met the man unexpectedly during a climbing holiday who would introduce him to the Secret Assembly (the Hermetic Order of the Golden Dawn) on his return to London. Unfortunately, our genius of letters wasn't impressed with the teaching methods. "The majority of old magical rituals are either purposely unintelligible or actually puerile nonsense. Those which are straightforward and workable are, as a rule, better adapted to the ambitions of love-sick agricultural labourers than those of educated people with a serious purpose."

This elitist snobbery and obtuse use of language is off-putting for the beginner and has served the purpose of the Thelemic Orders who prefer to keep Crowley's teaching under wraps. In reality, *he* cut through the 'red tape' of contemporary magical orders and later developed a system of teaching which enabled him to simplify his own eleven year mystical and magical training into a much shorter time scale. He reached the stage where he could promise any man or woman of average ability 'who has a germ of genuine aspiration, the essence of attainment within eight sessions'. This, of course, depended on each student to determine the details since some aspects of occult science lie outside the scope of particular people.

"I see the task of a magical teacher as being the magical development of the pupil and if the pupil does not develop their own magic (not my magic), then I have failed," wrote Chris in answer to the question. "I believe everyone can work magic, in the same way that everyone can do maths, whether they have a gift for it is a different matter, but even those with little natural ability can improve and do well if they are prepared to work at it."

Crowley also believed each one should fill in for themselves their own personal programme which meant that they could concentrate right from the onset of their training, the things pertinent to that particular individual. Cut through the waffle and even the rawest beginner can see the sense behind these sentiments - and they apply just as strongly to Craft teaching as to Ritual Magic. Ironically, many of the Pagan groups are less liberal and many a High Priestess would have a fit of the vapours by this advocation of 'pick-and-mix' style of occult study. Nevertheless, even Adepts of long years standing will confess to certain weaknesses - ***no one can be good at everything.***

Chris admits that she has problems in getting a 'presence' to manifest to full visual contact. "I know it's there because I can feel it but no matter how hard I've tried, I can't see the full form. Neither can I see the colours in an aura although I can 'feel' them," she added.

Graham on the other hand has difficulty in working within a strict ritualistic framework, preferring his own spontaneous shamanistic approach. "I've had to discipline myself to ritual but I prefer to work as the mood takes me."

"I'm hopeless when it comes to non-standard divination," admits Aeron. "If we're talking about anything other than Celtic or Northern Tradition then I pass it over to my Magister to sort out."

In reality, many of the books on occultism are less than useful if they are rigid and inflexible when it comes to teaching methods. More often than not many of the inaccuracies are repeated by other authors and the snowball of mis-information becomes uncontrollable. Crowley was quick to pounce on this deficiency when it came to American writings:

"The majority of writers on the subject bleat on from blunder to blunder ... Its objects and methods were either understood so vaguely as to be a mere variation on Sunday School sob stuff, or so distorted by dreams of the dollar or the dread of disease; their information being based on some book purporting to be the secret instruction of a particularly prominent yogi, but in fact the illiterate rubbish of an unsuccessful horse doctor from Idaho ... This illiterature is distributed indiscriminately ... There being no background of education, no standard of criticism, the reader has no means of distinguishing between the best and the worse. He has no means of forming a groundwork on which his mind might build."

On the other side of the coin, there are those with genuine magical knowledge who will exploit the ignorance or gullibility of the novice.

Often with an extremely wide experience in occultism, this type of magician practises what Chris has described as "Oh, er!" magic. This means using magical ability to produce cabaret tricks to impress and encouraging beginners to attempt workings for which they have not been trained. Both Chris and Graham have had plenty of experience in picking up the battered acolytes later abandoned by less reputable Adepts.

Beware of the teacher, is the warning from Raven.

"There are teachers who enjoy deliberately leading (or even more irresponsibly urging) their students to try things they are not magically mature enough to cope with. Some will even use a student to perform rituals in order to avoid a magical backlash," Graham explained.

"One case we have to sort out resulted from a teacher telling a student that she (the teacher) was being magically attacked by another person. The teacher explained that she needed all her magical energy to keep up her defences and that the student might consider directing energy against the third person - of course, the teacher added innocently, she knew this was not strictly white magic, but there would be no danger, since the third person would not know where the attack was coming from.

"The student, eager to help her poor, beleaguered teacher did the appropriate ritual and suffered appalling consequences. Lesson: magical defences do not need to know the source of any attack, they are designed to simply bounce energies back to the sender, and you get them back threefold!"

Some people are able to draw on the energies of others, i.e. in a vampiric way they can siphon off energy to enhance their own apparent magical abilities, or to cast a glamour, so that the victim actually desires more and more contact. This can often happen in certain teaching situations.

"Teachers of this kind usually prefer to have a number of pupils who they can draw off in turn," warned Chris. "This makes it less likely that any one student realises what is going on - they will simply put down the occasional tiredness after magical working, as the natural energy loss after doing vigorous work."

This second case from Raven's file involved a teacher confiding in one of her pupils that she was feeling particularly exhausted because of the magical work she was undertaking, which included the healing of a well-loved coven elder. The teacher told the pupil that she didn't want the elder to realise how much energy she was expending on his behalf, so asked the student if she could, confidentially, send energy to the teacher.

The young Witch was proud to have been asked to indirectly help with this important work, and arranged that at a certain hour each night she would raise power and transmit the energy to her teacher as requested. This was done in such a way that no-one but the student and teacher knew about the working.

Before long the husband of the student realised something was wrong with his wife, she seemed so pallid and exhausted, yet rest did not seem to help. He persistently asked what was going on, and after a little persuasion she told him about the pact with her teacher. The student's husband was also a magical practitioner, although on a slightly different Path, and realising what was happening, forbade his wife to continue with the experiment. Once his wife had recovered, she made careful enquiries with other former students and found she was not the first to fall victim to this ploy.

"We have often had to re-educate students who have tried courses from other groups," continued Chris. "The main complaint we have heard against other teachers is 'I never got any answers to the questions asked'. I usually tell them that this was probably because the teachers did not know the answers, but were too full of their own ego to say so."

Many teachers seem to take on students, not in order to teach, but to gain an admiring circle of acolytes. In other words, the pupils are there to prove just how wonderful the teacher is. "When they ask an awkward question a common response is: 'That is not something that we can tell you about now, you will learn it as you get to a higher grade'- what this means is that the pupil is showing greater intelligence and/or magical ability than the teacher can handle," Graham added.

"Even with so-called 'dangerous' magical techniques, there are ways of introducing a novice to the knowledge in a safe way. If someone asks about something they should be given a straight answer - and if the teacher doesn't know, they should say so."

Not answering a pupil's question is often a way that inexperienced teachers, or those with low magical ability (or even those who have never looked for magical knowledge outside their own particular Path) maintain control over the pupil. The student is usually told that the knowledge they require is only available at a higher level, i.e. they will find out about it when they have studied with that particular teacher or group for an unspecified time. Most knowledge of this kind is freely available from public libraries - it might take time to research, but no-one ever said gaining magical knowledge was easy.

Chris gave another example. "During a conversation with an Alexandrian Witch who wished to show off his arcane knowledge, I was told that the secret name of the Goddess used by the Alexandrians was never revealed to outsiders, but that it was Celtic and started with 'A'. "Arianrhod!" I said. The Alexandrian fell back in amazement. "How can you possibly know that!" he exclaimed, with large round eyes starting out of his head. Never having been through the coven system, I have had to find out things for myself - so I have read many books on the myths and legends of our forefathers, not only Celtic but Norse, Saxon, Greek, Egyptian, Amerindian, African, etc."

"Again, because we've had to do our own research into Wicca, and have managed not to get 'hooked' into one particular Tradition, we have been privileged to have been entrusted with knowledge and rituals of a number of different Wiccan 'families'," added Graham. "This means we can spot a fake, made-up Tradition at 40 paces. One of the best indicators is fake archaic language - and the best training for spotting this is to read and re-read the James I transliteration of the Bible."

Frater Asmodeus was also quick to add his ha'penny worth: "To teach well, you have to know your subject intimately and be able to stand up under close investigation. We have in this country all manner of High Priests, High Priestesses, Adepts, Magisters, Sadhus, Mullahs, Teachers and even Guru Witches. Some are genuine; some are always serious. Some, like Crowley, Sanders and others, play the fool to the general public and thereby attract only those with sufficient insight to pierce the disguise and the camouflage.

"We have, of course, the genuine bloody idiot; not to mention the apparent idiot who is still fully capable of rooking the gullible. Many newcomers will answer advertisements in Occult or pseudo-Occult magazines and, on finding they are being ripped off, will turn against its practitioners. This can only be bad for the Occult scene. No matter that karma will be stored up against the advertiser, or that the would-be student should not have been so easily discouraged, it is the general name and reputation of the Occult - our name and reputation, which suffers."

These stories are endorsed a hundred times over by Chris Bray at the Sorcerer's Apprentice and exposed time and time again in the occult magazine, *The Lamp of Thoth*. The S.A.F.F. (Sub-cultural Alternatives Freedom Foundation) Updates continuously warn against those who would bring Paganism and Occultism into disrepute by not offering the right sort of teaching and support for beginners. The message is loud and clear: ***choose your teacher carefully!***

Step into the Circle

Whatever tradition the seeker chooses, all working methods require the creation of a magical area and although very few can afford the luxury of a private temple, one room can be chosen for this purpose. In traditional Craft working the personal altar or shrine should be situated on the north wall - the place of power - in the form of a small table, chest or shelf. If you are unable to designate a special room of your own, make sure that part of the furniture includes a lockable cupboard or chest to contain your magical tools and regalia. For the Magus, the altar represents the solid basis of the magician's *own* fixed Will and the law under which s/he works. In Western Ritual Magic everything is kept within the altar, since everything is subject to law.

"The objects Witches place in their shrines are sometimes abstract, sometimes very personal, and may vary considerably," explains Chris. "The most common object you will find are candles as most Witches prefer to do their magical operations by candle light in the form of free standing night lights or those held in candle sticks. If, at this point, you have no other mystical or magical equipment, don't worry, you'll soon begin to acquire them!"

The smoke from incense has been used for thousands of years to carry the wishes and prayers of worshippers to their Gods. This enhances atmosphere and comes in many forms: cones, joss sticks and loose incense burned on a charcoal disc being the most popular. Each individual working requires its own corresponding 'perfume' and as the beginner gains confidence, it is possible to blend more personal combinations using loose incense. Be warned that charcoal gets very hot and is best burned in a special container well packed with sand.

Contrary to many contemporary occult books, magical regalia doesn't have to be 'virgin' - i.e. not previously used for any purpose. The knife (athame) doesn't have to be a plain black-handled blade painted with prescribed symbols. The altar need not sport a collection of tacky handmade pottery bowls and tinfoil dishes. Magical regalia can be whatever the seeker chooses and providing everything is ritually cleansed before being used - either by being held under running water, sprinkled with salt water or left in a circle of salt overnight before being consecrated - there should be no problem in using second-hand or antique magical tools. And car-boot sales can offer up some wonderful opportunities for obtaining the unusual.

There is, however, an unwritten law about acquiring magical equipment which Crowley always followed: "From the very beginning I made a point of carrying out the instructions of one of the old grimoires 'to buy a black egg without haggling' I always understood that spiritual and material wealth were incommensurable. If I wanted a book on Magick and it was offered me for ten times the proper price, I would buy it on the spot, even though I knew that I had only to go round the corner to find an honest tradesman."

In setting the scene for *Moon Magic,* Dion Fortune endorsed this belief when using 'ancient things from old temples' and 'lovely old oddments' but also warned of the old saying about that whatever was wanted for magical purposes must be bought without haggling.

Working with beautiful things is something Mélusine feels very strongly about. "I want the best I can afford for my temple and have collected pieces that give me pleasure to use. My knife is an antique Arabian one inlaid with jade, garnet and mother of pearl; the altar lamp a Victorian bronze; the thurible heavy brass and the altar covering black silk. This isn't being ostentatious since no one else sees it - it merely adds to the ambiance and richness of the atmosphere. The ancient Egyptians loved opulence so why should they have to settle for less in a modern 20th century temple?"

According to Graham, the knife is the most personal of all Witches' tools; even when working in a group, where all other tools are held to be common property, each Witch will use their own knife during a ritual. "The knife represents elemental fire and is linked to the southern direction and all strong passions such as love, hate, courage and the powers of action."

"The sword I can say with fair certainty was *not* a Witches' implement. It was a Magicians' certainly!" says Bob Clay-Egerton. "Ritual knives were used, and here I have been surprised by what I have discovered. Not only have the hafts, or handles, been grey or silver, but it seems that in addition to black they have been red, blue, copper coloured and gold; some for specific ritual use, others for more general purposes."

Aeron also gets irritated by those who try to set the rules for magical tools. "I usually point out that as our ancestors used flint and bone knives perhaps we should insist on these as being authentic. *I* use a sword in certain circles for several reasons. Firstly, both the Celtic and Norse people were martially-minded so I don't feel it is out of place; secondly, with a large gathering everyone can see exactly where a sword is pointing which can be difficult when using the traditional dagger and thirdly, being so diminutive, the sword gives me the appearance of authority."

The Sword, as far as the Magus is concerned, represents Reason. As Crowley points out in *Magick*, however, it is only in the *lower* forms of magical working that the sword becomes an important weapon - the dagger should be sufficient. Alex Sanders, founder of the Alexandrian Tradition was probably responsible for the introduction of the sword into Wicca and it is obviously now very much a question of personal choice. In times past, only people of a certain rank were allowed to carry a sword and so it is doubtful (from a historical point of view) whether most Witches would have been eligible. For the solitary worker, there is no one else to impress or hold sway over, so it would be an unnecessary piece of equipment.

In High or Western Ritual Magic, the primary instrument of the Magus is the magic wand. This is the tool which controls and directs elemental air and is associated with the eastern direction; its powers are associated with the god Mercury/Hermes/Tahuti. Most people will want to make their own because they are more magically potent if the user has played some part in the manufacture of the wand.

"Some Witches and ritual magicians transpose the elements associated with the knife/sword and wand, i.e. knife = air/wand = fire. So even these associations or correspondences can be turned to your own beliefs or understanding," added Chris.

The cup is the container and symbol of elemental water, whose station is in the western direction. Water is the element of the emotions, particularly of love, and of the subconscious. "In mystical terms," explains Chris, "all liquids are classed as manifestations of elemental water, which includes water itself, wine and any oil. The cup can be made from a variety of materials including metal, clay, glass, wood and horn."

In Book VI of *Magick*, Crowley explains that in the beginning the Cup of the student is almost empty; and even such truth as he receives may leak away, and be lost. "They say that the Venetians made glasses which changed colour if poison was put into them; of such a glass must the student make his Cup."

Many would be surprised to learn that the Pentagram is considered as a magical *tool*. It is the symbol of elemental earth which is invoked towards the north - the place of power, represented by a small dish of salt. Every magical working requires the use or display of the pentacle is some form as it implies the image of All (the true meaning of the name Pan, incidentally). The pentagram can be drawn on the floor as part of the circle; embroidered on an altar cloth; painted onto a platter or drawn in the air as an opening and banishing pentacle at the start and finish of the ceremony.

As Patrick Regan points out, however, there are many unthinking individuals who shun the inverted Horned God/ Goat's Head pentagram, believing it to be a satanic logo. "While it is true that a few satanic groups have in the last few years adopted this emblem," he explained, "its heritage as a sacred Pagan symbol stretches back much further in time than Hammer Horror type films, Christian medieval heresy and organisations like the Church of Satan."

The least important item but one that produces a considerable amount of ostentation is the choice of robe. Witches belonging to a group will probably find that there is a prescribed 'uniform' but the solitary practitioner has no such restrictions. The seeker can wear whatever s/he likes, providing it is comfortable but do bear in mind that if working in a confined area that lighted candles can be extremely dangerous.

Mélusine has an assortment of robes which are worn to correspond with the nature and time of the working. "These include a scarlet silk kimono from Japan; a blue embroidered caftan from Turkey, a white cotton jbellah from Tunisia and a specially-made Egyptian ceremonial robe. I wear what I like according to the working but it still a magical robe and not used for any other purpose.

"What I do object to, is the insistence of media-oriented Crafters who indulge their need to parade about in ceremonial robes for the benefit of press photographers. No wonder the public think we're barmy when all they see is a self-proclaimed High Priest/ess prancing about in a nightshirt, waving a sword around. The place for ceremonial robes and regalia is in the Circle, *not* posing for the tabloid newspapers."

Aeron has her own devil's advocate in the form of newcomer Hazel, who would be guaranteed to raise liver-spots on many a Wiccan High-Priestess. "What is it," she had asked, "that makes magic work and why are we trapped by the esoterically correct equipment trap? Why are we, as sane individuals, more inclined to believe that to be able to scry, we need that £150 solid glass ball in the Occult Emporium? Will it work better than the 50p glass fishing float at the car boot sale? Aesthetic value aside ... honestly, no, it won't. So why not try the fishing float first?

"While there is nothing wrong with purchasing vast amounts of occult paraphernalia with the intention of worshipping the Lord and Lady with the best there is, perhaps we should realise that even without all of the cauldrons, wands and swords available, you are already doing this. *You* are the essential piece of equipment within any circle, you are unique and perfect - you were after all created by them, and to deny your own value within that circle is an insult to them."

Before undertaking any form of mystical/magical working it is necessary to mention the question of ritual purity and consecration. "This is as much a state of mind as a physical condition," explains Chris. "Simply cleansing your body is not enough. The preparatory bath should not merely clean your flesh, it should be a ritual that strips away everyday cares and worries, and even your everyday self, so that you become your own priest/ess, your own channel to the god(s)."

Similarly, consecration is the ritual purification and setting aside of any physical item, which is intended for worship or magical practice. "Basically, anything you are going to use in your rituals should be magically purified and then consecrated. The purification wipes the object clean of any unwanted psychic vibrations, or 'memories', then the consecration 'programmes' the object by telling it what its new, magical, function is to be."

Whenever a Witch or Magician undertakes a magical working, they are protected by a magic circle. The casting of the circle creates a magical area which acts as a protective barrier against unwanted or disruptive influences or to hold and concentrate psychic powers, magical energy or a special, spiritual atmosphere. Once the circle is cast, the practitioner must not leave it, or even lean outside, as the psychic powers used to create it will be destroyed and negate any further magical working. The boundary of the sacred area should be marked in some way so that it is separate from the mundane world.

"There are many different rituals which can be used for setting up a sacred area depending on the individual's magical or mystical Path." Chris explains. "You will find that some rituals are complex and wordy, needing a variety of special magical tools, others need few or no words, and no magical tools. The ritual you will choose will depend on the magical or mystical tradition you wish to follow, and on your own beliefs in the matter."

It is essential to have an established and well-rehearsed rite for casting a circle of protection of some kind, as there are bound to be times when its presence is comforting, be it simply to keep out unpleasant influences, or to shield against ill-wishing or a psychic attack. Try to orient your sacred area so that you know where the four cardinal points of the compass are located and so your circle-casting becomes a reflex action.

Graham explained another way of creating a circle. "Part of the traditional costume of many Wiccans and Magicians is a cord which is worn around the waist. It is often marked with knots at certain intervals, which are used to measure the radii of different sized circles. The cord itself can be said to represent the Magic Circle, and when worn ensures that the Witch or Magician is always within his/her own Sacred Area."

The majority of prayers, spells and invocations used in modern-day magic are contemporary introductions since nothing pertaining to Traditional Craft was ever written down. Books on Wicca are keen to mention the *Book of Shadows* but as Bob Clay-Egerton points out: "I do not know of the keeping of a distinct *Book of Shadows*. True, some Witches in some Covens did keep notes of recipes for cooking or for medications, but I know of no record being kept of rituals, at least in the Craft."

The most popular legend surrounding the much-quoted *Book of Shadows* is that it was compiled by Gerald Gardner with a larger input from Aleister Crowley; much of it later re-written by Doreen Valiente because the Gardenerians did not want themselves associated with The Great Beast. This lack of real traditional material means that the Adept can use whatever he or she feels fit to convey the emotional or mystical need of the moment - a favourite piece of poetry or prose; invocations from the numerous books on the subject of Craft or magic; self composed chants specifically written for the purpose.

According to a passage in *The Eye In The Triangle*, Crowley realised that it was not so much the content of the invocation that was effective, as the intensity the celebrant can bring to it. On one occasion he recited "From Greenland's icy mountains ..." because for him, at that moment, it became effective. So long as the words can inflame, that "emotional intensity can hurl the soul over the precipice of everyday compulsive 'normality' into a purely poetic spiritual area, above the conflict-laden mind."

Despite all the elaborate ceremony and ritual, no-one can ever convince another, especially an outsider, that magic works. Neither can they get others to believe the possibility of being able to walk in other 'worlds', or communicate with the gods direct. "Until you have persevered and stepped into that timeless 'otherworld', it is impossible to convey the wonderful dimension that magical awakening opens up for the Adept," said Mélusine. "Those who walk away from it and dream up all sorts of weird or perverted happenings for the benefit of their therapists or the tabloid press, never even got across the threshold. It's sad fact that journalists would much rather talk to failed wannabee's than genuine Magicians."

The seeker, however, should be absolutely clear about what s/he expects from magical study - it is not going to elevate his position in the world nor bring great material wealth. It is not a passport to sexual licence or irresponsible control over others. Magical working is governed by strict Laws and the student or Adept who fails to abide by these disciplines will suffer the consequences. Even so, there are still those who expect magic to work wonders.

"One student asked if I could levitate items," grinned Chris. "I asked what he had in mind. He indicated his cigarettes and lighter which he'd left on the mantelpiece. I agreed to a demonstration and then called Graham, who was in the other room and couldn't hear the conversation. When he came in, I asked him to pass the boy his cigarettes and lighter, which was not, of course, what he'd had in mind. The lesson demonstrated three things: a) be specific in what you ask for; b) magic is an extra way to get things done in the physical world, either because 'normal' ways are closed to you, or to boost the effectiveness of your physical workings - it should not be routinely used instead of physical work. It's not for lazy people, it requires hard work, and c) there's more than one way to skin a cat!"

Chris also took a telephone call from a female student. "Can magic make me young?" she asked. Chris asked her to clarify exactly what she meant. "Can magic make me appear physically younger than my calendar age?" was the response.

"Yes, it can. You can cast a glamour so that people see you as being physically younger - it is impossible to keep up constantly (usually during sleep at the very least, your true self will be revealed)."

"But can I make my birth certificate show a different year?"

"Yes, certainly. Take a photocopy of your birth certificate. Tippex out the year on the copy and write in the year you desire, then re-photocopy it."

"But isn't that illegal? ..."

One of the most common questions asked by students is brusquely answered by Graham. "Do I have to have sex with the High Priest of the group I've contacted in order to become a Witch?"

"No, you do not! If you are happy about this, and believe all you read in the News of the World, then go ahead. But this is not part of the initiation ceremony of any genuine Wiccan Tradition."

As Crowley wrote on the subject: "Any religion must rest on revelation, and cannot be proved by reason or experience. It is at once necessary and impudent to claim the exercise of faith. From this it follows that religion must always be repugnant to reason, and its upholders must be prepared to be called charlatans ... Such is in fact the idea underlying initiation. It constitutes the absolute justification of the Path of the Wise, as indicated by the Adepts, whether of the Magical or Mystical schools."

Chapter 3
Earth Mysteries - *I Hear The Water Dreaming*

What exactly do we mean by Earth Mysteries? Is it an overwhelming love of the planet which has spawned charities, political parties, numerous magazines and countless green-eco groups? Is it part of the 1990s mega-myth that the Earth cannot fend for herself and that if world governments do not take heed of pollution and global warming, then Gaia is heading for destruction? Is it really taking part in an 'Earth Healing Day' by sitting in a meditative trance to channel combined energies into closing the wounds made through greed and commercial exploitation?

In 'The Pathway of Nuit' published in *Phoenix Magazine*, Dr Meriem Clay-Egerton took a more brutal and far-reaching view of humanity and its puny efforts to survive. "The planet is shaking itself free, initially to try and eradicate the parasites which are disturbing it ... All that homo sapiens could have produced now bucks, wavers and breaks down, and will finally disappear. It is no longer a bright and proud future, but dark and sullen. The Earth realises that to free herself she must destroy herself and start again with new building bricks. But she can't tell the guilty from the innocent, all will go as they must into infinity. The great pool of chaos.

"In the future, if there is any future to come - if this environmental niche has not been blown apart or torn to pieces by the so-called dominant animal species - what would an archaeologist find to say about us? Would he consider homo sapiens to be a worthy holder of the planet? Or would he be a noisome evil spreading blight, a parasite upon the planet's surface? In all charity he would see him as a dead end: unable to progress further; totally unable to comprehend what had happened to his world. Our present day archaeologists look this way at *homo neanderthalensis*, dubbing him as too primitive - in fact, subnormal! Only fit to be superseded by a newer, more intelligent species. It's modern man who's lost his roots. Unable to listen to the planet that bore him, he has total incomprehension of the silence that could give him new insights into his future."

Could it be that this arrogance of mankind - which implies that *he* can control and 'save' the planet is on a collision course for universal disaster? Scientific fact shows that Nature has already rid herself of one prototype - the dinosaur. Added to this, there are over 500 'flood myths' from the many different cultures around the world, indicating that mankind came dangerously near to extinction on a global scale at the dawn of its history. Are the Watchers or Light-bearers, those, who according to myth, stayed behind to help man rebuild society after the devastation of the Deluge, on the verge of washing their hands of the whole futile business?

The last person anyone would expect to find advocating care of the planet is The Great Beast himself. *Confessions*, published in 1929, stated quite categorically: "Men and women will never behave worthily as long as current morality interferes with the legitimate satisfaction of physiological needs. Nature always avenges herself on those who insult her. The individual is not to blame for the crime and insanity which are the explosions consequent on the clogging of the safety valve. The fault lies with the engineer. At the present moment, society is blowing up in larger or smaller spots all over the world, because it has failed to develop a system by which all its members can be adequately nourished without conflict and the waste products eliminated without discomfort."

But to return to the popular contemporary concept of Earth Mysteries. Before conjuring up the inevitable picture of some weird figure doing something 'strange in the woods', perhaps it is easier to refer to Shinto, the indigenous religion of Japan for a universally accepted and comparable example of a 'living' nature belief practised by a highly sophisticated and cultured modern people. Essentially a compound of ancestor and nature worship, Shinto's silent contemplation of a flower, stream, rock formation or sunset is, in itself, a normal, everyday act of private worship. As part of a national ritual, each year at the blossoming of the cherry trees, thousands of Japanese leave the city to enjoy the beauty of the short-lived flowering. Neither is it uncommon for a Japanese to spend a whole evening gazing at the moon; or sit for hours 'listening to the stones grow'. Inconsiderately, some might think, Shinto shrines are usually to be found in locations of breath-taking natural beauty - with little thought for the convenience of the worshipper.

For the traditional Japanese there is no dividing line between the divine and human since the forces that move in Nature, move in man, according to Zen teaching:

"When one looks at it, one cannot see it:
When one listens for it, one cannot hear it:
However, when one uses it, it is inexhaustible."

Even rocks are possessed of the divine spark and often form part of the intricate designs used to create those familiar Zen temple gardens for contemplation - reflecting the belief that the Buddha nature is immanent not only in man, but in everything that exists, animate or inanimate.

Patrick agrees with these sentiments. "Many folk will instinctively feel the divine spark of spirituality inherent in nature. A solitary walk by a beautiful river, a stroll through a wood in spring, or the awesome thrill of an approaching thunder storm in late summer. All these natural phenomena can make even the most ordinary person hanker for more of these feelings of elation that can grow from these experiences. Many years ago such feelings made me want to discover more of the euphoric 'at-one-ness' with magical nature.

"I discovered beauty of spirit in a spider's web, a nettle patch, a shoal of sticklebacks swimming in a brook. I found it throughout my early years in every aspect of the natural world to which I was exposed. Today, I have rediscovered magical nature anew in Pagan ritual in its many various forms."

Philip Heselton is an astrologer, prison chaplain for those of Pagan faith and author of several books on the subject [*Secret Places of the Goddess, Earth Mysteries - An Exploratory Introduction* and *The Elements of Earth Mysteries*], so who better to define what is meant by the term. "For me, Earth Mysteries is a living subject. It is not just a study of things in the past, but is something now, in the present, and moreover something that involves our own participation: we 'become' involved. The visiting of sites and our interaction with the landscape comes central to our belief.

"What we are dealing with in Earth Mysteries is a recognition that there are special places in the landscape that are in some way qualitatively special. Whilst we may not be able to define this exactly, we know when we visit them that this is true. Whether we can detect the energies present at such a site depends on many factors, particularly the cyclical nature of such energies in the landscape and in ourselves.

"One of the insights provided by Earth Mysteries is the finding of significance in one's 'local' landscape, to find contentment and happiness at one's local sacred sites and, for that moment, to put aside all desire to be elsewhere, be it Stonehenge, Glastonbury or wherever, and to know the truth that you are the centre of the universe and that wherever you are, is where you should be.

"There is an equivalent in terms of 'time'. It is a central part of all old philosophies that a key to living with the flow of the universe is to live in the 'present'. Most of the time, most of us don't do this - we are taken up with 'past regrets and future fears' and forget that there is no time but this present".

Mélusine was highly amused when she was first sent *Secret Places of the Goddess* for review because what was being outlined as a very simplistic approach to Nature worship was something that had been instinctive to her ever since she could walk. "Phil's book was telling me that what I considered to be a *natural* childhood affinity with woods and streams was, in fact, a magical/mystical rite. I was brought up 'pagan' (although the term wasn't in use then) because my father was a natural pagan himself and had no sympathy with church teaching. I grew up going barefoot amongst fields and hedgerows and was woken up at all hours of the day and night to be taken outside to watch some wonder of nature.

"By the time I started school I knew every god in the Greek and Egyptian pantheon but nothing at all about Christianity. I'm afraid the saints were a pretty colourless lot by comparison - there was no contest. My work has taken me away from my rural roots but on reflection I have to admit that when I go to the country for the weekend, there's no difficulty in 'walking softly' once I'm away from the rest of the crowd. It also means that I can't be in knee-bending awe of the Great God Pan - we've climbed too many trees, bloodied too many knees and crossed too many streams together for anything else other than camaraderie."

Graham still tends to find cities, grey and lifeless, but a piece of rock, a leaf, a marsh or mountain side, the flight of a bird, or even smoke curling and twisting out of a chimney pot - all these things can be rich in meaning for him. "If these things don't touch you, well, it's your loss I fear. Humans being as they are, tend to assume that if someone doesn't speak English, then they must be stupid. If an animal doesn't communicate in our language, well then obviously it can't speak at all. And as for trees or rocks - well, the idea that they may be sentient is just too silly for words.

"There's no wonder they don't communicate with us! Try to imagine the world from a tree's point of view ... think about it. It's hardly going to chat about the latest football score is it? But you can communicate all the same, a link is possible - and a view akin to that of another world is available to you. Just for a little effort and the belief that it is possible.

"It is said that the world of Faery, and the world of mankind are separated only by appearance. And according to those who are able to achieve conscious astral projection of their spirit bodies that the astral plane of existence is far brighter, more colourful, intense and 'real' than this plane of existence. It strikes me that we habitually view our world through dark glasses, and it may be that though we are generally intellectual, practical, rational beings, we miss out on a lot of the real beauty and meaning of being alive. The problem may be due simply to attitude."

Feasac is a appellation in Celtic Tradition for 'one who is aware' and it was obvious right from the start that all the Adepts who agreed to be interviewed had experienced this awareness, long before they realised the full implications of planetary vibrations, or considered some aspect of Paganism as an alternative form of religious belief.

"I rather think that I was a Witch when I was nine, though few others would agree," said Graham. "I've always loved the countryside, the raw elements, wind, rain, sunshine, the smell of the earth, the strange 'deep' time at dusk which belongs to neither day nor night. That's my sort of magic. I think I had to do all my studies to discover what wasn't magical as far as I was concerned. It seems that even taking the wrong Path can be enlightening."

"One of the easiest ways of 'plugging-in' to earth energies is to bond with something that reaches right down, deep into the ground, a standing stone or old trees, for example," Mélusine offered. "It's rather alarming the first time it happens because usually it's an unintentional, unexpected and highly physical experience. Leaning back against the tree or rock you become aware of this terrifically strong pulse-beat and the immediate reaction is to move because you think you're pressing on a nerve. You shift your position and the pulse-beat is still there; you re-arrange yourself but the beat goes on, as they say in the words of the jazz-men.

"Having recognised that it *is* an 'outside' sensation, you

should be able to feel the pulsations with your hands, just as if you were placing the palms of your hand against the rib cage of an extremely large animal. It's a simple method of coming to terms with the fact that the trees and rocks are 'alive' with a inner core of vibrant energy."

Everyone is acquainted with Inquisitional accusations against witches' familiars in the form of animal companions but little is written about the Witch's or magician's use of 'totem' animals. "The main difference between a totem animal and a familiar is a very personal one," explained Chris. "A totem animal is chosen for its 'tribe', i.e. if your totem animal is a stag, than any stag that you come across can be a representative of your totem. However, if your goldfish Ivan is your familiar, then only Ivan will do for acting as a magical messenger - no other goldfish has the same capacity."

Way back in our remote history, a totem animal was the one associated with either a family, clan or magical group as a means of identification. From the second quarter of the 12th century 'heraldry' was used as 'distinguishing marks of an individual and his heirs' and a considerable number included an animal or bird as part of the device. In this guise, clan symbolism has persisted from the Stone Age into the high-tech Space/Computer Age.

This new-found natural awareness of earth mysteries give the Adept the ability to recognise his or her own totem animal. Some practitioners prefer to choose their own, while others wait to be 'acquired' by the form of some mystical link. For example, at times of decision or mental/emotional upheaval many people find that a walk in the woods or countryside helps to relieve some of the daily pressure. Animals or birds appearing under unusual circumstances, (i.e. bats, owls or foxes during daylight hours) or sighted more frequently than the seeker would consider normal, identify themselves as a possible totem. Alternatively a totem animal can reveal itself by appearing with unusual or distinctive colouring.

"Often white or albino animals are magical signs of your

particular totem and these might appear in meditation, dreams, or even caught for an instant in the glare of your headlights as you drive through the countryside at night," explained Chris. "If a particular totem animal hasn't made itself known to you in any of these ways, then it is possible for you to choose one which seems appropriate either to your magical aspirations, or something you feel an affinity with. Your totem animal can be from a species which has a physical existence on this plane, or it can even be a mythical beast."

This magical awareness also brings greater rewards in a closer affinity with the animal kingdom as Mélusine relates. "One very early April morning, I was walking the dog in the high fields above the house when a single swallow flew overhead. This wasn't the familiar, erratic fighter-pilot flight - this was a determined little body who flew as straight as an arrow towards the house. I idly wondered whether it was one of *my* swallows returning from the previous year but when I eventually got back to the house, it was sitting on the telephone wire, preening itself. What are the odds of being there just at the right moment to see a solitary bird, whose journey has brought it all the way from Africa, return to its nesting site? Co-incidence? I don't know - but I don't really care because it was an intensely precious moment for me because this particular bird is part of my Tradition."

The Wildwood

Everyone is familiar with the term 'Wildwood' even if only from a half-remembered, half-forgotten adventure in *The Wind In The Willows*. Richard Cavendish wrote that "the uncanny quality of woods is part of the lore of childhood" but for the Witch and Pagan, woodlands are not places of fairy-tale and terror, they are gateways where physical and mystical Nature become inseparable.

Philip Hesleton explained this curious phenomena. "To whatever Pagan tradition we belong, I have found over the years, through reading accounts in books and articles, and above all, talking to people, that many of us had our first experience of the numinous - that living spirit which lies behind physical form - through walking in the woods. Indeed, this is so universal in those I have talked to, that I suspect it to be of a fundamental and archetypal nature. Certain woods have that quality which marks out those special places where we can more easily make contact with the Goddess and the God. If we can allow ourselves to feel and act instinctively, we should fairly quickly become aware that trees and woods are one of these special places."

Philip recommends Peter Marren's book *The Wild Woods,* as an attempt by the author to chronicle the locations of surviving ancient woodlands in Britain. This is a useful guide to those who are drawn to those places which have never known the plough (and apparently many of the still surviving secret ritual sites are in such places). More than just a nature guide, and not just a cold catalogue of forestry locations, the book is 'both warm and evocative' with some remarkable photographs.

"What is happening when we walk through the woods? The trees themselves cut us off from the outside world - they make us look at close quarters - both at the wood itself and ourselves." he continues. "Robin Ellis has, very perceptively, mentioned the frequent sense of disorientation ('The Woods Between the Worlds' *Phoenix Magazine*), even on the part of those, who like myself, generally have a very good sense of direction.

"The wood is alive. As a consequence it changes with the seasons and over a longer time-span as well. It is deceptive in that, for example, you think it is going to be ever so easy to find that particular tree again, perhaps the one you have chosen for a special purpose. But then, when you go back some time later, things are subtly different - the trees seem to have moved and you can be left confused and uncertain, unless you accept this as part of the nature of the woods - their own way of protecting their secrets.

"Our senses become attuned and, as a consequence, we can be changed, usually in a very positive way. We use all our senses, including the subtler ones, hearing the different sounds and echoes in different parts of the wood, and become aware of the variety of scents which can be detected, merging to create an aromatic environment which causes adjustments to our subtle being.

"On entering a wood it is always as well to be aware of the portal or gateway - that point where we naturally stop and, if we are wise, ask permission to go forward. We must always be prepared to receive the answer 'no' otherwise the action becomes a meaningless sham. When that answer is given it is unmistakeable and must be taken seriously. More frequently, however, the answer is a friendly welcome, accompanied by a raising of the spirit."

Robin Ellis also detailed one of these 'special places' located within Sherwood Forest in Nottinghamshire; although normally associated with the Robin Hood legend, it is highly unlikely he ever set foot in the place. Over the years the Forest has developed an odd sort of reputation. It has been the haunt of Merlin and there are numerous folk tales about elemental beings like Robin Goodfellow.

Savernake Forest, once covering half of Wiltshire, still occupies 2000 acres of haunted woodland. With its share of ghosts, headless horsemen, white wraiths floating through the trees and the large black dog that appears on lonely forest tracks. This is also one of the places to meet Herne the Hunter, Lord of the Wildwood, even though Craft legend normally associates him with Windsor Great Park.

Windsor Forest is the *historical* home of Herne, Horned God of the Craft with sightings of him recorded for over 400 years. Legend tells that he was hanged from an oak in the Forest which suggests the 'dying god' sacrifice but there is little to suppose that 'he ever had any real existence in the world of men'. He wears horns like those of a stag on his head and during the course of time his legend has changed little from medieval times. According to *Man, Myth & Magic,* the stories told within this century speak of him as hunting by night through the Forest and across the common at Cookham Dean near Maidenhead. In this guise he is the Wild Huntsman, who rides at the head of an invisible pack of hounds of the Wild Hunt.

There are only sparse remnants left of the old 'Whittlewood', Whittlebury Forest in Northamptonshire, which once covered some 32 square miles, or 20,430 acres. A royal hunting forest from medieval times, the Whittlewood itself is much older with historians suggesting that the last battle between the Romans and Boudicca's Iceni took place in the area. The area originally covered by the ancient woodland has its fair share of Celtic, Roman and Saxon ghosts and buried treasure although now all that remains is a small tract of woodland and clumps of old oak trees running alongside the old Watling Street (A5).

"Working in 'managed' woodland has a totally different feel to 'wildwood'," explained Aeron. "The medieval woodland pays little heed to your comings and goings, being far more interested in 'doing its own thing'. Whereas the trees in the coppiced area would quite happily lift up their roots and scarper (if they could) at the approach of a human. The brooding nature of trees used to 'surgery *sans* anaesthetic' can make even the strongest of tree-Witches blanch. The webs of energy between individual trees or groups, give the impression of you being watched with unfriendly intent. Light a fire and you can almost watch the stampede!"

Those who have witnessed the destruction of woodland will empathise with the sentiments of Dr Meriem Clay-Egerton recalling a childhood memory: "One day I went to the woods as normal and, horror of horrors, all that was left was a mass of torn up ground, and tattered scraps of branches and leaves. I experienced a terrible crying, surging lament for all the life that had perished. Here the presence or essence of the woodland hung like a miasma over the torn remains.

"I was told by adults that the land had been sold to developers to build houses on ... that day I felt totally riven apart, and realised innocence was no protection against the madness of men, and their addiction to money. Neither beauty nor life was of any use in a world where blindness was a ripe, fitting companion to destruction."

If legends and folklore survive amongst the trees, many more traditional folk festivals trace ancient lineage back to Celtic times (some may even be older) and have defied the attempts of the clergy to stamp them out or totally submerge them within the Christian calendar.

Chris gives an example of how these old beliefs have survived: "Outside early agricultural boundaries, the forests and moorland were still wild and untamed. The god of the woodlands is still so much part of our lives: he is simply known as the Green Man, or Jack-in-the-Green, strongly linked to the ancient springtime festivals representing rebirth and renewal. At this time of year the hawthorn (or may) blossoms and 'Bringing in the May' was a custom celebrated up to the beginning of the 20th century. Because of the connections with fertility and sexuality, this custom was frowned on by the clergy. May became 'unlucky' and in many country areas people will not allow may flowers into the house for fear of ill-luck. These 'evil' connotations were recorded by monks as early as the 12th century."

May Day is the great festival of rebirth and renewal; an occasion of great feasting and celebration among the common people of Europe which had been superimposed upon the ancient Beltane. The focus of celebration was the may pole or May tree, and the election of a Queen of the May which is believed to be connected to the ancient Scandinavian custom. The famous maypole in London's Strand, which was 134 feet tall, was later transferred to Wanstead in Essex as a telescope support! One feature of the English ceremony is a dance of the Morris Men featuring characters from the Robin Hood legend - all symbolic of primitive ceremonial magic. Traditional May Day and maypole celebrations were banned by Cromwell since it's phallic and fun-loving celebrations offended Puritan sensibilities.

Re-emerging after the Restoration, a May Day celebration in Lewisham in 1894 recorded a Jack-in-the-Green as part of the celebrations; he was encased in a tall framework covered with ivy leaves and crowned with paper roses while the May Queen and her attendants danced around him. An earlier record of 18th century London tells of 'the black-faced chimney sweeps' dancing on May Day, led by a Jack-in-the-Green who was also hidden inside a framework of evergreen, with flowers and ribbons on top.

Most holy wells were originally Pagan sacred springs which were re-dedicated by Christian missionaries; some are prophetic, others therapeutic while some had the power to work evil. Paying homage to the particular deity of the well or spring is an ancient custom and is still celebrated in the form of elaborate well-dressing ceremonies the length and breadth of the country around Ascension Day at the beginning of May.

Probably the most well-known folk-festival in Britain is the Helston 'Furry Dance' or Flora Dance held in Cornwall each May. In essence it is one of the great May Day folk customs of antiquity according to *Man, Myth & Magic* formerly celebrated on the 1st May. In more recent times it has been held on 8th May, the feast of Helston's patron St Michael. This shift of date and emphasis from pagan tradition to Christian feast suggests another adoption by the Church of an ancient pre-Christian celebration.

Although little was left of oak worship by the 17th century but isolated rural superstitions, the Restoration changed all that. Having hidden himself in the Boscobel oak to escape the Parliamentarians after the Battle of Worcester, Charles II's return gave rise to Royal Oak-Apple Day on the 29th May which was his birthday and the end of exile. It is suggested, however that this is a much older ceremony to terminate the May rituals of Jack-in-the-Green or the King of the May who was destined to be sacrificed. The leaves usually carved around 'those curious heads to be seen in many churches, which represent the Green Man' are usually oak leaves.

In various parts of the British Isles, particularly Cornwall, bonfires are still lit on Midsummer Eve. Originally these blazed across Europe to mark the summer solstice on the 21st June but the early Church altered the date to coincide with the feast of St John some three days later. In Celtic times the vigour and extent of the crops were believed to be governed by the distance from which the fires were visible.

Abbots Bromley is the location of the annual Horn Dance in September; no one knows how old the dance is but its closest parallels are the ritual dances of primitive societies, reaching back to the Stone Age. On the Monday after the first Sunday after 4th September, a group of men gather in the church of St Nicholas to receive six sets of reindeer horns, the hobby horse, the crossbow and other items required for the Horn Dance which is unique in these islands. This same set of horns has been used for centuries although reindeer have been extinct in the British Isles for many hundreds of years, indicating the great antiquity of the ritual.

Around the Autumn Equinox there are hundreds of livestock fairs like the Nottingham Goose Fair or the Corby Sheep Fair in Lincolnshire. These were annual events for disposing of surplus stock before winter set in and to acquire essential goods to see families through the cold months ahead. Local tourist information centres can provide dates and details of celebrations and festivals of regional interest. If any regional events claim long historical antecedents, then it is highly possible that the origins pre-date Christianity since, as Dion Fortune records, the old pagan Britons were in the habit of having fairs when they were assembled at their holy centres for the big sun festivals.

"The fairs went on just the same, whether they were pagan or Christian, and the missionary centres grew up where the crowds came together. The common people never knew the difference. They went for the fun of the fair and took part in the ceremonies to bring good luck and make the fields fertile. How were they to know the difference between Good Friday and the spring ploughing festival? If you want to get on the track of the Old Gods," concluded Fortune, "you sniff round the heels of the dean and chapter because you know they won't be very far off."

The popular theme of bringing home the Yule log

depicted on Victorian Christmas cards, symbolises the old Norse winter fire festival over which the god Odin presided. The Yule log should be brought into the house on Christmas Eve, together with evergreen decorations, and lighted from a piece of the previous year's log, which has been kept all year to preserve the luck of the household. As the Roman Empire spread its influences across Europe, they introduced the feast of Saturnalia. During the 'holiday' gifts were made to the poor in remembrance of the 'golden age of liberty' when Saturn ruled the whole world. The combined festival was too firmly entrenched to be abolished and so the Church finally recognised that if it couldn't be suppressed then it should be absorbed into the Christian calendar. According to *Man, Myth & Magic*, it was only in the 4th century that 25th December was officially decreed to be the birth date of Christ and it was "another 500 years before the term Midwinter Feast was abandoned in favour of the word Christmas".

Holy places and sacred sites

Anyone who has become fascinated by ley-lines will have a copy of Alfred Watkin's *The Old Straight Track.* First published in 1925 it caused violent controversy in archaeological circles due to the fact that Watkins claimed to have identified an ancient system of straight tracks (or leys) that criss-crossed the British Isles and which was old when the Romans came to Britain. First in his native Herefordshire, and later across the entire British countryside, Watkins noticed that beacon hills, mounds, earthworks, moats and old churches built on pagan sites seemed to follow straight lines.

His lengthy investigations alleged that these islands were covered by a vast web of straight tracks, aligned with either the sun or the path of a star. The mysteries and principles behind the ley system, however, still elude scientists who cannot disprove their origins as a 'legacy of prehistoric knowledge which is all but lost' or whether their purpose was spiritual or temporal.

"Ley lines and earth energies can't be scientifically defined because the energy-flow waxes and wanes," explained Chris. "They change polarity, they ebb and flow like the tides and may even change their character with the seasons. To complicate things even further, our own perception of these energies can change and colour them, influenced by such things as our current state of mind, our convictions and beliefs, and even the weather! It's not surprising that the hardened sceptic experiences no revelation in a stone circle.

"And when the scientists' 'magnetic anomaly detector' gives one reading one day, and an entirely different reading a week later, it is easy to dismiss the results as meaningless. The perception of earth energies is unique to each observer. At sacred sites there is an abundance of 'energy' available, to reinforce whatever views and strongly held beliefs we may unconsciously use to channel those energies through."

"Science cannot, as yet, explain how Leys work or what they are and therefore tend to dismiss the whole idea as mere superstition," says Graham, himself of scientific bent. "Actually science doesn't know how a light bulb works either; it has theories about how some aspects of it appears to work, and scientists are more than happy to use such theories as though they were proven fact. We don't know how dowsing rods, the principle tool used in finding and measuring leys and earth energies, work - but we do understand how to make good use of them."

"It is necessary to understand the difference between a 'place of power' and a sacred site," explains Aeron. "Many people have treated ancient earthworks as either 'power or sacred sites'. Without any evidence of religious antecedents or appeal to the gods for their pardon for against any offence, such modern activities are on a par with worshipping at a castle moat or neolithic flint quarry! Simply because something is old does not mean it has, or had, a religious or ritual usage.

"In human terms, a power site may have been as mundane as the boundary between two neighbouring peoples.

Such places became endowed with the appellation 'powerful' and, through time, assigned deities and genus loci (spirit of place) thereby becoming in our eyes holy - sacred. Not only would they become sacred but eventually sacred to a particular god/dess. That is to say, set aside for the use of the deity, or a place where, should the god be so inclined, the individual might be blessed with a visitation. Alternatively they could be blasted by them or the natural forces they control - human presence is not always welcome at some sites of power."

A great deal of national newspaper publicity is given to Pagans wishing to visit various standing stones and sacred sites to celebrate various religious festivals as though it were something weird, wonderful - and totally unreasonable. It would not be difficult to imagine the furore if Westminster Abbey or St Paul's Cathedral were suddenly made unavailable for worship and the National Heritage committee decided to treat the buildings as museums, with access restricted to a fee paying-public.

For most Pagans, the banning of religious ceremonies at places such as Stonehenge is the worst form of discrimination for not only do the celebrants draw power from the site, the continuous act of mass worship replenishes energy that has leaked away. The excuse for fencing off the monument is that the site is suffering from erosion due to the number of visitors each year. Regular religious ceremonies might help to repair some of the damage but in the meantime, the majority of Pagan worshippers are forbidden access to one of the most sacred sites in the British Isles.

For Melusine, however, there is no desire to revisit Stonehenge. "The last time was many years ago, in the early morning around Winter Solstice. The Plain was white with hoar-frost and in the scarlet glow of the rising sun the stones glistened with moisture. It was magnificent and it's an image that will never leave me. When I visualise Stonehenge, it is set in a surrealist landscape of scarlet and grey - and it's one thing the National Trust can never take away with their petty restrictions and their theme park mentality."

Establishment bodies, of course, would dismiss this as nonsense on the grounds that ancient monuments have no connection with modern Paganism. This argument can be counter-balanced by referring to the massive stone formations found on the American northern plains, known as medicine wheels. According to Alvin M. Josephy in *500 Nations*, the medicine wheels were constructed with "piles of rocks laid out on the ground in a pattern of concentric circles or ovals intersected by spokes radiating out from a central cairn".

Archaeologists suggest that these rock formations, some a hundred feet in diameter, were used by the Plains people for religious purposes as well an annual calendar and maps. Most of the medicine wheels are located on elevated sites and the spokes point out "toward major landmarks and toward other medicine wheels on far-off peaks." The Native American Indian has a culture that goes back over thousands of years and today's Plain's people *still* consider them to be sacred. As Josephy observed, it is hard to imagine otherwise. "In their silence and timelessness, the medicine wheels have connected people with the supernatural, the land, and with one another through uncounted generations."

"Sacred sites become sacred by a dedicated usage while other places may have been consecrated for a specific use," Aeron explained. "The building of megalithic monuments such as the West Kennet (Wiltshire) and New Grange (Ireland) burial sites are prime examples. Rituals held in the past would have been purely dedicated to the cult of ancestors and the deities deemed to have been concerned with death and possibly rebirth. It seems unlikely that such sites would have been visited for anything other than the rites for which they were designed.

"A couple of my acquaintance decided to work a ritual at an ancient site in the hope that they would have a child. Unfortunately the place they chose was a burial site and during the following two years they lost four babies through miscarriage. Coincidence? Maybe, but if we consider the generations of 'magical' overlay on the site and the deities to whom the souls of the dead may have been commended, I for one, am not surprised at the tragic outcome. I also believe that if they had no other alternative than to work there, they may have stood a better chance if they had re-worded their ritual to include such things as 'gateway to a new physical life'."

It is not always necessary to go to the 'actual' power centre of Glastonbury, Avebury or Stonehenge to draw from the leys since accessibility and a lack of privacy could make working difficult. Using an Ordnance Survey map to locate the ancient/natural/historic sites; draw a straight line from the main site to any other place where there are the remains of ancient worship, and anywhere along that line will be good for tapping into earth-energy. Dion Fortune explained that the lines of force between the power centres serve a better purpose as the Adept can access quite enough power without being overwhelmed by it. Standing stones trace the lines on high ground while hammer-pools are located on low ground "because water shows up in a valley bottom among trees, where stones wouldn't" to get a dead straight line across country.

Writing in *Phoenix Magazine*, John Billingsley recorded the visit made by Earth Mysteries artist Monica Sjoo, to the Calderdale Earth Mysteries Group to give a slide presentation and talk. Sjoo's work depicts ancient sites and visualisations of 'the experience of the Goddess'; many feel that her art is of primary relevance to all those involved in Earth Mysteries, men as well as women, researchers as well as Adepts. During her visit, John Billingsley escorted her to some of the ancient sacred sites and asked her for her impressions.

He recorded that the Iron Age hill-fort at Castle Hill produced a totally negative response due to the location of the ugly Victorian tower, which she felt desecrated the place "in much the same way as the still-standing church tower on Glastonbury Tor does". The trek across Ilkley Moor to look for the famous Badger Stone was much more exhilarating but the artist reacted strongly to the ugly 'imprisoning' fence surrounding the Swastika Stone on Rombalds Moor. "Again a sense of desecration and none of the power and wild beauty of the land above."

The following day, however, when she visited the incredible rock formation above Todmorden, known as the Bridestone her imagination was stirred enough to inspire a painting. "There is something entirely eerie and otherworldly about, not only the forms of the rocks, but also their darkness, intermingling with streaks of golden ochre. I have visited many extremely powerful rock formations ... but I felt that the Bridestones have a special and uncanny power."

The Bridestones aren't the only place to inspire artistic senses as Mélusine discovered when "purely by accident, whilst amusing a visiting sculptor, we came across an old slate mine which had been abandoned as late as 1920 following an outbreak of typhoid and a subsequent flooding of the row of cottages which had housed the remaining miners. It was a brilliantly sunny day but the mine workings were in permanent black shadow - the *genius loci* had been working overtime to produce a tremendous sense of desolation, even though there were dozens of people on the beach."

Next to Stonehenge, the next most famous 'pagan' site must be Glastonbury, a place so steeped in myth and legend that the very name conjures up the mists of Avalon. Even in Celtic times, Glastonbury was a strange place - an entrance to the Otherworld - and it is from Celtic bards that the mysteries of the Tor have survived. But the mysteries of Glastonbury are not confined to myth. There are the very obvious physical sensations that can afflict those climbing the Tor and weather conditions produce some extremely weird phenomena.

According to Robin Ellis ('Dreams of Avalon' - *Phoenix Magazine*), there is a long tradition that some immense power lies hidden deep within the Tor. Some believe it to exist deep within the Crystalline Cave that lies behind the sealed entrance close to the Blue Pool. The sacredness of the site is also suggested by the excavated remains of yew trees, dating back to Celtic times.

With such an excess of 'psychic' energy on tap, discipline should be the watchword of anyone attempting a magical operation at a sacred site. "Anyone who intends using earth energies for 'negative' purposes should be very wary," warns Chris. "This isn't simple moralising. Any magical intention which is based on a negative emotion such as greed, envy or hate is an aspect of impurity within ourselves - we all have such thoughts and feelings, it's giving them expression which can be dangerous - and aiming to channel such strong negative energies through leys ... Well, let's hope the operation simply fails, as the consequences could be seriously disturbing at the very least."

Many Pagans believe that sacred sites have their own 'guardians' to prevent amateurs making improper use of site-energies. In *Needles of Stone*, Tom Graves cites the group of students who acquired a grimoire (spell book) and decided to perform a magical working on top of an ancient earth barrow at night - for a joke.

Whatever happened spooked the group so badly that they panicked and ran. According to Graves it was impossible to get an exact description of what suddenly appeared on top of the barrow, as its appearance was slightly different for each of the students involved but as an Adept would realise, this is a characteristic of 'guardians' and many other kinds of nature elemental.

For days afterwards the students were plagued by the fear of being stalked, some even requiring psychiatric counselling before they were able to overcome the fear of being followed. This is not the 'black magic' of fictional horror; no demons being conjured up from the Abyss. It is merely a natural safety-value to stop inexperienced or foolish people from coming into contact with forces they cannot control or understand.

But it's not just psychic vandalism that affects an ancient site. "Fires set at the base of rocks damage by encouraging cracking and splitting," recalls Aeron in *Dagger & The Plough*. "Surface fires and fire pits are disruptive for archaeologists and geophysicists; painted graffiti changes the chemicals on the surface of the rocks and kills lichen; incised markings remain for countless generations while litter, broken glass and candle wax pose health hazards to livestock, wildlife and humans."

Natural sites also have guardians which, as Philip Heselton explains in *Secret Places of the Goddess*, can be sensed by both physical and Otherworld components. "Often you will find your eye drawn to some feature, a tree which is distinctive in some way or a rock formation. You certainly get human guardians of some sites who appear from nowhere - the woman walking her dog, the old labourer, even a child. Animal guardians can also be striking - a wild animal that comes surprisingly close and watches you for longer than seems natural."

While on a recent visit to Castlerigg stone circle, Aeron took the opportunity to chat to other visitors about why they were there. "With only one exception the answer was 'Because it's a sacred site'. When questioned further not one could explain to whom sacred nor why. Nevertheless they still all agreed that it was an impressive ring of stones set in beautiful countryside and that they had a feeling that an undefined 'something should happen to them."

Writing in *The Lamp of Thoth* about his visit to the prehistoric Hypogeum on Malta, Frater Marabas described his experiences in the impressive and beautiful subterranean temple. 'The Great Goddess Rediscovered' tells how he was able to strip away all previous archaeological theories and reveal (to himself) the true secrets of this mysterious place.

"The Hypogeum is bursting with unexplained enigmatic mysteries. The deepest part of the site is 40 feet below ground reached via a series of steps, narrow ledges and deep pits. The innermost chamber is a high vaulted room about nine feet in diameter and cut into the walls at floor level are five small arch-like openings just large enough to admit an adult which lead into circular pits about three feet deep which archaeologists have described as burial pits or storage for grain."

During his visit Frater Marabas found himself alone in what is termed 'The Oracle Room' by the guidebooks, standing by an arch-shaped hollow at face level approximately 14" across x 18" high x 12" in depth. The hollow has a curved top but straight bottom. When a man speaks into this chamber a resonance is set up that reverberates not only in the Oracle Room but throughout the Temple. If a woman speaks into the chamber, nothing occurs.

"Archaeologists (working on the principle that the priests of old were charlatans leading a cretinous mass) say that this accidental or lucky design was used to frighten the congregation into subservience and belief of the oracle's power. The reverberation produced is certainly impressive indeed and would put to shame an electronic synthesizer, so great is its power.

"Being an occultist and sensitive to ethereal vibrations, it soon became obvious that a mystical happening was about to occur. I was standing alone in the Oracle Room trying to appreciate how these so-called 'primitives' could have known how to obtain such a fantastic sonic effect when I began to receive information that brought insight from the inner planes. Moving to the lip of rock opposite the reverberation chamber, I pressed my shoulder against the end of it and could see straight into the chamber. This was how the Oracle worked - there was no need to stick your head into the chamber; it was more perfect than the archaeologists knew."

Humming in a deep voice Frater Marabas directed it across the room into the reverberation chamber and the reverberations picked up instantly; this time much louder than the effect of speaking directly into the chamber. There was more to discover - there was an oscillation there and humming again for a longer period, the oscillation built up into a rhythm.

"My head began to buzz and in an instant I knew what I had to do. This overlooked Oracle Room was a mantra resonator which had been specifically designed to effectively and speedily jack up the High Priest's consciousness (and that of others in the rest of the Temple in a secondary way). Anybody in the Oracle Room would have been 'gone' in several minutes. The congregation probably stood in the main chamber and got the side effects.

"Then it hit me. The High Priest wouldn't just mumble any old rubbish; it would be the basic phonetic mantra of the Cult. It would be 'ma' and I began to reiterate this most fundamental of sound concept ideas and the room came alive. Within a couple of minutes I was in a semi-trance state and in a flash she was there. Over in the first chamber, the High Priestess, curled up in embryonic pose. From my position, without altering my gaze or mantra, I could see right into the chamber that was the obvious Womb of the Mother Goddess. For a split second *She* was there!

"It was perfect; the reverberation could only work with a masculine voice. The priest organised the thing but the priestess was the only one who could divine the Will of the Goddess and reach full possession state. Via the masculinity of the Priest's voice, the potency of the sound activated the trance state in the Priestess and she received the guidance of the gods. It was sacred."

Without his occult training Frater Marabas would probably not have been able to 'tune-in' to the psychic vibrations emanating from the underground chamber; an inexperienced person making the same discovery by accident would more than likely have been terrified out of their wits. Despite his vast experience of psychic phenomena, however, it still took about four hours for Frater Marabas to totally regain his equilibrium.

Angela's further experience of these 'earth forces' occurred whilst visiting the inland holiday resort, Volkenburg (meaning Falcon Castle) which is built on and around the only hill in Holland - although they refer to it as a mountain. Beneath this hill are miles of catacombs extending into Belgium which were used as an escape route during WWII. During a visit to a friend's flat located on this 'mountain-side'... "We were overwhelmed by an immense presence of energy that completely filled the room and lingered for some 10 minutes. My friends were literally terrified but I recognised it as being similar to the experience of my own energy flow discussed previously, although of a much greater strength."

Angela was intrigued - even more so because the local people had 'witch dolls' hung in every house. In fact, local shops specialised in them as part of the traditional holiday trade. "I began to wonder - did this energy flow have a connection with Witchcraft? I had been taught that Witchcraft was the Devil's work, but how could it be when I had experienced this same feeling while avidly pursuing Christ's work? And so once again the search was on ... This energy flow is there for all to tap into, I was just lucky enough to have a natural sensitivity and awareness of it and I have come to appreciate that a prayer is a simple form of spell!"

The Earth's Riches

Although popular as items of jewellery in the Victorian era, amber and jet are the traditional adornments for Witches because of their magical properties and their use as 'stones of power' go back to prehistoric times. Crude amber ornaments were made as long ago as the Paeleolithic Period with evidence of this proven by excavations in many caves containing Stone Age remains.

Like amber, jet is a 'natural' substance, in that it is the product of fossilised plant life entombed in the earth for centuries. While amber comes from the resin of the *pinus succinfera,* jet is closely related to coal and more brittle than amber. Jet beaded necklaces have also been found in prehistoric graves. Amber is solar, positive and emanates positive energy on a psychic level - jet is lunar and absorbs negative psychic energy and so protects its wearer. It was therefore logical (if not consciously realised) that Victorians wore jet mourning jewellery given its ability to absorb negative energy emanated during the grieving process.

As a 20th century occultist and geologist, Dr Meriem Clay-Egerton is fascinated by the fact that for over millennia, humanity and quartz have interacted with each other. "That they used quartz deliberately, becomes evident if one studies its usage, not region by region, but over the entire area of England, Scotland, Ireland and Wales. Everywhere one looks there are clear, distinct traces. To people who know its potential, it was clearly no accidental employment of any material to hand. It was sought out for use. Why?

"It is the most common constituent of rock; a basic silicate dioxide, having three molecules arranged in either a right-hand or left-handed spiral form which has the power of polarising light in more than one direction. When light enters a crystal it splits into two beams, due to the differing speeds of the light's velocity being refracted back from the different vibration of the crystal's lattices, and their own individual refracting indices. In certain circumstances, the crystals can act as 'windows' to ultra-violet and infra-red wavelengths. In addition to these scientific points, we may also hear quartz crystals 'hum' or 'sing'. We can also see quartz crystals displaying piezo- electric effects.

"These may well be modern, scientific terms for what our ancestors saw or knew. Burial chambers with quartz kerbstones were commonplace, as were the pits used for inhumations, which were sprinkled with quartz chippings, both whole and broken. (It is now thought that these were used to either keep the individuals concerned safely at rest, or to permit the living to contact spirit entities when they were in a correctly attuned states.

"Standing stones (some of which are made of quartz, others may contain a high percentage of it), are accepted by psychics as being able to act as conductors of 'earth-force', such as that encountered at nodal points for energy lines. If they are acting like natural 'acupuncture needles', then it is not surprising that they should be as pure a substance as possible and with natural powers of their own. Many circles in the South-West of England appear to have been originally constructed with a central point; other phases being tacked on afterwards. A quartz stone, or stones with a high quartz content, will often appear in such a prominent position, having superseded the original wooden post.

"Nowadays, we protect our water with chemicals to make it fit for us to drink, but in ancient times folk made offerings to the guardians of the holy wells. Some were simple things, others valuable objects which had been ceremoniously broken; it is strange how often white stones, and quartz in particular, figured highly on the list of offerings. As the wells were quite often used in fertility and healing rites, then I suppose we should naturally expect quartz to be a frequent gift. Today, crystal healing is still practised; and quartz plain or coloured, is one of the principal stones used - yet another relic of our past."

Echoing these sentiments expressed earlier about 'shop bought' equipment, Hazel takes her observations out into the wild to examine the natural treasure trove at our disposal. "Why do we assume that natural gifts and wonders such as hag stones and agates, have to be purchased from a shop, when they are washed up in abundance around the British coastline, or found in stream beds? Even having found them, we toss them aside for the £30 crystal in the Gem Shop, believing it to be more effective because it doesn't have any flaws.

"The ebony and silver wand is more glamourous to wave about than a bit of decorated dowel, but is it really more effective? Does the fact that it probably cost £60, give as much pleasure as finding yourself wandering down a tiny woodland path, in search of the right tree or bush from which to cut your own wand? Does removing the ebony wand from the shelf in the shop give as much feeling of inner peace and well-being, as would communicating with the trees under their leafy canopy? Does the handing over of your hard earned cash please you as much as offering a libation of thanks (be it mead or lemonade) to a fellow planet dweller? By the cutting of your own wand, you have communicated with the natural realm and thus practised one of the principle lessons of paganism."

Philip Heselton also has his own views on natural wands. "The wand, traditionally cut from hazel, (though other woods can be used, each conveying its own distinctive character) is probably the most basic and primitive magical tool - certainly more ancient than the knife or *athame*. It is for directing energy and concentrating power.

"The way I acquired my own wand is interesting. I had been wanting a wand, but the time hadn't seemed right since I had been told that, according to a particular tradition, wands can only be cut at a certain time of day on only two specific days in the year. Some time later, I was driving to a conference at the other end of the country and wanting a rest, drove off the motorway and found a nice quite lane. I took a short walk and, not far from where I have parked the car, I found myself looking at a magnificent hazel tree.

"I began to think that there were some good branches there suitable for a wand and that it was a pity I was not there in the two moments in the year that wands could be cut. It took me some time before I realised that, in fact, it was actually within minutes of being one of those key moments in the year. As the realisation spread in me, I had this overwhelming feeling that this was meant to be and that I could cut my wand. I did so - it came away easily. I gave thanks to the tree and the wand has been a most powerful tool and is still growing in power."

Whether you keep your wand in its natural state or remove its bark, smooth and polish it thoroughly, depends on personal choice. Philip keeps his in its natural state with very little additional work. He does, however, keep it wrapped up and it only sees the light of day (or more often, moonlight) when he is actually using it. One tradition claims that a wand should be kept wrapped and buried in the ground when not in use which possibly maintains its charge of Earth power - or is a throwback to a practical precaution during times of persecution.

Historically, hazel was one of the main woods used for wands and also royal sceptres. It is found as such in Hebrew, classical and Nordic mythology; in Scandinavia it was sacred to Thor while the Romans believed Mercury to have been given a hazel rod by Apollo. This ancient winged staff (caduceus) 'girt with serpents' was inherited by Aesculapius to become a symbol of the medical profession. On a more mundane level, hazel was used in divination with Pliny explaining its use for the discovery of underground springs.

It's not surprising then, that hazel is still traditionally chosen by Adepts for their own wands, although Mélusine (also acquiring her wand purely by chance) has a different kind. "I'd always been told that you never cut yew although it does provide an extremely powerful mystical tool. While out walking with the dog, I discovered a branch had been ripped from a very old yew tree. It's the oldest yew in the village judging by its size, and stands on the edge of our garden. As daft as it sounds, that branch demanded to be taken home - superstition or not and it's proved to be an extremely effective magical wand."

Traditions which lend themselves to a closer affinity with Earth Mysteries is the relative new-comer on the occult scene, the Hedge-witch - and those with shamanistic leanings. Drawing heavily on the 'natural' elements of communing with Nature, both Traditions at present appear to be suffering from the onset of a fashionable 'mind, body & spirit' syndrome which threatens to distort traditional teaching.

Chris explained that a Hedge-witch is someone who works intimately with nature, gathering plants and raw materials from the wild to work her special magic - magic directed at helping the community in which she lives. "It can be very personal magic, and often involves spells of healing; it may also involve counselling, or simply being a sympathetic ear, or divining the future - yes, fortune telling!

"It is the magic of everyday life. If you go to a Hedge-witch because your broken leg isn't healing properly, yes, she will perform a healing spell and put special healing energies directly into the wound. In addition she'll also give you a comfry compress, or liquid to infuse through the plaster cast, or a bottle of something to sip, to take the emotional shock away and let your own body have the space to do its own healing."

Chris was quick to point out, however, that she is not talking about something airy-fairy and toothless. "We're not talking about sitting around in a circle meditating on 'healing the earth', we are talking about practical solutions to immediate and more temporal problems."

The epithet 'hedge-witch' was coined by Rae Beth in her book *Hedgewitch - A Guide to Solitary Witchcraft,* using it as a short-cut to describe the traditional and perhaps most common variety of Witch. This is a person, male or female, doing most of their magical work alone, who has to rely on their own wits, knowledge and ability to make the best use of conditions and material readily to hand.

"The term was leapt upon with glee by many folks who wanted some sort of official title for what they were, i.e. a solitary Witch," concluded Chris. "It was also used by *groups* of people who wanted to organise solitary Witches - surely a contradiction of terms! - and appeared in the naming of The Hedgewitch Association. I do think, however, that the term is now used indiscriminately without any thought given to what being a Hedge-witch is about."

Shamanism is also becoming more widely known and talked about these days, laments Graham. "Regrettably so, I feel, because we all tend to suffer from 'I've read it in a book so it must be true' syndrome, plus the fact that we now tend to learn everything from books (or computers) - i.e. theory is held to be more important than practice.

"Witchcraft, true traditional Witchcraft is shamanistic in essence. Any book which tells you "This is shamanism" is giving you a very narrow view of what it really is. There is an endless stream of experts out there, all of whom will do their damndest to tell you that their own particular method of teaching is the one and only true version. But as true shamanism doesn't easily translate into intellectual terms - how on earth do you really describe the experience of seeing a leaf? Man has tried to dress it up with Ritual Magic, full of instructions and theory, but devoid of feeling and life.

"Essentially shamanism is unique to each and every practitioner; there may be similarities, but there is no such animal as the right, or wrong, way to do it. Nowadays you will find lots of New Agey waffy people describing themselves as shamans. This is a modern phenomena, with the label or badge being more important than what you actually are. Never mind the names and labels, theory and categorisation - do something spontaneous and discover the difference!"

To Graham's way of thinking, a good parallel expression of shamanism is to be found in Zen and Taoism, both of which going beyond intellectualising and lead back to direct experience of the universe. "Such experiences are not impressive to the intellect but they are real, as opposed to illusion. The shaman seeks to find the deepest connections between her or himself and nature, they are seeking personal spiritual paths which lead from the physical world to the spirit realms.

"Unfortunately due to the way we are educated it often seems almost impossible to learn anything by direct experience. We are forced to study the way other people do things, regardless of the bearing it may (or may not) have on the direction our own magical workings will take. So do away with all images of deity which rise up before you, and find out what it real for yourself. To me, this means sod the theory - do something and whatever you do experience, however insignificant it may seem - it is your own reality to be treasured.

"The main reason why shamanism is popular today is simply fashion - the true witch, the true shaman and the true scientist are as rare today as they ever were. I think it will serve shamanism well when this particular trend eventually lapses."

Because of the *personal* power of the shaman, the use of Power Objects is especially crucial. These Objects are themselves very personal and it is difficult if not impossible to pass them on to another. The true shaman will spend a considerable amount of time and effort seeking out Power Objects, or contacting entities who will either give them or reveal their whereabouts. Amongst the Native Americans, these Power Objects would be kept together, wrapped in soft leather or cloth and known as a Medicine Bundle.

A Power Object is an item which gives the user power or helps to release the power within. It can be virtually anything, and very often will be an apparently ordinary natural object such as a pebble. Similar pebbles won't do, just that one that will have a special meaning for the user. In every case, a Power Object is something which adds to the shaman's personal power, and any item which gives off negative vibrations, i.e. feels unpleasant, will not be suitable for magical working.

"We all tend to be 'glamoured' by beautiful crystals and ancient indecipherable talismans," concluded Graham, "which is a pity because we could find genuine power in a pebble or a leaf. Far too many idiots seem to think that you simply must have elaborate, expensive 'magical' equipment but it was never like that in the old days - the Stone Age when shamanism started out."

It is fairly obvious to Graham that there is a whole lot more than meets the eye to this world of ours. "Even without resorting to a magical view, there is far more out there, just waiting to be experienced, than any of us ever usually comprehend. The dedicated gardener gets much more pleasure and meaningful experience from his labours than one who views gardening as a chore. The artist 'sees' a far richer world; certainly more than the materialist who only sees things in terms of their practical and/or financial value. Lovers also have their own unique view of the world. Contrary to the well known adage, I believe that it is ugliness, and not beauty, which is in the eye of the beholder."

Perhaps it is necessary to change our *own* rosy-tinged view of the world and accept that in order to survive, the human race must surely rid itself of the arrogant belief that its efforts alone can save the planet. It may, however, be already too late.

An even greater danger signal than global warming is the research being carried out by British scientists at BT's Advanced Applications & Technologies Laboratories which indicates that humans may have reached the limit of their intelligence [which brings us back to Dr Clay-Egerton's theory]: "There is no incremental improvement path available to the brain, which makes evolution difficult," a member of the team told *The Daily Telegraph*.

A report by the Medical Research Council's Institute for Environment & Health on the subject of falling sperm-counts led to an alarming conclusion that, at the current rate of decline, the human race could be wiped out by the year 2050! The additional threat of AIDS, BSC and the flesh-eating streptococcus A, may be the warning signs that humans have outlived their usefulness and that it is time for them to be swept away to make room for another species to evolve.

The latest horror is *pfisteria piscicida*, a plant-like cyst that 'snoozed inoffensively in shallow water for millions of years' and which is now a rampaging, mutilating monster of microscopic proportions which attacks both sea-life and humans. As Tom Mangold shrewdly observed in *Esquire* when reporting on the possible links between this 'cell from hell' and pollution: "Insult Mother Nature enough and she doesn't collapse sobbing into her spoilt environment. Insult Mother Nature enough and you'll suddenly be the bad guy facing Robocop."

Chapter 4
Coven Magic - *A String Around Autumn*

Witches belong to covens, everyone knows that. From the medieval Inquisition to the modern-day tabloid press, every Witch is automatically labelled as a coven member. In reality, however, the reverse is true. The majority of practising Witches work alone or with a partner/tutor, and covens, like almost every other aspect of Craft, have been misrepresented and distorted out of all proportion.

Even those few reported upon more objectively by the media don't do themselves any favours when it comes down to representing the Craft as Graham points out: "It seems that all the 'good' witches (here 'good' is taken to mean 'those having a brain in their heads') don't belong to covens, they've obviously better things to do with their time. But for sure, you simply must belong to a coven in order to be a proper witch! We've all read it in the papers and in books written by experts, seen it on the telly and heard all the stories, haven't we - Witches belong to covens!"

What is a coven?

Aeron Medbh-Mara is Priestess and Lady of a Clan (i.e a group of several different covens or hives) in the Midlands. In her book, *Life-Rites,* she explains that the coven system exists to protect and further the Craft and the particular tradition it follows; also for the mutual support and training of its members and, more often than not, as an extended family. The benefits of joining a covenstead include the company of like-minded people with whom the novice can discuss Pagan philosophy and belief; obtain support if there are problems with family or just if life gets too difficult; not to mention access to training and teaching material. "This becomes a way of life," added Aeron, "and not just something we do of an evening to be forgotten the rest of the week."

Realistically, she points out coven life is not to everyone's liking, nor accessible to everyone who seeks it. "There are more people looking for covens and tutors at the moment than there appears to be covens to join. This inaccessibility could be for several reasons, including locality and coven secrecy regarding contacts and locations. It could also be that a covenstead has its full complement of people and no vacancies exist at present."

Joining a coven can perhaps be likened to joining the army and before jumping in blindfolded, with both feet and hands bound, the would-be Witch should fully understand what commitments they might be expected to make. The coven system works in many different ways across a variety of Traditions and interpretation of rituals can differ enormously from group to group. If a recruit wants to join the regiment it means being honour-bound to abide by their laws, customs, traditions and rituals. If a group (and many do) work skyclad, i.e. naked and the would-be witch is uncomfortable with this aspect, then it would be inadvisable to pursue an application to join that particular group.

As a 'new kid on the block' the status of the novice is a very lowly one and, like army life, the first thing anyone must learn is to accept the orders of those more advanced in the hierarchy of the coven - even if they happen to be younger, or considered intellectually or socially inferior by the newcomer. This form of discipline can vary from painting the High Priestess's outside lavatory or acting as tea-boy for the rest of the group. Then there are pages of ritual to be learned by rote with which everyone else but the newcomer appears to be fully conversant.

Responsible Witches are fully aware that there are more

than a fair number of suspect covens and Aeron has her own set of guidelines which she suggests everyone adopts when approaching a group for the first time. "When and if you've been invited to meet with members of a coven, arrange the meeting in a public place - quiet pub lounges are ideal. If you don't like the look of them (or they you), either party can leave without causing offence. Such a meeting also prevents the awkwardness of official 'interviews', the surroundings being more convivial. ***Never*** arrange secret meetings in unknown places, and if this is suggested then immediately be on your guard."

Ideally the would-be Witch should never approach a group without some form of prior introduction or recommendation. A responsible coven leader (usually the High Priest or Priestess) will not mind being questioned about the way their coven operates but don't expect them to divulge the secrets of the universe at a first, second or even third meeting. The sensible beginner will have made a list of pertinent questions of a more practical nature. How often does the group meet? Does it meet in a private house and are there any house rules? Does the group use real names? Is the coven robed? Are robes bought or made? Is there a monetary fee involved? Is there any recommended reading material?

The speed or delay by which an application is processed should allay or increase suspicion. If the beginner is pitched straight into a full-scale ritual working then it could all end in tears. Having explained a little about the Tradition of that particular group, the coven leader should then suggest a recommended reading list, possibly request some personal verbal or written view of what the interested party perceives Craft to be, before issuing an invitation to take part in a social evening with the rest of the group. Any short-cuts at this stage should be treated with extreme caution - if not downright suspicion.

"Obviously one does not take a newcomer into the group and expect them within half an hour to not only grasp each concept or symbolism, but perform publicly and correctly each ritual and gesture," explained Aeron. "Unfortunately, experience does not always come cheap, and there is more than simply counting the cost of a weekend course in crystal use or a mismanaged spell. Time and effort are required alongside meditation and experimentation. What does happen if Circle is breached? Can this actually happen? What would be the effect of taking someone into a badly prepared Pathworking? What could be the end result if someone messes around with incense while people are on asthma medication?"

The fully experienced coven leader will understand the difficulties in coping with what is intrinsically the first steps towards a brand new religious worship because covens aren't just about weaving magic and charming warts. Every coven is dedicated to the god/dess of that particular Tradition, and it can be an extremely daunting prospect to offer up an invocation to some strange and unfamiliar deity.

The dubious covens, on the other hand, have about as much spiritual integrity as Rentokil, basing their whole coven system on inflated ego and a desire to impress. Since introducing their basic Wiccan teaching course, Graham and Chris have experienced countless cases of having to re-educate students who have been misled and mis-informed by the play-acting and posturing of the so-called High-Priesthood.

This mis-representation of Craft is something Graham feels very strongly about having experienced first-hand the damage caused by poor teaching. "Some covens appear to be composed almost entirely of the human equivalent of sheep. Most of them are more or less brain dead and have sought after the title 'Witch' in order to pretend that they do in fact have a life.

"Others are simply deluded, 'glamoured' (highly impressed for no good reason, i.e. gullible) by how the other coven members 'see wonderful visions', 'cast powerful spells', 'foretell the future' and generally behave in a sad fashion - and they copy them! In most of these cases there's a wolf running the group, High Priests and Priestesses alike. No matter how democratic and equal everyone is supposed to be in a modern coven, there's invariably some idiot who, being genuinely less important and even more sad than all the others, thinks this means that they really ought to be leader."

Stepping into the Circle

Circle working can, of course, be a very daunting prospect and the beginner, by becoming part of a coven has a more effective safety net than the solitary practitioner should anything go wrong. On the plus side, working with a group of people can generate an extremely high level of magical energy to channel into the spell and the newcomer isn't called upon to prove his or her capabilities, being able to just go with the flow.

Possibly the most adroit and honest representation of coven working is the book by Evan John Jones, *Witchcraft - A Tradition Renewed.* Having first learned about Witchcraft and the occult in the early 1960s, he belonged to the coven of the enigmatic Robert Cochrane. Jones gives a revelatory insight into age-old rites which have been recalled and reworked for the present day. His excellent book is based on teachings that have passed down through generations, rather than the more modern Gardnerian and Alexandrian versions of popular Wicca.

All covens work according to the four Great Sabbats although some may delay their celebrations by about nine days to keep in line with the old Julian calendar. Evan John Jones gives an brief introduction to each Sabbat but if the student is keen to discover more about the actual working of Hereditary coven rituals, they should buy the book to study, since it is probably the most accessible text ever produced for explaining Craft procedure and symbolism.

Candlemas/Imbolc on 2nd February

Traditionally this ritual should be held outdoors and is the time to drive out the spirit of the old year. This is done within the circle, and after the banishing ritual has been performed the site is cleansed with salt. Today most covens will hold this ritual indoors but the celebratory feast should be taken outside - weather permitting - with everyone joining in for a good time.

May Eve/Beltane/Walpurgis Night on 30th April

This is also the time of enjoyment and pleasure. Being the time of welcome to the coming summer, the ritual has a light-hearted approach, as a thanksgiving for what is received from the circle. Evan John Jones cites the old folk-tune *The Lincolnshire Poacher* being used for the circle dance during the rite. As this is an old Celtic fire festival an outside bonfire would be appropriate.

Lammas/Lughnasad on 1st August

A time of thanksgiving for all that the year has brought to the coven and part of the celebration can be a harvest home ritual as well as a time of contemplation for the season of growth is over. When the rite is completed, food and drink are brought out and everyone joins in the feast.

Hallowe'en/Samhain on 31st October

The festival of the beginning of winter which is the ancient Pagan festival of remembering and communicating with the dead. For Jones's coven, on this occasion only, twin circles are laid out - one for the living and one for the dead. For Hallowe'en the ritual differs greatly from those of the other rituals of the year and is more sombre by nature.

According to Jones, in Hereditary practice the full coven membership should be fixed at thirteen people, preferably an equal divide of male and female. "The thirteenth person should be female, and she will stand apart from the rest of the coven. She is known as 'the Lady' and holds her office by selection and occupies it for as long as she feels able and willing to do so; but she must renew her oath of office every seven years."

At any time a fully initiated member can claim the right to set up their own group within the Tradition; any member wishing to do so should be encouraged and assisted by all members of the main coven. The only condition to this aid is that the member concerned must take a pledge in front of the full coven, to hold firm to the aims, ideas and workings of what now becomes the clan.

Both Evan John Jones and Aeron Medbh-Mara have spent most of their adult years within the coven system and they know that, properly organised, the system works for everyone's benefit. Each new member is carefully schooled and coached to reveal his or her own special personal talents in magical working. Carefully supervised and encouraged the beginner quickly learns to tread carefully onto the Path, knowing that there is that safety net provided in the form of a watchful tutor.

On the minus side, the newcomer who joins a coven with no antecedents will gain little faith in their own magical abilities and need never put themselves to the test. This lack of confidence arises from poor teaching and the limited knowledge of the tutor. It is a problem more widespread than is actually suspected; this type of group is usually self-taught, self-initiated and self-obsessed. More often than not, it means that the leader hasn't received a thorough grounding in any tradition and as a result, the whole system is a mishmash of Gardnerian, Alexandrian, Native American Indian, Buddhist - with smatterings of Crowley. The rituals are complex, confusing, predominated by the visual effects of robes and regalia and are probably magically sterile.

This type of coven can offer little or no opportunity for individual expression as Philip Heselton has discovered. "Probably one of the main points of difference between pagan groups is the extent to which their rituals are planned in advance. At one extreme, everyone has a text and their own part to perform, which they read in turn until the last page - very much like amateur dramatics.

"At its best, I am sure such ceremonies can be meaningful and moving, but in my experience the emphasis is too often on the 'amateur'. Lines are forgotten (I am certainly not innocent of this myself!), your place in the script is lost and, having put down the paper at some critical point in the ritual, it proceeds to blow away. Gathering gloom after sunset means that the latter pages are unreadable, and so on ...

"I know I exaggerate somewhat, but it seems to me that if you are calling on the Goddess to inspire you, then you have to be prepared to allow that to happen. It is very much a question of direction. Do you want to direct the ritual, or do you want to put yourself in the hands of the Goddess? Whilst a set form of words can be limiting to a ritual, words themselves can be immensely powerful. The answer to this apparent dilemma may lie in having a stock of short and powerful things which can be said if appropriate, coupled with spontaneous utterances. In fact, many of the most moving rituals I have taken part in have been largely silent."

Graham isn't impressed with coven ritual - "'There really ought to be as many different groups as there are Pagans' to quote Julia Day in *Patchwork of Magic* and it's a view I agree with wholeheartedly. Unfortunately humans seem to suffer from a deep seated desire to be clones. I appreciate we all have to learn, we all need to start somewhere, but why, oh why, do the majority of us completely fail to make any *real* progress?

"Many years ago we were in touch with a group of strict Gardnerians, everyone of whom had memorised every word of every rite they ever performed. They never varied their rituals, everything was strictly Gardnerian and nothing else was allowed. Despite being fully aware that we were not of their Tradition, they still used to be astonished by our views, and found it amazing that we could cast a circle in a different way to the prescribed method they used. Perhaps that's why Gerald Gardner introduced flagellation into the Tradition, he was trying to beat some sense into his followers!

"When Gardner largely 'invented' modern Wicca, little did he know that thousands upon thousands of people would believe every single word he wrote as the absolute truth. They didn't (and still don't) realise that it's the spirit behind the words and rituals that matters. A ritual is only any good if it does something for you, and no matter how many words of power you utter, pentagrams you draw or invocations you memorise, it's all a waste of time unless it has *real meaning for you.* Witchcraft wasn't originally a fixed and stereotyped system; no two Witches ever work exactly alike. Something I always tell people is that they ought to be searching for their own magic! Look at lots of ideas, the many different ways of working, and from that personalised study seek to develop their own ways."

As far as Aeron is concerned her position of 'Lady' brings the added responsibility of protecting the existing members of her clan from infiltration by the wrong people. For this reason her teaching sessions rarely bring the 'babies' into contact with the 'grown-ups' as far as ritual and magical working is concerned. Having been a tutor for more years than she cares to admit, she has seen literally hundreds of eager-beaver wannabe's cross her threshold anxiously wanting to be engulfed by a spectacle straight out of a Hammer House of Horror film.

Disappointment is often the reaction to a group of people sitting around in jeans and sweaters, drinking coffee - it just isn't their idea of Witchcraft. Experience also shows that many of the so-called exposés in the tabloids stem from this kind of disappointment because the eager-beaver feels as though 'he's been had' and these aren't proper Witches, so he sells his story to the press with a few embellishments to tickle public interest. In the public mind, coven rituals are still flaming flambeau, billowing clouds of incense, stone altars and naked maidens. "And sex with the High Priestess," added Aeron wearily.

Some covens do offer a more spectacular approach as Graham is well aware. "Many find satin robes, perfumed incense, words of power and overtly sexual God and Goddess worship a distinct turn on, much in the same way as dedicated shoe fetishists perversely find themselves more excited by a female's shoe than the female herself. There's simply oodles of "Oh, er gulp!" (not to mention "COR!") for the right sort of mind in many a coven.

"This isn't true of all covens, of course, but for a great many groups it seems that the average 'Witch' is more content to go through the motions of their 'authentic and traditional' coven rituals whilst being about as genuinely magical as a Snickers bar. The robes, the magical weapons, the words of power, ritual dances, initiations, etc., are all forms of magic spells and as they don't know any better, the average coven member thinks to themselves, "I'm doing 'spells' therefore I'm doing magic!"

"No one has ever taught them, certainly not the High Priest/ess, that any spell is only a method, a technique for expressing your own magic. No spell casts itself, no spell is in itself magical - the individual is the real magical centre - the spell is just one way of expressing that magic. Not all 'traditional' (the word is meaningless really) spells work for everyone, and if you don't happen to get on with the particular spells your group uses, you'd better keep quiet about it, or you'll be made to look very silly indeed. Perhaps you find that memorising the banishing rite of the lesser pentagram doesn't make you feel inspired? Well you'll just have to pretend if you want to stay in the group."

Although Crowley was initiated into the Hermetic Order of the Golden Dawn he considered (at the time) the initiatory period an insult to his intelligence. He expected 'devastating, priceless secrets' and was given the Hebrew alphabet, the names of the planets with their attribution to the days of the week, and the ten Sephiroth of the Qabalah, all of which he had known for months. Later he admitted that the basic groundwork *was* necessary, since the aspirant must be 'absolutely familiar with the terminology and theory of Magick from a strictly intellectual standpoint'. A valid point, he thought that the basic course of study should precede initiation and not be mixed up with it.

He does, however, give an insight into the Order's methods of working, which is, in fact, more liberal than many of today's covens. "The oath of the probationer involves no difficulties of any sort; no penalties are stated or implied; the aspirant merely pledges himself 'to perform the Great Work, which is to obtain the knowledge of the nature and powers of my own being'. He is not required to reach any particular stage of knowledge by the end of his probation; he is free to choose such practises as appeal to him; and, provided that his record shows that he has devoted a reasonable proportion of his spare time to the Work, he is unhesitatingly passed to the degree of neophyte. It sounds as if it were impossible for anyone to fail. Yet, actually, only eight per cent manage to get through the year of probation. The reason is that no sooner does a man make up his mind to enter the Path of the Wise than he rouses automatically the supreme hostility of every force, internal or external, in his sphere."

Chris endorsed those sentiments. "We have noticed ourselves how true this is. Initiations, major commitments, or decisions made on your magical path are often heralded by, or followed by various upheavals in your normal, everyday life. Anything that can go wrong, probably will - this can include physical accidents, rows with your loving spouse, trouble at work, a large bill suddenly demanding payment. It is often as if, because you are making a new start in a magical way, many aspects of your old life also have to be cleared away, or cleaned up and attended to. Unfortunately, it all usually happens at once, just when you are feeling especially vulnerable."

Despite his liberal views on training, Crowley would have disapproved of 'the extended family' concept of modern covens, maintaining that members should not know each other save officially and have as little to do with each other as possible. Theoretically, he believed that a member should only know his introducer and those whom he himself introduces. Today, Pagan groups interact with one another at conferences and camps but this doesn't seem to present much of a problem.

Like Aeron, Janval Phagan is a High Priestess: "Some groups, especially those who meet irregularly, or which contain those of varying degrees of awareness or skill, use a method of gauging and balancing energies called 'attunement'. This often involves everyone holding hands in a Circle in order to collectively both 'ground and centre', and give permission to be in each others space and aura.

"Others, like ourselves, use one-to-one physical contact (hugs) before entering Circle to give and receive permission to enter the aura, exchange energies - and to establish/renew bonds of friendship, love and trust between members of the same group. These hugs are not confined to opposite sex members, but are exchanged across the board, male to male, female to male, Initiate to pre-Initiate. Some males feel uncomfortable at first with such overt physical contact, but with time and effort come to give and receive it in the manner in which it is meant.

"When two or more covens or groups (who meet regularly on their own), come together for a festival or other gathering, the separate energies of the groups are almost palpable and one can, with a little observation, tell to which group any individual 'belongs'. Their aura and energies are those of their group or coven - however, after a few minutes they and the people with whom they make physical contact, will balance their energies. No matter what their personal likes or dislikes, effects of the day (row with the boss/husband/wife), all is set aside for the work in hand."

Skyclad:

The decision to join a group that practises ritual nudity should be the free choice of the individual concerned but if that happens to be their tradition, the novice must conform to the dictates of the coven elders. The tabloid press is obsessed with Witches working naked but it is an inescapable fact that at some stage during a Witch's life, s/he, alone or in a group, will chose to undertake a magical ritual minus his/her clothes.

For the true Witch this is as normal as breathing but it doesn't mean that the removal of one's clothes for a magical purpose is tantamount to orgy.

Philip Heselton giving his 'Thoughts & Feelings on Going Skyclad' in *Phoenix Magazine* wrote: "I have often experienced the walk over fields and through wild woods to some secret sacred site, perhaps with a companion in the Old Ways, sometimes with several. Having prepared the site for the coming ritual we, almost instinctively, remove our clothes. No longer (if I ever did), do I feel in the slightest bit embarrassed by this: it is merely the final part of the preparation. But immediately I take off my clothes, a great joy seems to surge through me. Even the slightest breeze can be felt on the skin - there is a freedom which is impossible to describe to those who have never experienced it but, above all, there is a feeling of *rightness.* In this natural place, all I am doing is removing those trappings of civilisation for a brief period and drawing closer to the beings who surround me in that natural site.

"As one who has had some contact with what might be called 'traditional Witchcraft', I am aware that some traditions do not practice nudity. Equally certain, however, others do. Going skyclad is emphatically not, as is often stated, the invention of Gerald Gardner, who was a practising naturist. A careful reading of his books reveals that the New Forest witches with whom he first made contact in 1938 practised ritual nudity. Also Leland, in his book *Aradia*, or the *Gospel of the Witches* (1890), makes it quite clear that nakedness was a central part of their rites: "And as the sign that ye are truly free, ye shall be naked in your rites ..."

"I am not asking anyone to change the way they do things, but if they have not gone to some remote spot and removed their clothes at midnight under a full moon as an act of worship of the Goddess, then I would suggest that they might be missing something."

'Robed or Skyclad?' - esoteric author Bernard King joined in the *Phoenix* debate. "This special attire, or lack of it, is an added ritual means of setting the mind apart from mundane tasks and obligations, and persuading it to recognise the occasion as something apart form normal activity. The two alternatives, simply stated, are robes or nothing.

"Robes are the ideal solution to working out of doors in either (or both) the British climate or an urban environment. Many of today's pagans are urban dwellers, often with only a small, overlooked patio on which to practice outdoor rites and nudity would shock the neighbours even more than working robes. True they don't have to look but that hasn't prevented the floods of letters complaining about sex and violence from TV viewers, who could change channels much more easily than changing the directions in which their windows face.

"Those working indoors also find robes appropriate, though for difference reasons. Robes cover physical scars and imperfections, and will offer confidence to those who remain conscious of their bodies. Robes provide a means of dressing apart for ritual magic or worship - but they are also a means of instituting a species of class difference.

"Some will have used the old sheet method to make their robes. Other will have had them made out of crushed velvet or some other exotic material by a girlfriend or even a professional seamstress or tailor. Even old-sheeters may have bought some gold braid to tart up the plainness of their ritual garb. A situation thus arises whereby the mind may be diverted by mundane considerations of envy or pride from the real purpose at hand, even in the best-cast of circles.

"The astute leader will be able to avoid this problem by specifying the material and cut of the groups' robes. Ideally there will be a member of the group who can make the robes for the others, and sufficient funds to have bought the material in bulk. Yet all this care will go for nothing if there is no guidance as to jewellery to be worn with the robes - which can cause the same problems which common ritual dress has sought to circumvent.

"Another problem with robes arises when we consider that the majority of rituals take place in smallish indoor rooms.

Nobody intends to let the hem brush against that quarter- or altar-candle, but it can still happen This is not to say that working robed is either a bad thing or impractical. It can work well in a sensibly-planned environment and is, for many pagans, the only viable option. For others, however, there is a real alternative.

"Working skyclad gets round the fire hazards; the possibility of envy and the wrong argument, which is that the power is found within us and robes hamper its release. If this were true, a thin cotton sheet would be waterproof. Power will flow when it's there, whether through polycotton, paper or cast-iron. Another popular objection comes from men: "I might get an embarrassing erection." Honest - it simply doesn't happen. The unclad human body is rarely erotic. Hardly any of them are perfect, despite the examples on page three of some tabloids. And, in the ritual context, being skyclad is exactly the same as wearing robes because it is a means of dressing apart. It is mostly our unfortunate confusion of nudity with eroticism which has created the barriers to its acceptance."

Talking about 'sky-clad' working automatically leads to the question of scandalous goings-on of a sexual nature in coven circles. The most notorious being, of course, the initiation rites which are the staple diet of the Sunday tabloids. In a serious group, the initiation is no more than a ceremony formally welcoming the new Witch into the next stage of learning, usually having been a neophyte for a year and day. *Witchcraft - A Tradition Renewed* describes such a coven celebration of the Hereditary Craft during which the new Witch carries a lighted candle into the Circle representing the past life. The candle is then extinguished, with the initiate relighting it from the Circle fire to symbolise a new life 'your chosen one, one that you have freely selected and freely entered into'.

Again both Evan John Jones and Aeron Medbh-Mara are practitioners of Old Craft (i.e. pre-Gardnerian/Alexandrian) and their respective books *Witchcraft - A Tradition Renewed* and *Life-Rites,* give an honest and inside appraisal of the rituals and teaching of their own particular Traditions. Both are used to strict coven administration but this does not detract from their enjoyment of Craft working or passing on the thrill of learning to their fellow members. Unfortunately, these are not the examples that have been brought to Graham's notice in his capacity as a Craft tutor.

"Hierarchy is a powerful element of a large number of covens: who's which grade, who's the most psychic (or who boasts the most) and who's got the best body during sky-clad rituals. The High Priesthood definitely knows how to impress and/or frighten the lesser members of their group. The same methods are used to attract potential members into the coven to start with, though at this stage they tend to concentrate on the carrot as opposed to the whip. 'Ah,' they will say to you, in all seriousness and with heavy occult overtones, 'Of course, if you were initiated, we'd be able to teach you all sorts of things!' Curiosity and gullibility often go hand in hand. Once you've been initiated, you'll then find it's not so easy to withdraw from this type of group as it was to join it.

"What they didn't tell you when they were so humbly offering initiation was that the 'all sorts' that they're going to teach you after initiation, largely consists of a pile of wordy rituals that they wrote themselves a few years ago, plus some other unattributed bits they copied out of a book last week which they hope you haven't read.

"The High Priesthood will use any method they can maintain to boost their authority over their coven, including sex. It's not unheard of for a High Priest/ess to have sex with members of the group in order to keep them under their control. Boasts of magical power and hidden knowledge (which they might possibly reveal but only to the right person), are also common. Whatever else they might be, this kind of High Priest/ess are definitely good actors."

While researching material for this book, the author was introduced to Simon and Emma, a young married couple from

Wiltshire who had fallen under the influence of a similar High Priest and Priestess. An attractive, intelligent pair, they had originally been working solitary but after embarking on a distance learning course they were invited to take part in an initiation ceremony.

Curiosity and gullibility certainly took over and they found themselves in a situation from which they found it impossible to escape. Neither had any problem in undergoing the sky-clad ritual but as a happily married couple they declined the offer of a sexually explicit Great Rite which involved intercourse with the High Priest/ess as part of a combined First and Second Degree. "I said I felt I couldn't do anything to hurt my husband and that we would both prefer the First Degree ordinary initiation," said Emma. "To which he [the High Priest] said 'That's fine, there's no pressure. That's okay by me if you want a half-baked job'."

With hindsight both Simon and Emma now realised that in their eagerness to be accepted as 'real Witches' they allowed themselves to be convinced that it wouldn't be a 'proper' initiation if they didn't go through with the ritual. "I *wanted* to be accepted, I *wanted* to be with the Horned God. I asked whether or not we could bring the ritual to that conclusion but invoke the gods in us, so that Simon and I could celebrate together." The response was that it wouldn't be appropriate, despite the fact that the couple were being initiated at the same time.

The sexual athletics for both of them involved blindfolding, binding, scourging and branding with Emma feeling such distress and discomfort that she was totally unable to maintain her trance state because of the chains digging into her back. "I wasn't prepared," continued Emma tearfully. "I did not receive the Goddess into me but he [the High Priest] still proceeded with sexual intercourse. Even though, I would have thought, even outside a magical circle, it would have been rather obvious that I wasn't properly prepared for it."

Neither Simon nor Emma are stupid people. They'd spent a long time as solitary witches and were extremely well-read in Craft lore. So much so that they spotted anomalies in parts of the course but they were so desperate for some way of endorsing their commitment to the God/dess that they fell prey to an unscrupulous High Priest who said 'Come and be one of us! I offer you knowledge.'

Needless to say, the aftermath of the initiation caused serious damage to their marriage. "I can't describe how I felt," said Emma. "It was guilt, humiliation, disappointment in myself, disappointment in them. When Simon and I got home things were so bad between us that I telephoned the High Priest and told him how distressed we both were. He told me that I should rise above it, that it was all about caring and sharing, which made me feel that it was me that was at fault, that I couldn't have given enough."

"Neither of them [both the High Priest and Priestess involved] have any idea of the damage they've caused and we're obviously not the only ones," added Simon. "We feel that it is important to stress the potential damage that can be caused by incorrect teachings and practises carried out in the name of the Craft. After undergoing our initiations we were even more disturbed to hear that they expected us to open our marriage to include them."

At the conclusion of Simon's initiation he was marked on the forehead by the High Priestess and told that having been joined to her as one of her Priests, he would be expected to go to her without questioning. Simon found this deeply distressing as it was an unexpected intrusion into his marriage, and one which he refused absolutely to accept, even though the demand was continued via 'phone calls from the High Priestess for some time after he and Emma had returned home.

The High Priest approached the subject from a different angle insisting that Emma was sworn to him during initiation which included a promise to retake her vows with the High Priest every year. Upon her refusal to accept this, she was told that she was 'obviously still bound by Christian morality' and made to feel once again, that she was failing as a true Witch.

"It made me so angry when I heard about the way this couple had been treated," stormed the normally placid Chris who was, by now, spitting feathers. "And as for referring to the symbolic Great Rite as a 'half-baked job' - ***words fail me!*** This is obvious someone who doesn't know his stang from his athame and should never, *never* be allowed to peddle this sort of trash as genuine coven working. It's this sort of garbage that brings real Craft into disrepute."

Melusine found it "... unforgivable that anyone should be left feeling this way after what should have been be the experience of a lifetime. The sexual aspects of the affair are irrelevant. Initiation, and it doesn't matter whether it's self- or group initiation, should leave the participants with the sensation of riding on the tail of the Hale-Bopp comet. The fact that they only felt humiliated and degraded merely illustrates what unmitigated cowboys this so-called High Priest and his cohort must be in using sex by coercion for their own gratification. Renegades like this should be shunned by any genuine Adept."

Ever the stickler for coven etiquette, Aeron debunked the claim that it was inappropriate for the couple to invoke the gods into themselves. "In my rather extensive experience, I have *never* known the Great Rite to be performed at a First or Second Degree ritual. Neither have I come across a combined First and Second Degree ritual [which Simon and Emma were told they had undergone] since a beginner wouldn't be schooled enough to take a Second Degree. And if a couple are taking the Third Degree at the same ceremony then it would be *normal* practice for them to perform the Great Rite together - privately."

"I must have had hundreds of people come to me with complaints over the years, about 'Wiccan Elders' who insist that beginners must be sexually initiated in order to enter the coven," Graham added. "If sexual initiation is what you're after then that's fine, but you don't need Witchcraft as an excuse to have sex. True power can be passed sexually but it isn't the only way no matter what anyone else may tell you.

And anyone who does insist that sexual initiation is essential is on a power trip. They are lying and just like touching up pretty women (or young men) in a strange ritualistic manner. The number of people out there who are simply on power trips in unbelievable and, like the pair to whom Simon and Emma refer, an awful lot of them are 'leaders' of covens.

"If, however, the idea of being stripped naked in front of a group of complete strangers whilst being blindfolded, tied-up and terrified, not to mention screwed stupid by the High Priest, gives you a thrill, then so be it. Just don't kid yourself that you're only doing it for the sake of the Craft. There must be some good covens out there, but if you really insist on joining a group, do try and find out what you're getting into. Even ask them *why they want you* before you turn up for initiation only to discover the press, a truckload of complete strangers, and a High Priest with an undisguised swelling between his legs."

Fortunately, despite their unpleasant experiences, Simon and Emma never lost their faith in the God/dess and having coped with a long period of personal distress they are now working with an experienced Craft healer. Because both found it impossible to work together with any conviction after their ordeal and their magical working suffered considerably as a result. To their credit, there are no excuses that drugs or drink had been the cause of their humiliation and both freely admit that they should have read the warning signs long before they got themselves into a situation they just couldn't handle.

There could, of course, have been an entirely different outcome. If the couple had been less committed to Craft their story would probably have appeared in the tabloid press as another example of 'satanic survivors'. It should be stressed that neither the High Priest or Priestess have committed any illegal act and the initiation was carried out between consenting adults BUT - and it's a very large **BUT** - the manipulative mind-games employed by this pair to coerce a normal, decent, happily married couple to indulge in tawdry bedroom athletics is *not* accepted Craft practice.

Since Simon and Emma took their courage in both hands and told their story to the *Comhairli Cairde,* several people have attempted to trace the antecedents of the High Priest/ess involved through Craft contacts. To date, no one can be found to vouch for them, which suggests that they belong to the ranks of the self-taught, self-initiated and self-obsessed. Nevertheless, as a safeguard, signed sworn statements giving dates, times and names have been lodged with a solicitor should Simon and Emma have any further problems with this couple.

Treachery of a different nature threatened Marget's Scottish coven when, having attended her meetings for some nine months, one of her students turned informer. The next thing Marget knew, the banner headlines in a Sunday tabloid announced that 'Satan Gran's Coven is a Cauldron of Sin' with the subheading of 'Naked witches hold orgies near Macbeth's grave'.

"We actually practice very little magic during our meetings," she told the author. "Mostly we perform healing spells or offer up prayers. And what the reporter saw fit to leave out is the fact that I'm a prison chaplain which means I've been thoroughly screened by the Home Office."

Marget was angry enough to fire off a complaint against the newspaper to the Press Complaints Commission because two of her group were named, photographed without their consent and their places of employment clearly identified. There are dozens of cases on file at the SAFF of Pagans being targeted by fundamentalists following this type of media exposure and Marget asked that the newspaper be censored for its misleading and inaccurate reporting which could have endangered her group. The lewd behaviour described in the article was, in fact, carried out by the reporter's own girlfriend, who had come along, presumably, for the ride!

Despite the fact that a well-balanced piece on Marget's coven had appeared in the local press, a letter to the Press Complaints Commission from the national newspaper sneeringly referred to the former article which "painted her and other coven members out to be white than white" and "... Mrs Inglis and her wondrous works". The tone of the letter suggests that the newspaper reporters set out to discredit the group right from the start, regardless of the truth.

The dearth of truth in newspaper reporting and the apathetic response by establishment bodies to complaints by Pagans had been chronicled in some depth in *Malleus Satani - The Hammer of Satan,* so it came as no real surprise that the PCC failed to uphold Marget's complaint. Despite its Code of Practice which the PCC 'is charged with enforcing', it still upheld the tabloid's right to compromise the Codes of accuracy, privacy and misrepresentation without censor. Only 1% of complaints are ever upheld by the PCC and despite some lengthy correspondence with the *Comhairli Cairde* - who made it known that full details of the report would be made known, the PCC refused to re-examine Marget's case.

Those who wish to join a coven must accept that this type of infiltration makes for 'good news' in the eyes of the media. Should coven security be breached, there is the very real possibility of seeing the group's individual members named and photographed by reporters. Despite the fact that it is not illegal to hold and practice an alternative religious belief, this is where personal courage is called into account; when the media accuse Witches of all manner of 'vile and evil practises' and there is no interest in reporting the true facts. Accept that in the eyes of establishment bodies, Pagans do not appear to be able to demand the same rights as other minority religious or ethnic groups.

For Pagans who enjoy working within an extended family group, the coven does provide the opportunity to join with others for celebrations and festivals, as well for worship. And as with all families there are more personal 'rites of passage'- birth, deaths and marriages - all of which are celebrated under the auspices of the God and Goddess. In *Life-Rites,* Aeron describes the types of rituals employed in her own coven to cover all aspects from the cradle to the grave. "It was necessary to produce a guidebook to address issues which, although often overlooked, are important when attempting to organise a reasonably large community of varying ages. By design, it illustrates a coven working on a mundane level rather than being an attempt at revealing any of the Mysteries of the initiated Craft. It also shows that we're just an ordinary social group once the robes are exchanged for our normal, everyday clothes."

Neither is it all social affairs and celebration since Janval, Marget Inglis and Philip Heselton all act as Prison Chaplains if called upon by the Home Office to visit an inmate who is of the Pagan faith. This acceptance by one Government Department, in adding Paganism to the list of permitted religions in jail, is the first positive step forward for many a year, giving it a new status amongst alternative religious beliefs. This does not, however, prevent both tabloid press and religious fundamentalists from continuing their attacks in the media and accusing Witches of all manner of indecent practicses - without a grain of evidence to support their allegations.

As a result of these attacks, there is also a strong, ongoing debate within the Pagan press, over the advisability of including children in coven gatherings; especially with a legion of teachers and social workers waiting in the wings to report on any alleged unseemly behaviour. Aeron gave her opinion which is based on years of coven administration: "Generally speaking, I see no value in excluding them from those celebrations where other 'non-initiates' are welcome. Such events would include those to which a parent would normally expect to be able to take their children, irrespective of religious beliefs.

"Events covering conservation, relationships with others, nature lore, etc., where the 'religion' plays little or no part should also be made available to them. Such knowledge is increasingly emphasised in schools and in the media and it would be folly to exclude them from our own activities in these areas. For those meetings which would be unsuitable for children, i.e. with a strong religious or magical content, parents should arrange for a child-minder."

Social Intolerance

In view of the Church's intolerant reaction against homosexuality, it appears that there are also personal prejudices surfacing within the Craft. Among some peoples, homosexuality is one of the distinguishing marks of a shaman or medicine man. The Algonquin Indians believed that those showing homosexual tendencies, because of their 'abnormalities' were closer to the spirit world than ordinary men and could therefore act as intermediaries, while Navaho shamans sometimes thought of themselves as magically transformed into women and often dressed in women's clothing.

Chris and Graham received a letter from a distressed young man who had joined a group, having first informed them that he was gay. This didn't seem to matter at first, but gradually pressure was brought to bear on him. He was originally 'paired off' with one of the young women in the group, simply as two students learning together and then later, as magical working partners. Eventually he was taken aside and told that he wasn't helping himself, and that he should be making more effort to desire the girl sexually.

"It was pointed out to him that as a fertility religion Wicca depended on the (sexual) interaction of male and female; that male with male did not work because the 'polarity' wasn't there," explained Chris. "He was told that homosexuality was an aberration, but that it could be 'cured' if he was prepared to work at it - that is, if he had sex with women he would eventually get to like it and his attraction to his own sex would be overcome!

"I was both shocked and horrified that this attitude should still be prevalent in society, but particularly in Wicca where, I believed, that even if practitioners were ignorant of the magical significance of homosexuality, they should have at least (as 'outsiders' themselves) been more tolerant of the young man's sexuality and kept their prejudice to themselves. The Witches in this case should have considered themselves 'blessed' that a homosexual had asked to join their group, since there is much anthropological evidence to suggest that rather than being thought of as in some way lacking, homosexuals were believed to have the divine essence of both male and female spirits."

Concern was publicly expressed by Bob Clay-Egerton when he found a leading Pagan journal stating that homosexuals could not be Witches. "When I first commenced my studies in the days of illegal Witchcraft, I was taught before my initiation that anyone who commenced the practice of Craft in sincerity, formal initiate or not, was a Witch. This would imply that a homosexual can be a Witch. The homosexual, or trans-sexual will probably find major obstacles put in their path if attempting to join a coven and may find it easier, I suspect, to find acceptance among magicians than they will among Witches.

"Sexuality, to my mind, is not a physical but a mental and instinctual thing. The problem is not in the mind of the trans- or homosexual Pagan but in the early conditioning by socio-religious mores of Pagans not yet sufficiently advanced to be able to stand apart and look with the eye - not of morality and sexuality - but with the eye of spirituality. The question must, in all fairness, be examined as much as possible without personal beliefs being allowed to interfere.

"I only have some 50 odd years of occult study to my credit and have merely scratched the outermost surface of knowledge but I dare wonder if we all, male and female, do not have quite a bit of both sexes in our individual makeup. I do know personally, however, of one High Priestess who, from first hand practical experience of working with both homo- and heterosexual members, is prepared to consider such applications for admittance into the Craft based on ability rather than gender."

"To my knowledge there should be no deliberate exclusion of homosexuals - whether male or female - from Craft but I know it does happen," added Aeron, confirming the point made by Bob Clay-Egerton. "After twenty-one years of interacting with all sorts of people within Circle, I've never known an individual's sex to make any different whatsoever to any ritual or magical working."

Bob Clay-Egerton also has evidence of a different kind of censor within the Craft. "A Witch of my acquaintance recently told me of her experiences when trying to join a local coven. Her application for membership was swiftly rejected in an extremely terse manner on the grounds that she was 'entirely unsuitable'. It seems this was the only reason or explanation which was to be forthcoming but the lady persisted and applied to two other groups in the vicinity. Again she was rejected, even without a meeting with the High Priesthood of either coven.

"What was the reason for this young woman being deemed unsuitable for membership of a coven of modern Witches? It was quite simple. Her name had appeared in print as having been involved in prostitution; she had used physical attractions for the purpose of making money. It was due to this that she had been judged unsuitable and other covens had been warned about her desire to join one of their number. She had been asked nothing about her aspiration, her desires, or why she had chosen that life.

"In my view this is unethical, to say the least. A meeting should have been arranged and a personal assessment of suitability could have been made rather than an automatic acceptance of a second-hand opinion. Who would have suffered so greatly if it had been known this young woman was a member? Who would have been likely to know? Only other Witches, for we are usually a secretive lot and protect our own. Fortunately, the tale has a positive note and today this person does belong to a coven which does not judge her past."

If, on joining a coven, newcomers find themselves subjected to prejudice or censor, then the best course of action is to leave. There's plenty of evidence to suggest that the gods throw 'bad' teachers in the student's path as a sort of psychic obstacle course, in order that the student develops persistence and dedication to overcome the difficulties presented by misleading or inadequate tutoring. An old occult adage states that the right teacher comes along when the student has proved him (or her) self ready, so don't be afraid to leave a group and join a new one - even if it means working solitary for a time.

Magpie found changing covens certainly broadened his own outlook. "There are probably a lot of us who have wondered about the advantages of joining a coven at one stage or another - whether it be at the outset of one's Craft life, or after some period as a solitary. Mind you, there are those already in groups who 'still' wonder about it. There are some strange people around. Psychic fairs draw a lot of them, though some of us actually discover them in our own circle of 'acquaintances'. The type who wax lyrical about nice Mr Crowley but haven't quite cottoned on to his sense of humour. Or pontificate about chaos but, when pressed, believe the chaos current to probably involve a couple of batteries and a light-bulb. Listening to such self-congratulatory ramblings can merely compound any existing feelings of loneliness despite being part of a group.

"This is when you get to wondering what life would be like in a 'real' coven. Perhaps you feel you've taken it as far as you can with your present group and need further teaching. Or maybe you're just curious as to just how big the Craft world is beyond your books, and how much more lies beyond what's written. It could be that you've started to doubt your own objectivity, or even sanity, being unable to share experiences with anyone who might advise on a path of further development. Or even, try as you might, you just don't appear to be getting along as you feel you should."

After much deliberation, Magpie found a compatible covenstead. "One very bizarre aspect of the Craft world is how everybody seems so familiar, even though there's no possible way one could have met them before. There's no such thing as a typical Witch. On the whole they seem painted in stronger colours than most other folks and are possessed of an honesty and integrity so very rare in the world without. Admittedly this can take some adjustment since trust is a risky commodity these days, but the rewards are more than worth it. Any good coven is as much a family as a working group and the love shared is both comforting and empowering.

"Group life can be intense, to say the least, and it quickly becomes part of one's life, warts and all. For the average neophyte the most common question uttered must be a silent 'who are these people?' It's also disturbing to realise that the next generation of neophytes will be wondering the same about you!"

Everyone needs to feel comfortable in the company of members who form the working group and Hazel's 'essential guide to Witch-hunting in your area' written for *The Broom Cupboard* demonstrates the camaraderie prevalent in a well-run coven - although her High Priestess might not appreciate her revelations.

"There is a myth in current circulation that, now the image of a little old lass in a pointy hat is no longer in fashion, the modern Witch is in fact a thin vegan student; who knocks about in star-spangled dungarees and is frequently spotted in Sainsbury's, dragging bead decorated dreadlocks through the fruit and purchasing herbal teas. This myth is actively encouraged by Witches ... those to whom I refer love to think that the rest of the Pagan world hasn't sussed them out. They delight and revel in the thought that this hippie 'peace for all' version is shielding a deeper and darker secret that could turn modern Witchcraft, as it is known and written about, on its head."

Hazel reports that the unsuspecting will not spot a real Witch in Sainsbury's by a shopping list. No healthy alternative here, strictly tiramisu, lardy cake and half a dead cow go into the Witch's trolley; not to mention the half barrel of brandy (a medicinal requirement for dealing with neophytes), and some six large jars of coffee - just to get them through the weekend. "It is best to observe at a distance, from where you will see that those shifty, crafty eyes are ringed with dark circles. There's nothing particularly mystical here; it is not elaborate make-up, fairy salve or the result of a rampant Wiccan orgy that the press love to write about. It is, in truth, due to the fact that Witches rarely sleep, having 'far too much to do' and spend half the night feeding their caffeine habit.

"If you are outdoors, then Witch-spotting is a different matter - for, in the great wide open, you will more often than not hear them before they hove into view. It isn't that they are clumsy and crash through the undergrowth ... Oh, no: Witches are as stealthy as cats, but they mutter and threaten the realm of Nature as they make their way to their meeting place. And there's not a lot about them that resembles a human, I'm afraid.

"Not a pastel robe amongst them, not a nude body in sight. It can best be described as the entire contents of the army surplus store, brought to life and heading your way, muttering and shaking a very big stick. The whole magnificent regalia consists of at least one set of thermals, t-shirt, shirt, sweater, thick woolly jumper, two pairs of trousers, waterproof trousers and coat; thick woolly hat, scarf, gloves, two pairs of socks and, depending on how cold it is - ear muffs. Apart from the fact that it is mid-July and everybody else is out in minimal clothing makes no odds and, should anyone be foolish enough to sneer at them ... well, it rains so they can sneer right back.

"Accompanying the High Priestess is usually some scantily clad being with a nervous twitch - this is a neophyte and they live in fear absolute of getting themselves noticed by The Multi-Layered One. Gone are the days of legend, of the familiar; this pathetic being has replaced them - after all cats just don't make coffee quite as well as a neophyte. It isn't that the Witches have gone out of their way to terrify these poor individuals. Imagine one moment visualising Witches robed in pastels, dispensing love and white light to all - and the next, being dragged through the undergrowth by a creature appearing more interested in the chicken sandwich in their hand than the pretty butterflies floating around their head ..."

The reasons for joining a coven or group remain fairly evenly balanced although it would appear on the law of averages, that the student is more likely to encounter a bad coven than a good one. A large number of people thrive and expand their mystical abilities under the tutorage of an experienced High Priesthood but as Aeron pointed out at the beginning of the chapter, there are more people looking for covens to join than covensteads with vacant places. However, for guidance she points out the pros and cons of coven v solitary working; not forgetting that members of a coven spend (on average) only 0.84% of their time in a group situation and therefore 99.16% working alone.

In favour of solitary working

A. There's no one to nag at your idleness, save your own conscience.

B. There's no one there to laugh at your mistakes.

C. You can't feel 'blackmailed' into doing something you don't feel ready for, or 'up to' today.

D. You don't have to be anywhere.

E. You don't have to wait for others to arrive.

F. You're not going to offend anyone other than the deity involved if you go in for a spot of blackmail yourself.

G. There's nothing to stop you from calling the Goddess 'Sandra' if that's how she appears to you.

H. Private things stay private.

I. No-one borrows your stuff and forgets to return it.

J. You don't feel as though taking two hours to do some thing is wasting anyone else's time.

K. You don't have to explain anything to anyone - such as why you keep your incense in your sock drawer.

L. You don't have to agree on the pronunciation of athamé - you can call it a knife, blade, dagger, or not use one at all!

M. It doesn't have to be forever.

In favour of working with others (even if only occasionally)

A. You can't teach yourself what you don't know exists.

B. Books are expensive and authors can't cover everything in one volume. So you can borrow from someone else.

C. It's impossible to identify 'bad' habits when you don't know bad from good.

D. There's encouragement or praise when something is achieved.

E. There are suggested 'short-cuts', or helpful observations.

F. There's someone to talk common sense when, in enthusiasm, it dribbles out of your ears.

G. It's useful to compare notes - even if it's on different subjects.

H. A trusted partner can drum for longer than a CD, refill incense, drive you home, and do all the things for which you haven't a spare pair of hands.

I. There's always something new to discuss.

J. There's always someone who knows something about it.

K. It's almost guaranteed they'll call 'it' something different.

L. There's someone with whom to share.

M. A good tutor or group will always let you learn, practice and leave if you wish.

N. It doesn't have to be forever.

There are always alternative methods of exploring the world of magic as Graham points out. "Through reading various books on the Craft, all written by 'expert authorities', you certainly can get the impression that in order to be a Witch you simply have to join a coven. In reality the greater number of Witches either always remain solitary, or work with one or two very close friends who are on the same wavelength. The number of Witches who don't belong to a coven greatly out number those who seem to believe that you have to be a joiner/follower, instead of being yourself! If you still want to belong to a group - well, create an informal one of your own. There's a lot of fellow seekers out there and you could do much better than a lot of covens."

Chapter 5
The Solitary Path - *A Way A Lone*

Disagreeing with Israel Regardie's view, Aeron opened the discussion on solitary working on a contentious note. "I'm not sure who first made the comment that 'Witchcraft is a religion', but I am sure that I disagree with them," she said. "I have met and worked with very able Witches who are avowed atheists, agnostics, Christians, followers of the various Celtic, Nordic and Germanic tribal traditions (and probably more besides). Therefore, I have had to come to the same conclusion as Marian Green, that Witchcraft in its more hidden form pays little heed to any particular form of religious belief."

This opening paragraph would probably bring screams of 'heretic' from staunch members of established Traditions but they are wise words and ones that potential solitary practitioners should ponder upon for a while. The would-be Witch on joining an established coven is expected to conform to the rituals of worship directed at the particular god(s) under whose auspices the group work. The solitary is free of such restrictions and as there are so many different deities and Traditions to choose from, it is rather obvious that precise religious devotion and magical ability need not necessarily always go hand in hand.

The explanations Aeron prefers to give in *The Dagger & The Plough* are those of Operative and Ritual Witchcraft. "The first, Operative, is the natural and unsought ability to see, change, understand or have a 'feel for' and/or control that and those around in a manner beyond that which is currently classed as 'natural'. Ritual Witchcraft is the system of beliefs and ritual that underpin the above and while most areas of this can almost be taught by rote - true Operative Craft cannot A tutor may take the raw gifts and abilities of a 'novice' and by working with the individual may guide them towards their full potential but they cannot 'make' someone without a magical aptitude a Witch."

According to Aeron's theory, the 'witchiness' of an individual is therefore not dependent upon which god/dess or pantheon is adopted; this depends on the ability to manipulate matter through the agency of mind. "Through the possession of a deep understanding of the universal principles they can set in motion corresponding events on the physical level - sometimes known as sympathetic magic - but these abilities, being inherent in their makeup are not dependent on the existence, presence or intervention of a deity."

So why does the beginner need to find or be 'chosen' by a particular deity before stepping onto the magical or mystical Path? In all honesty the true answer is that they *don't!* Folk are usually drawn towards Witchcraft because they already have had some form of psychic awakening, even if they don't always recognise it as such.

In addition to this, the 'big three' - i.e. Christianity, Islam and Judaism are unsympathetic to Witchcraft and magic (despite Christianity openly having its own Mystery Tradition). And since mankind has been conditioned to work within some form of religious belief system, the beginner is left with little alternative than to turn to the multi-pagan traditions of the Old Ways.

Mélusine finds much of Aeron's teaching in accordance with her own experience. "I suppose I'm what is known as a 'natural' because much of what I later discovered was considered to be magical ability, I already possessed, albeit in a totally undisciplined form. The discipline that came from working with my tutor enabled me to channel those abilities in a more positive and controlled manner. Having said that, it is important not to confuse what one means by magical and mystical.

"I'd been introduced to classical Egypt at a very early age and as I knew 'all the other kids in the gang' it wasn't necessary for me to learn about the various deities. Now working in the Egyptian Magical Tradition, I just look upon it all as having come full circle, since this is the fundamental basis for the majority of Western religions anyway. The real question is, can one attain the *mystical experience* of calling down the god-form without the use of *magical knowledge*? I agree one doesn't need a god-form to be able to work magic, but does one need to acquire a certain magical ability before achieving mystical enlightenment? There are those who would say not, but I personally find it more satisfying to work with the god-forms than without them."

The solitary worker has a doubly difficult path, according to Israel Regardie writing in *The Eye in the Triangle*. "The whole area of mystical experience with its close relation to occultism and physical phenomena is difficult for the average person to handle ... They must never acknowledge the existence of anything that might briefly challenge the narrow view they have formed of life. A larger, wider outlook must be positively frightening to them. It is safer to ridicule and condemn."

The solitary must therefore learn to explore the magical world alone and often refrain from discussing the details of their discoveries for fear of being carted off to a therapist or clergyman by a well-meaning member of the family or friend! Even those who attempt to meet critics halfway are still held up to ridicule as the followers of Odin discovered when they presented a petition to the House of Lords against the proposed rail-link being routed only yards away from their sacred White Horse Stone. Despite the fact that the group from the Odinic Rite bowed to Westminster tradition and respectfully appeared before the committee in suits, the newspapers still failed to treat them or their religious beliefs in a serious and rational manner.

And despite what one hears about Interfaith groups, the newcomer must accept that any form of 'concession' towards

Paganism is frowned upon by the Anglican clergy as the Archbishop of Canterbury found when he gave his endorsement to the Sacred Land Project in 1997. The project, to mark and conserve more than 2,000 holy sites across Britain, is backed by Prince Philip, the World Wide Fund for Nature and major faiths across the country. Critics of the scheme, however, maintained that it would lead people towards 'counterfeit, misleading and misguided beliefs', regardless of the fact that the majority of the sites are pre-Christian and considered sacred by the Pagan community who resent being referred to as fraudulent, misled and misguided.

The Learning Process:

As Aeron observes in her latest book, each environment be it moor, bog, forest, heathland, fen, arctic tundra, desert and mountain, etc., posed different problems for the indigenous population. Each people had their own deities concerned with the various aspects of life, climate, circumstance and death. "True, in some cases we may be faced with a relatively modern landscape for, as we have colonised each area we have subtly or otherwise attempted to change the environment to meet any current need. As these changes have come about so the interaction with the gods may have changed, perhaps even the gods themselves, as they have been replaced or asked to take on 'extra responsibilities'?"

The solitary, working without the guidance of a coven leader or a set of preordained rules, should thoroughly familiarise themselves with the particular Path or Tradition which draws them. Ideally, a considerable amount of time should be spent with *academic* textbooks (as up to date as possible), which will give authenticated historical background information for the culture under investigation. *Why?* Because as far as a great deal of so-called Pagan teaching is concerned, there is a vast amount on library and bookshops shelves which is inaccurate, misleading or downright garbage. The historical reference books won't be painting any rosy pictures of life in a

Celtic settlement inhabited by a hunter-warrior race; the potentially serious Witch or magician won't want a fluffy bunnies and carpet-slippers approach to occult knowledge.

Whether the Pagan community likes to admit it, or not, there are now two distinct approaches to Pagan worship. One is the cleaned-up, politically correct, socially respectable form of neo-goddess-worship which hails the deity as an insipid madonna-like creature. An amalgam of Virgin Mary/Diana/Gaia/Isis representing the maiden/mother and totally rejecting the image of the crone/destroyer. There is often little, or no mention of the god, since his image is more difficult to render impotent - it is incongruous to depict the Horned God skipping around in a fairy-ring and therefore his image is suppressed even by the males of the neo-Pagan species. Unfortunately this is increasingly becoming the generalised public face of Paganism because traditionalists, i.e. those who prefer not to sanitise their deities, are retreating back into the shadows through sheer exasperation at the trivialisation of the religion.

As explained previously, the traditional approach to deity acknowledges the dual importance of both male *and* female elements which is essential to effective magical working. There are few apologists among the ranks of the traditionalists since their uncompromising attitude is governed by certainty; ***they know who they are and what is expected of them.*** They appear less frequently on television and, more often than not, decline to give interviews for the national press decked out in flowing robes and flowers or waving a sword around. Neither do the traditionalists have any problems with the identity of their deity since there is only one Creator and the male/female images merely differing aspects of the One. This One, however, often presents a darker, less benign countenance but it is part of natural magical working and can only be ignored at the Adept's peril.

Twenty years ago there were hardly any books on occultism which were *actually written* by occultists and initially the publication of genuine material was often left to eccentrics and attention seekers who now appear to be an embarrassment to some of the current leaders of Paganism. In those days, when a *genuine* book appeared on the shelves, written by a *genuine* occultist, it became famous overnight. Chris Bray of the Sorcerer's Apprentice, the country's premier supplier of serious occult reading matter, understands only too well what is happening in the Pagan community.

"This occult revival, which began as an intelligent, almost scientific, investigation of the supernatural, now appears to have taken second place to a rebirth of superstition. The popularising of occult ideas and methodology has enabled people who are not really ready to make the self-transformations demanded of initiates, adopt an occult persona and salve their anxieties by relying on occult junk.

"Occultism is not for everyone and genuine occultists do not proselytise but our emphasis at the Sorcerer's Apprentice has always been on educating clients to learn how to apply genuine magic for themselves. We attempt to destroy superstition wherever we meet it.

"Unfortunately few of the hundreds of other occult suppliers and teachers will do the same and so, particularly in the past decade, there has been a significant increase in people who rely on superstition, and who lack discernment. The same result is reached in Paganism by another form of superstition: that of an unquestioning belief in Paganism as a religion *per se*. Recently, far too many people have adopted Paganism as a belief far too quickly. Instead of developing discernment and an appreciation of the difference between Paganism and orthodox religion, they have brought their Old Aeon religious superstitious baggage with them, only to clutter up and confuse the development of Paganism - as well as themselves."

Which, of course, brings us to the popular pick 'n' mix belief system that is currently emerging out of neo-pagan belief. Much of the fault for this lies with the abundance of books which, although purporting to instruct on the intricacies of Craft, include hefty dollops of (usually unaccredited) Native American shamanism, Oriental philosophy, tarot, Qabalah and (*always* unaccredited) Crowley. Whatever the tradition, karma creeps in, although this is essentially Hindu/ Buddhist philosophy and on occasions the Akashic Record has been aligned with Egyptian Tradition without any further explanation that it derives from *akasha*, the Sanskrit word meaning 'primary substance' and therefore could not be indigenous to ancient Egypt. Although not quite the same as karma, Northern Tradition has its *wyrd* and the Celts *dàn,* which equates with destiny; Egypt has its 42 assessors in the Hall of Judgement and its Register of Doom.

There is nothing wrong with using different philosophies as analogies, of course, but whether it be the fault of author or publisher, it merely adds to the inaccurate material available to the solitary worker if quotations and examples aren't accredited correctly in the text. Another instance of this type of misinformation can be found in the working papers from a popular correspondence course on 'traditional Witchcraft' which included lengthy passages from the Qabalah, tarot and unaccredited quotes from Crowley. When a student questioned the validity of the sources in connection with pure Craft working, the instructors turned nasty!

"Why," asks Aeron, "are people so intent on amalgamating our indigenous beliefs into one that is 'acceptable' to everyone else? Would we insist on the Jews and Muslims to 'pick'n'mix' their faiths to make one new one simply because they originated in the same geographical space. What if a rose by another name doesn't smell so sweet to the Gods of our tribes and they finally abandon us to our fate?"

It is now easy to see why the beginner who has a firm grounding in historical references will have a more positive attitude towards what is, and what is not correct, when it comes to magical 'parasites' that have latched themselves onto an author's ego-trip to make a book appear more involved and/ or interesting. With the growing need in mainstream publishing for 'mind, body and spirit' titles, it will become more and more difficult for the student to find serious studies of magical instruction and so this academic grounding begins to take on a more important and vital aspect.

"What I find positively frightening about new esoteric books coming to me for review is the level of triteness to which the authors descend to produce books of a marketable quality," complained Mélusine. "Today's consumer wants sound-bites, scrappy bits of information that enable them to pass themselves off as knowledgeable beings. Added to that, the authors have all sorts of background qualifications to support their writing - all but the most important thing: a thorough grounding in *magical* experience. Nowadays, if you want serious books on magical subjects, you've really got to know where to look and, as a result, the prices of many second-hand occult books are no longer affordable."

Aeron and Chris also showed concern about the watered-down versions of Paganism that appear to be the only reading matter now readily available which, to quote Dion Fortune, isn't Paganism but 'decomposing Christianity'. Throwing another spanner in the tutorial works, Aeron was highly critical of the 'mind, body & spirit' approach which distorts the newcomer's initial understanding of what true Paganism is all about. "From experience I've found that folk always return to the influences that first attracted them to Pagan exploration. It doesn't matter what else they read, that first 'hook' is the important and formative one."

Mélusine and Chris were quick to protest but on reflection, had to agree that Aeron did have a valid point. Those who had experienced natural psychic leanings from childhood were more than likely to be drawn to traditional Craft teachings, having an instinctive ability to cut through the waffle. As a result, no matter what in-depth study they've made of other esoteric subjects in the years between, they remained firmly 'grounded' in traditional Craft learning. In fact, this type of Pagan has the ability to move freely between Traditions and can, if and when necessary, be called upon to lend extra psychic energies to a magical/healing ritual, even though they have not been formally instructed in that other Tradition's working methods.

"At first glance it looks as though Aeron is maintaining that people don't move on from their original point of entry but this isn't what she means at all," explained Mélusine. "I've certainly returned to my 'roots' but I now view them from a completely different perspective. Perhaps the T. S. Eliot quote from *Little Gidding* sums up what Aeron means:

"***We shall not cease from exploration***
And the end of all our exploring
Will be to arrive where we started
And know the place for the first time."

"I don't think occultists can afford to ignore what is going on in mainstream publishing. Before long there won't be any authentic books for the potential Witch or magician to study and the whole Pagan religion will be massaged to fit into a neat neo-Pagan-Christian social chapter that excludes traditional Crafters. Personally speaking, I don't want to be part of it but I'm fully aware of the potential dangers; it won't take much for neo-Pagan-Christianity to start openly accusing traditional practitioners as being 'black'. This already is the case as anyone will see if they bother to read the various magazines that come out in the Pagan press."

The Simple Path:

In a previous chapter, we saw how the solitary Witch, shaman or magician is forced to work alone for a variety of reasons. Some are self-taught, natural or intuitive; people who feel the confines of group workings would be stifling to their independent methods of psychic exploration. Others live in rural areas where the simple question of logistics makes contact with others a problem. Then there are those who are reluctant to draw attention to themselves because their urban surroundings could prove hostile if their beliefs became public knowledge. Many more intensely private folk celebrate Pagan festivals with a partner and don't require any other stimulus. While the remainder work solo under the guidance of a more experienced tutor.

Mélusine works solo because she has yet to meet a suitable partner with a grounding in the Primitive Egyptian Tradition. "There are lots of folk about working within the later Graeco-Osirian/Isian Tradition but I find this too dogmatic and compartmentalised. The earlier forms didn't require logic or uniformity; in fact very little is taught about the original myths from Greek sources usually quoted in magical books. Although the most important aspect of the individual's way of life, the old religion wasn't bogged down in doctrinal credo. It was a more creative approach and each worshipper was required to use his own imagination in his overtures to the gods.

"On a purely personal level I would find working within a group an absolute nightmare since I don't have any herding instinct. All my rituals are performed solo but having said that, I do have a couple of more highly experienced people I do work with on occasion. As for the future, if the right partner came along, and the timing was right, I wouldn't reject him."

Chris and Graham have been magical partners for over 15 years although they have slightly different interests. "From my mid twenties my magical studies concentrated almost totally on Wicca," explained Graham. "By this I mean 'The Old Religion' which isn't necessarily the same thing as modern Wicca. Modern Wicca is often portrayed as a rather stereotyped system, whereas the Old Religion was probably much more varied and colourful. It probably had strong elements of shamanism, unlike some forms of modern Wicca which bear strong similarities to Ritual Magic."

Chris on the other hand has a diverse knowledge of herbal and healing very much along the lines of the 'hedge-witchery' outlined previously. "Most Witches by their very nature are loners. They have to rely on their own knowledge and in consequence are often found in libraries, or ploughing through thick herbals in search of a special healing plant. And when they have found the information they need, they will convert that new-found knowledge into action."

There is often a great emphasis given in herbals and magical manuals as to the way in which certain herbs should be gathered. If a grimoire states that a certain plant should be gathered before sunrise, without using any iron implements, then you will find a Hedge-Witch out in the darkness with a wooden pick, or even a special tool made from a pre-decimal copper penny set in a wooden handle, to gather that particular plant - even if she normally never rises before noon! This behaviour isn't as wacky as it may first appear as Chris explains:

"There is a set of eight traditional herb gathering rules which are the instructions for collecting plants in general, however, certain plants have their own very specific ritual instructions. In some cases, these rules apply only to a herb gathered for a very specific purpose; at other times they refer to the way in which a certain herb must always be gathered to maintain its maximum magical 'charge'. These instructions may include certain ritual actions, such as inscribing a circle around the plant before starting to dig it up, or cut it. The instructions may also refer to which part of the plant will be used, e.g. the flowers, all of the plant above the ground, or the roots, and so on.

"Common instructions include 'gather the plant just after the first cockcrow' or 'with the dew still upon the leaves', or 'as soon as the dew has lifted in the morning'. One frequent instruction is that a specific plant should be harvested without the use of iron. This may well hint at the pre-Iron Age roots of this knowledge; it is often said that the 'cold iron' is anathema to fairy folk, ghosts and spirits, etc., (i.e. these creatures can be dispersed by throwing an iron nail at them). This is well attested in folklore and spell instructions too, and may be a good indication that iron has a marked effect on certain subtle emanations."

This all sounds rather vague and perhaps still not a good enough reason to avoid iron implements to our 'logical and scientific' modern western minds. It has, however, been confirmed by scientific experiment that certain trace elements and minerals found in some plants can be distorted, or even destroyed, by iron. Possibly it is the specific combination of minerals and elements which gives the plant its power for healing (or whatever) and in this case it would be advisable to preserve that blend as intact as possible. What Chris finds equally as fascinating is the fact that our ancient ancestors apparently knew this thousands of years ago, and the information was ancient then - so where did the original 'learning' come from?

"All the instructions for magical herb gathering are given in order to preserve the highest concentration of the plant's magical energies. These instructions were not there to make the Witch the laughing stock of the neighbourhood, they were given for very practical reasons, and if you want to work effective magic you follow them.

"Some of the rules are there to impress on you that what you are doing is a very special ritual in itself. So it will often be specified that you should be in a state of ritual purity, wearing new/clean clothes, or even nude. But this is not only for ritual purposes - you are aiming to ensure that the herbs you collect will be in as pure and uncontaminated state as possible and you must not contaminate them yourself. Another common instruction is for the harvested herb to be laid on a clean white cloth. This again is to avoid contaminating the magical ingredient by keeping its energies as pure as possible.

"An important detail is the age of the moon, or the season (or even a specific date in the year), or that a certain star or constellation should be visible - again indicating the time of the year when the particular energies you wish to utilise will be at their strongest. Although these rules and regulations appear to be 'magical', herb gathering in former times was the same for spell working, a medicinal healing infusion or poultice. The people who were the doctors of the tribe, whether magician, priest, witch or shaman, used the process of healing the body, which was considered such a mysterious thing that it must be magic!"

Shamanism and the Solitary

As with many of the other non-indigenous Traditions embraced by Pagans, the majority of serious writers on modern shamanism often use correspondences that do not fit snugly along side the traditional roots of European Witchcraft. The authors have gained their knowledge and/or training through contact with Native teachers of either South or North America and so the students take the attitude of "I've read it in a book by an expert, so it must be true".

Traditionally there are three ways of becoming a shaman according to author Mircea Eliade (*Shamanism: Archaic Techniques of Ecstasy*): (1) by spontaneous vocation, (2) by hereditary transmission or (3) by personal quest. Whatever method s/he follows, a shaman must have received two kinds of instruction or experience, firstly through visions and/or trances and secondly through traditional study. This twofold teaching can be imparted by a genuine teacher or through the spirits. Eliade is, however, adamant that the lack of public ritual no way implies the lack of initiation since this can be performed or achieved in the candidate's dreams or personal ecstatic experiences.

Whilst he can appreciate that book-learning is often the first step to discovering a different Path, Graham is firm in his belief that book contents should not be treated as gospel. "How many of those foolish modern shamans go out into the magical world and discover their own correspondences from scratch. In the end, if we wish to progress, this is exactly what we must do. Discover and develop our own magic, not copy someone else's.

"When working alone you simply choose the correspondences which feel best to you. We've all read the tables of correspondences in books on magic which unerringly tell us exactly what herb comes under which planet, and which hour of the day 'vibrates' to which deity ... all of which is of no real value to the shaman. (I maintain that it's of no real use to the true Witch or Magus either!) Of course the thought immediately leaps to mind 'But what if I get it wrong? What if my own choice of correspondence is wrong?' If you're sincere and really mean what you're doing, as opposed to merely dabbling, you can't go wrong. If you associate the dark of the moon with healing, then you will be able to use the dark of the moon for healing, regardless of what anyone else may say."

Shamanism is very much a personal Path and even the best teacher can only give pointers to the various methods of working; each student must find their own Path and walk it alone. Graham feels that if many more modern Wiccans would grasp this particular nettle, they would come to realise that the same is true for their Path. "No teacher, no matter how enlightened, can do your learning for you. Shamans do work together from time to time, but even when going through a ritual together, each one will be using their own archetypes, keys and triggers - you can't become a shaman by copying someone else."

Since their unfortunate escapade, Simon and Emma have gone back to working as solitary practitioners although Emma feels that she's merely returned to her roots of a small family farm environment. Her grandparents, who still lived with the family, were still doing things the 'old fashioned way' and so from an early age she was taught about folklore, herbs, home-cures and the ways of Nature.

"I'm not making wild claims of hereditary blood but we were a true pagan family, in its original context. When aged 14 years, I refused to take religious study at school on the grounds that I was a Witch, my Mother never batted an eyelid; she did, however, advise me to pretend I'd turned Catholic as this would cause less fuss! With this quiet parental approval I bought myself a book by the late Sybil Leek, and as soon as I read it I felt wonderful because I found there were other people who knew the things I wanted to know.

"I showed the book to my best friend and, enlisting the somewhat nervous company of a third girl, we had what we called our coven. In those days, of course, the Craft was still quite secretive - and so were we. Everything we used was hidden in the tack-room and our few working tools were unbelievably revered and precious. In our innocence we couldn't understand a lot of what we read but our meetings produced a fabulous atmosphere and our simple spells worked! We adored the Goddess (the Horned God was slightly more difficult to attune to) and Granny's old recipes were valued as never before. I still have her book to this day, though age and use have made it fragile."

The solitary practitioner, working strictly by instinct or gut reaction, can feel at a disadvantage from having no one to turn to for guidance if there is something that is unclear or uncomfortable about a working. Emma points out, quite correctly, 'that the gods must surely prefer well-intentioned, simple 'true to thine-self' attempts, as opposed to magic which is clouded and cloaked with the thoughts and opinions of others'. It's a simple philosophy but a sound one to keep in mind when the beginner begins to wonder whether it is a magical result - or merely wishful thinking.

Crowley, as usual, had an answer: "Shallow critics argue that because the average untrained man cannot evoke a spirit, the ritual which purports to enable him to do so must be at fault. Magick is one of the subtlest and most difficult of the sciences and arts. There is more opportunity for errors of comprehension, judgement and practice than in any other branch of physics."

Working solitary means that the Witch or Magus has the disadvantage of not having a 'power-pack' in the form of other group members to generate the necessary energy to work magic. Despite this drawback, however, there are various means by which positive results can be achieved by a relative beginner. Having said that, there are no short cuts to magical results, especially for those working alone or as a pair. Whatever form the ritual is to take, it is necessary to make all the necessary arrangements of consecrating magical equipment, studying the right correspondences, preparing the circle and observing the rules of ritual purity.

"One of the wonders of working alone," confesses Mélusine, "is that it *does* enable you to take short cuts - but only once you know what you're doing. Like a lot of other disciplines, it is necessary to fully understand the rules before you break them. Some folk can take hours of preparation before they can lock into their contacts, others can achieve it is seconds. It's all a matter of practice but even the most experienced will admit - if they're honest enough - that it doesn't work every time. I would be highly suspicious of anyone who boasted a 100% success rate."

Breaking the rules:

If we're going to talk about breaking the rules, we'd better think about why they are there in the first place, and what is the point of making rules if you can break them. "In magical working, as in building construction, rules give you a framework which you can use to devise your own magical working system," explained Chris. "Think of it this way. There, are many different 'languages' which are used to create computer programmes. Each of these languages has its own rules and as long as you stick to those rules, a skilled programmer will be able to use any of those languages to tell a computer to perform a certain set of functions, e.g. to create a game, word process, create files, or whatever you desire. Any computer will respond to a number of different languages as long as you follow the rules of each. But if you use some of the rules from one language, and some from another, the result will be chaos - or simply a blank screen.

"The rules of magic are actually a form of language which we use to raise our own spiritual awareness, plug into the psychic world and also enables us to communicate with other entities. Whichever system of magic you use can be looked on as a different language. Using the complete system, which takes practice and study, leads inevitably to fluency. Using bits of several magical systems gives a sort of 'pidgin' magic. Only if you are first fluent in the different magical systems can you see the 'words' which are universal, or inter- changeable. At this point - *and only at this point* - should you cautiously attempt to break the magical rules.

"The main problem most dabblers have is that they complain of getting no results, no matter which system of magic they use. You cannot sit someone down at a computer and expect them to write a programme after having glanced at a couple of manuals and picked bits out of them at random. There's no getting around the simple fact that if you want results from your magic, you are going to have to work at it - and this means magical practice, not just reading books!"

Aeron believes you should only break the rules if you have a reliable safety net provided by an experienced tutor. "All the books tell you about the *tools* of Craft - the divination, scrying, bits of 'common magic', but they don't say anything about how to work with your own abilities. They don't act as a mirror for the soul - only another person can do that. Someone who knows you through and through and will tell you that you've got the damn thing upside down. Someone who wants you to be the best you can, who'll see you through everything and still encourage you to greater heights; who'll watch and pass the TCP when needed.

"I know folk would rather have knowledge and experience second-hand through a book and hope that the author copied it down right - remember that infamous book where the details are wrong? That book's been in print for years and it's never been corrected. I wonder how many folk can't understand why their talismans aren't working as a result? Books give you the how, but not the why. So give me a live tutor any day. One who will explain six other ways of achieving the same result using only half the time and energy. One who will show how to get the best from your skills and abilities - not how they do it. Someone to guide you in a working ritual and act as a check, so you can't delude yourself that you've done or seen something you haven't.

"You need someone with whom you can compare results, the right the wrong and the nearly there, and celebrate like fury when you understand something new. Someone to share the most precious times, both good and bad - who can assist you in making the correct connections with the Old Ones so that any initiation/mystery is lived and not play acted."

The obvious real advantage of working alone is, of course, that the Adept is free to explore whatever Path or system appeals to him/her, without contravening traditional coven teaching methods. There aren't any set lessons to be learned, although as already discussed, it would be extremely foolish to assume that by reading a couple of books on the subject has prepared the would-be Witch for the physical surprises waiting in store. The world of magic is extremely *physical* in its manifestations so it's best to keep it simple until the unfamiliar becomes familiar and comfortable.

Simple Magical Exercises:

Meditation:

According to Chris there is an old Celtic riddle which asks: "Where is the centre of the Universe?" - the answer is "Here," since we are all the centre of our very own universe. "The more simplistic forms of meditation merely teach you to control your thought processes in order to focus the mind, to enter into altered states of consciousness, or simply as an aid to relaxation. Meditation can, however, be used for many other purposes including learning to hone your magical Will, opening the mind to revelations whether from your own subconscious, or from other discarnate entities, and as a preliminary to astral travel, or other magical workings."

Starting the practice of meditation couldn't be simpler and it doesn't necessarily involve complicated (and uncomfortable) Eastern postures to achieve it - sitting or lying down is a matter of personal preference. Create a relaxing atmosphere by the use of dim lighting, perfumed candles or joss sticks and, since few of us can guarantee complete silence from extraneous noises, gentle background music.

There are three simple meditative exercises which can be used to start to channel concentration: (1) try to keep your mind completely blank for two minutes. Close your eyes and visualise a blank area in front of you, pushing thoughts away as they intrude in the darkness, or (2) visualise the brightest star in the night sky and, ignoring the rest, let it pull you towards the brightness. Alternatively (3) by identifying each of the chakras (energy points of the body) with a colour of the rainbow: genitals - red; navel - orange; solar plexus - yellow; heart - green; throat - light blue; forehead - dark blue and crown of the head - violet. Visualise a warm red light rising slowly from the genitals, changing to orange as it reaches the navel, continuing up until the top of the head is bathed in a warm violet glow.

Gradually increase the amount of time spent on each exercise. Initially, during exercises two and three, the target will be reached very quickly but as the concentration develops the body will float more slowly towards the star, or the light will take longer between the changes of colour it moves through the body. It is when the body reaches the state of total relaxation that the mind opens up to outside thoughts and experiences. Chris advises that if you find yourself progressing more rapidly on one exercise than on the others, concentrate on the harder exercises and keep the easy one as a form of recreation.

These are only simple exercises to prepare the beginner for more serious undertakings of a magical/mystical nature but they remain in the Witch's armoury of knowledge. More effective than '40-winks' or a 'catnap' these exercises can be used as a pick-me-up whenever stress or tiredness creep in at awkward moments. For example, an important business dinner after a really stinking day at the office: 15-30 minutes using any one of these techniques and you'll be able to boogy all night. Magical knowledge has its practical uses in addition to the sublime.

Candle Magic:
The use of special colours with magical significance is a very old art, although the main use of colour in ritual these days is in the art of candle magic. Again Chris explains "It is a form of magic which is easy to master and yet can have great subtlety. When starting it is best to stick to single strong shades of colour although this can be developed into an extremely effective magical system with study. Use the following colour correspondences as a guide to start with but bear in mind that the colour must mean something to you. If you associate green with happiness and white with sorrow, then use those colours to express your magical intentions."

White/Silver:
Psychic development, purity, truth, clairvoyance, astral travel, lunar powers, new beginnings, initiation, inspiration.

Yellow/Gold:
Attraction, intellect, intelligence, wit, strength of mind, solar powers, fulfilment, optimism, riches.

Red:
Strength, power, strong emotions of love and hate, courage, violence, life, bloodshed, passion, sexual energies.

Blue:
Protection, healing, cooling emotions, patience, occult power, foresight.

Green:
Growth, luck, accumulation of wealth, business matters, generosity, fertility, prosperity, firmness, authority.

Pink:
Love, gentleness, friendship, self-awareness, single mindedness, happiness.

Violet/Purple:
Magical/spiritual power and their development, clairvoyance, idealism, calmness, justice, nemesis.

Black:
Darkness, communication with the Mighty Dead/Ancestor spirits, telepathy, divination, retribution, stillness.

This simple ritual simply requires a candle of the appropriate colour for the rite and anointing oil of your choice. The easiest method for anointing is that to attract something to you, or to make something increase, you should start at the top of the candle and stroke the oil downwards in one long, continuous movement to the base of the candle. To make something decrease, or to get rid of something, anoint from the base up towards the tip.

Write on a small slip of paper the object of the rite and place it beneath the candle holder. Then light the candle to draw your desires towards it like a moth to the flame.

Chris added a word of warning: "If you extinguish your object candle, it can only be used to perform the same function again. This may be useful if you intend to perform a series of rites for the same purpose over a number of days, as you can use the same candle as a link between the rites. If you need to dispose of the candle wash it in cold running water for five minutes before pushing it well down in the rubbish sack. Running water effectively wipes clean any psychic vibrations and makes it safe should another person handle it by accident."

Cord Magic:

"Working magic with cords and threads is one of the most traditional forms of Wiccan magic and also perhaps one of the most neglected," explains Chris. "On many traditional altars you will find several different cords of various lengths, and in different colours, and these cords are often detailed as one of the essential magical tools of the Witch."

There are many uses for cords in magical workings and the most common is the one found in many different books of spells - the Witches Ladder - the cord with nine knots. This spell can be performed for any number of purposes, the individual's magical intention being the main ingredient, although the use of colour symbolism can be used to enhance the working. A spell for love could be carried out using a pink or red cord; one for money requires a green cord symbolising growth; purple (for the powers of Jupiter) or gold (to symbolise wealth); a spell for protection needs a blue or white cord.

"You can, of course, simply buy a piece of cord of an appropriate colour, but it is always a good idea to remember the magical idea that the more you put into a spell, the more you will get out of it," added Chris. "The Witches Ladders we make are always hand-plaited from appropriate coloured embroidery silks. We sometimes plait different but complementary colours together for an even greater magical effect. For example, if plaiting a Ladder for wealth, why not use a strand of purple, one of green and one of gold, then you have all the influences detailed above in one spell!"

Taking That First Step:

The first ritual performed as a solitary practitioner is extremely nerve-wracking as one of the Raven students (who wishes to remain anonymous) found out to her cost. She had worked out the appropriate planetary hours, the correct phase of the moon, made herself a magical robe, gathered her magical tools, memorised the 'correct' words as best she could and made sure she wouldn't be disturbed.

"In all honesty, she hadn't been feeling well for some days, which was probably a sign that she should have tried something less ambitious, or even abandoned the ritual and tried another night," explained Graham. "She was, however, quite determined that nothing was going to put her off. The circle was set out with a cord, cast and empowered as she'd learned to do. Picking up a roll of charcoal by the wrong end and scattering charcoal over the cream carpet, she nevertheless gritted her teeth and forged ahead.

"Her cat watched bemused as she lit candles and got the charcoal burning; she realised she's forgotten the ink and would have to visualise a talisman of Jupiter. Stepping back she tripped over her robe and fell backwards, her foot catching the altar with a hefty blow scattered burning candles and red-hot charcoal over the carpet. As panic set in and she stamped on the charcoal with bare feet, the terrified cat shot to the door yowling loudly to be let out.

"Still she ploughed on, ignoring the cat (which was almost impossible) she apologises to Jupiter for the disturbance. Unfortunately the cat didn't appreciate the pressing need to sell the house and went from merely terrified to utterly hysterical and was now making an incredible din and trying to claw its way through the door. She couldn't stand it any longer and broke the circle, finally admitting defeat. A complete waste of time, or so she thought."

In the cold light of day, other little mysteries of ritual working revealed themselves. How had the wall candles managed to burn as if they'd been blown by a strong horizontal wind, scattering melted wax all over the carpet and music centre below when she had double glazing? All the windows had been tightly shut and there had been no draughts. Obviously Jupiter was showing how thoroughly displeased he was!

"We finally managed to convince her that it was nothing to do with Jupiter's displeasure with her efforts, but rather that she was simply much too 'uptight' about the whole thing. Now she adopts a much more relaxed approach to her rituals and enjoys them."

Anyone wishing to include a pet animal as part of their working should first ascertain whether the animal has the correct temperament. Not all animals react the same way to magical practises. For example: some cats actively seek out magic and appear to enjoy being in close proximity to a magical working, interested in all that's going on, while other animals make it perfectly clear that the last place they want to be is anywhere near where psychic work of any kind is carried out.

"My cats show distinct boredom for ritual," Mélusine has found. "It's the dog strangely enough who actively insists on taking his place in the circle. Unfortunately, we've had instances where he's nodded off and his snoring has blown out the candles, or he's had an attack of wind which doesn't blend too well with the incense. Minor distractions but nothing compared with having to complete a ritual standing on one leg with the other keeping the door shut, because he's been left outside and is now demanding entry in the middle of a working!"

Unless those who recognise their own abilities from an early age, meet up with a partner and can use the relationship to help expand their psychic horizons, the solitary can often spend years in a magical wilderness. Up until the time Graham and Chris met through a Pagan organisation when they were in their early twenties, they had both worked solo, although Chris had been fortunate in receiving tuition from a high ranking Adept in the Craft. The wide experience they've gained has enabled them to instruct beginners in the Way of the Wise, although they find it increasingly more necessary to strip away all the misconceptions before the student can be offered a clean slate.

Mélusine took a different and much longer route. "A high-powered career in London took me away from my roots but the magic was always there - pushed onto the back burner, so to speak, where it stayed for 20 years. Every so often I'd meet up with people who claimed to be Witches but somehow the claims never seemed convincing and I did nothing about it. Journalistic opportunities during the last anti-occult campaign finally brought me into contact with 'real' occultists when I met my present tutor who convinced me that I should open up my contacts again. It was surprisingly easy to resume the mental alertness and magical perception."

Emma's childhood coven fell apart when one friend emigrated to New Zealand with her parents and the other discovered boys. "Marriage and children took up fifteen years of my life; then I was afflicted with years of ill-health which left me almost bedridden. It was during one of those periods when I was zonked out on painkillers that I rediscovered the Goddess. When I woke up, I felt positive for the first time in ages; I was determined to get well and I did. Within weeks I could sit up - stand up - walk and finally totter about. Late one night I crept into the garden and sobbed, letting all my unhappiness drain into the earth. I knew for certain that I'd found the Goddess again and that she was happy to take me back."

As shown in Chapter Two, it is extremely easy for solitary practitioners to fall prey to selfish or unscrupulous tutors. Emma had prior knowledge of a couple of groups with excellent reputations but these were 'family' groups of long standing; it was probably the solid reputations of these closed groups that stimulated her need to belong to something larger and more organised. With hindsight, she believes the trouble with many of the bigger groups lies in their eagerness to accept just about anyone, without allowing time for friendship and trust to develop.

Emma didn't know Simon was a Witch when they met but after a few months she decided to come clean and was pleasantly surprised when Simon admitted that he'd also recognised the signs. "We worked quite happily together for a couple of years but since neither of us had any formal training, it was a hotch-potch of instinct and limited knowledge but the magic was there and working well.

"Human nature being what it is, we soon wanted to increase that knowledge and spread our wings a bit. I began to be increasingly more dissatisfied with our beautiful, simple magic, I wanted proper training. Goodness knows why. My intention was honest enough, I just wanted to be taught the deeper Mysteries; I was worried that we were somehow missing something."

From thereon in, Simon and Emma stepped onto the roller-coaster that would eventually throw them on the mercy of the group described in an earlier chapter. It all started simply enough. They saw an advertisement in a Pagan magazine for a course of postal tuition, sent for the material and, liking what they read, joined up. Despite making lots of pen-friends with whom they still remain in contact, the time came when their natural abilities forced them to question some of the teachings. As a result they were both unceremoniously booted out. Undaunted they tried again - and this time fell into the clutches of a High Priesthood which almost wrecked their marriage.

"It ruined our magic but we have accepted our part of the responsibility - we should have been content with what we had," said Simon. "Fortunately, we're finding our way back, having come full circle and starting a fresh with a recommended tutor who is helping to rebuild our magical confidence. Now we're happier being two solitary Witches who happen to be married and who can work together when necessary."

Good, solid tuition stood one of Graham's students in good stead when she was drawn to a large beautiful crystal at a craft fair. The vendor was extolling the virtues of the crystal which, he alleged, had been consecrated at Glastonbury and placed on one of the stones at Stonehenge - a snip of a price at £300!

"Everyone was picking it up and handling it. Passing it from hand to hand and admiring the sheer beauty of the thing. I was really envious until I suddenly thought, 'Hold on a minute! If all these people are mauling it about, shouldn't it be cleansed before use? And wouldn't that remove any Glastonbury/ Stonehenge aura it might have had?' By the end of the afternoon someone had paid the price but I didn't feel envious any more, I felt rather pleased with myself that I knew better."

A Question of Self-initiation.

The biggest bone of contention between group and solo working is the validity of the solitary practitioner's claim to be an Initiate. There are those, like Simon and Emma, who are so desperate for acceptance that they will submit to the most incredible rituals in the belief that this is the only way to commit to the God/dess. The traditional High Priesthood across the board is largely responsible for this reaction because (and rightly so) they don't want 'amateurs' setting up groups and peddling inaccurate and misleading information about Craft working.

On the minus side, many refuse to even acknowledge an Initiate if that individual works outside their own particular Tradition or even outside their particular group. This does, of course, lead to accusations of snobbery and elitism but there isn't a more reliable method of checking up on the antecedents of the claimant in an attempt to ensure that those in teaching situations are qualified to do so. From the solitary's point of view, unless for reasons of vanity, initiation should remain a matter between the individual and his or her chosen deity.

What exactly is Initiation and what does it entail?

In nearly all forms of religious rite there is a ceremony suggesting a spiritual rebirth as part of the process of assuming full status as a Witch or Magus. According to *Man, Myth & Magic*, "a transcendent existence, and the powers that go with it, replace the mere human condition." During these ceremonies some demonstration of magical, divine or shamanic power by the initiate is looked for as a sign that he or she has attained the appropriate characteristics of a god, animal or spirit.

As we have seen in an earlier chapter, Bob Clay-Egerton was originally initiated into a coven when he was very young but it doesn't prevent him from accepting self-initiation as a natural progression. "An initiation is an acceptance, symbolically, into a new order, group or condition, as the initiation of qualified apprentices into a guild or other group of craftsmen. Initiation into an occult order is similar. It implies that the initiate becomes a new person, a new man or woman. In occult terms, it implies the 'death' or suppression of the old ego and the birth, or supercedence, of a new dominant ego. In normal initiations the ceremony is conducted by persons already initiated but in occult ceremonies the ritual is performed between the would-be initiate and the presiding entity/deity of the tradition s/he wishes to enter. This being the case, there is no bar to self- initiation. The deity concerned and the would-be initiate are the only entities concerned with the validity of the ceremony.

"The essentials for self-initiation are a certainty about what you are being initiated into; to be sincere in your intentions and to be aware that initiation may cause changes (a) in your personality and attitudes to life due to the actions of your new persona and (b) in the attitude of others to you. If you are intent on self-initiation then a simple ceremony can be performed which will establish you as a Priest/ess in the service of your chosen deity."

Graham also has little difficulty in accepting self-initiation: "When I was 25 I was initiated by Chris at my own request, despite her insistence that it wasn't necessary. It takes a while to really appreciate that self-initiation is just as valid, and maybe more so, than so-called 'proper' initiation by another witch. There are many in the Craft who would still deny that I'm a Witch now, as I wasn't initiated according to their own particular system."

Chris, in her own inimitable way, went for the belt-and-braces approach. "Following my sojourn in the convent, I quickly went through my own ritual of self-dedication and to my mind, I was a Witch. Around this time I came in contact with a very special teacher who was rather mysterious because I only knew him by a single initial but he was extremely supportive and helpful, supplying me with tapes of Wiccan rituals and psychic exercises. He never indicated in any way that my self-initiation was any less valid than any other form of Wiccan initiation, on the contrary, he was happy for me that I had found my spiritual path and that I had made my commitment to it. This has also been the reaction of other subsequent Wiccan teachers. A Traditional (hereditary) Witch even taking the very special step of accepting myself and Graham into her own group - by performing a ritual of making us 'of her blood'."

After years of experience and tutoring, however, Aeron isn't at all happy about the increasing number of people who make wild claims about self-tuition and initiation.

"I'd love to know how they do it," she says, "I mean, it's like teaching yourself brain-surgery, isn't it? 'I want to be a shaman/witch so I'll read this book and get on with it; I'm sure no one will notice if I make a mistake - after all, I can always have the instructions in front of me, can't I?'. How can you self-initiate yourself into something you've only got half the instructions for? How can you self-initiate into a Mystery Tradition where its very nature means it can't be written about - mysteries are shown and experienced through the soul, not learned from a page. However it's accomplished there has to be a huge change and it's between you and your god(s). There has to be a leap of faith, fear, hope; the whole gamut - the chance of not coming out at all, or of coming out mad or inspired."

Mélusine, however, is adamant about the validity of her own status. "If The Old Man [Crowley] held that self-initiation was acceptable then that's good enough argument for me. He maintained that the law is for all and as early as 1900 and despite his own elaborate initiation into the Hermetic Order of the Golden Dawn, devised a Ritual of Self-Initiation based upon the Formula of the Neophyte which was later published as *Liber Pyramidos DCLXXI*.

"'Who art thou?' is the first question which is put to any candidate seeking initiation - it is also the last. In the middle comes - 'Why art thou here?.' I've answered those questions to the satisfaction of the god of my particular Tradition and I can't really see any Wiccan High Priestess arguing the toss with Him. Crowley maintained that there was no question that those initiation rituals of neophyte and Adept weren't genuine if they contained the true formula of a sincere intention. His proof was that they could be made to work by those who understood and knew how to apply them.

"Having said all that, I would still question the validity of many self-initiates. A large number of those who claim this status for themselves usually refrain from entering into any in-depth discussion with Initiates because they are painfully aware of their own inadequacies. Initiation isn't a pretty little ceremony with a recital of something taken from a book - it's an extremely frightening and awe-inspiring moment, or it was to me! I *know* when someone's been through that experience - and so do other Initiates but it's not something that is discussed because it is highly personal. I don't dismiss the theory of self-initiation but even if you do perform the actual ritual alone, it should be conducted under the prolonged guidance of a more experienced Witch or Magus, to whom you can go back to and say - ***'It didn't half hurt, Mum***!'"

"Unfortunately too many people (including those running covens) have a very blinkered view as to just what constitutes being a Witch," said Graham. "There are idiots who argue about what is the 'correct' method to cast a circle; over what constitutes 'proper' initiation; and most of all, over just who is a 'genuine' Witch and who isn't. If you are genuine in your heart, the Lord and Lady will recognise you and that is far, far more meaningful than gaining the recognition of a group of clones. Anyone with half a brain can easily see that there is no one 'proper' way of being initiated, that any method of casting a circle is perfectly valid and no-one can say 'I'm a proper Witch but you're not!'"

Proper Witches or not, the various occult Paths are littered with people who admit to the strangest things and wonder why genuine Initiates suddenly turn away, scratching their heads in wonderment. "I recently heard someone describe themselves as a healer," said Aeron. "When I asked how they worked, they explained they'd never actually done any healing 'cause they didn't want anyone to know they're Pagan.

Then there was the chap who'd worshipped Isis in a space dedicated to Brighdhe and couldn't understand why he felt peculiar. Silly idiot couldn't grasp the idea of the goddess of the place not liking this foreign bint's energy."

Janval Phagan even had a man claim to her face that he was of her Tradition. He'd never worked with her or her Clan but claimed association on the grounds that he'd read something of her's in a magazine. "The look on his face when someone explained his gaffe was a sight to behold. Good job the Old Ones know who 'is' and who's role playing, isn't it?"

Despite the disagreements, a strange attitude to solitaries is the magnetic appeal that their way of working often has for some 'groupies'. Many a solitary has been invited to a Pagan gathering (usually by a third party) to witness the High Priesthood strutting its stuff, only to discover that after a few minutes of conversation they're being invited to join in more *private* workings. As we've shown, many solitaries can and *do* work with others, as and when called upon; a group of people from completely different Traditions can effectively generate a considerable amount of power whatever the purists may claim to the contrary.

Unfortunately this does not always go well as Simon discovered. "Emma and I were invited to work with someone whom we believed to be an experienced occultist and who needed to perform a ritual to help another member of her group. We carefully listened to the whole story and decided there was no reason not to lend a hand. At the appointed time we decided that, as it was her show, we'd let the High Priestess direct operations once we'd taken part in building the circle.

"To avoid a situation of too many chiefs and not enough indians, we quietly concentrated our energies into the person we were helping. While the High Priestess carried out the invocation, we acted as batteries - chanting, drawing down, pouring high amounts of energy into the operation - resulting in the recipient having a powerful magical experience.

"To our amazement we were criticised for our energies being too 'heavy' although in the next breath we were told we didn't contribute enough verbally - even though it was our house, catering, magical equipment, not to mention our energy in and out of the circle. Personally, I think our combined energy unnerved her and that the only way she could cope with the discomfort was to belittle our contribution. This sort of discourtesy certainly convinces us more and more that going it alone is the only sure way to know and understand pure magic - unspoiled and genuine. A solo Witch has no one else to blame if things go wrong. It makes a man of you, so to speak."

For this reason a large proportion of solitary workers are highly suspicious of the magical capabilities of many in the coven system. If there is any form of elitism, it actually tends to be on the side of the *solitary* Adepts who feel that their magical and spiritual development actually outstrips that of many a coven member. It often transpires that the High Priest/ess who appeared so keen at the outset, becomes almost fearful of the energy generated by their new working partner(s). If this reaction does manifest, then it becomes painfully and embarrassingly obvious that the High Priest/ess is inadequately trained in dealing with this type of natural force. The next thing the solitary Adept knows, whispers are circulating that they're into 'black magic' which is the only convincing reason the High Priest/ess can give for not maintaining contact.

"The High Priesthood can be highly efficient at sniffing out naturally powerful solitaries as well as the frauds," admits Mélusine. "They don't openly acknowledge our capabilities or accord us any formal recognition but they sure as hell want to tap into the power source. The added difficulties arise when they realise that the solitary (or couple) quite comfortably work with the dark Shadow, or fourth face, of the goddess. Few covens even acknowledge that deity has a hidden face but it merely serves to demonstrate the sterility of their magical/spiritual abilities. The best thing to do is smile sweetly - and look thick! They soon leave you alone."

Now working with a sympathetic tutor, Simon and Emma are now much happier with their situation. "As far as magical experience goes, I can only speak from my own, though having discussed this group v solo theme with a couple of close friends, it seems to be a popular response that solo working brings the greatest rewards. Agreed there might not be the drama but our magic, although quieter, is certainly not weaker. Neither is it spoilt by pride, ego or one-up-manship. Now we feel our magic is truer, and because it's deeply personal, i.e. just us and our god(s), we know when we find a truth that it's our truth," said Emma.

"I think we've now seen enough poor teaching to be able to see the warning signs early on and when all is said and done, it's far better to go it alone unless a well-respected teacher is recommended," added Simon. "A poor teacher can do untold damage, so to anyone who feels strongly that they need to join a group, or seek a teacher, I would say tread warily. Watch as you walk in the woods; it's better to be in the dark with the gods than in the light with fools."

Whichever way an individual's Pagan tendencies manifest themselves is an intensely private matter but it is obvious from discussions with committed Adepts that they do not look on their faith as a compromise or merely spicy alternative to Christianity. Nevertheless, the path to Adepthood is strewn with those whose Pagan persona is based purely on one-act plays, from the 'High Episcopagan and the Priest/ess of Politikal Korrectness to the Childe Ov Kaos and Crowley-in-a-Past-Life' (*Pagan-spotting - A Field Guide*). This play-acting is usually a cover for those who are self-taught without the benefit of any other form of tutoring.

Bluff Your Way In The Occult, although written tongue-in-cheek offers another valuable 'field-guide' to pseudo-Craft practitioners and the fancy jargon that accompanies the even fancier robes and regalia. The author warns the unsuspecting to be wary of those pompous and impressive sounding names in Egyptian, Latin or Hebrew. "English words can only be used if they're really archaic or really long."

"One of the best ways of recognising the pseuds *can* be learned by the book," offers Mélusine. "*The Bluffers Guide to the Occult* was written in jest, but believe me I've actually heard the various terms and phrases being used in the context that Alexander Rae wrote about them. The longer and louder they talk, the more your suspicions should be aroused. Genuine Adepts will let *you* do the talking, so they accurately assess the level of *your* knowledge before offering any indication of their own interests or capabilities. It's probably the one who looks least like a Witch, who's the one to watch."

"On a serious note, there are many reasons why Witches are they way they are," explained Hazel. "Foremost, they know how to turn off the television. They actually appreciate life and love living it; they are not frightened to be themselves; to walk in the rain, wind and snow. They love to feel free. These are people who cannot stand to feel their spirits trapped; they don't mind doing what the rest of humanity considers 'silly' - like sitting out all night watching the moon - and they don't fear their dreams or turn down the chance of achieving them. So, if you want to spot a real witch, look for someone whose mind is on earth, but whose spirit soars with the comets."

From a more practical viewpoint Chris concludes "Being a solitary Witch means that you must have self-discipline, because you will have to motivate yourself to get your magic done. There is no-one else to chivvy you along and remind you that 'we're doing a circle next Thursday, so you bring the wine, because Adrian is fetching quiche'. If you need to do a working on a Thursday with the moon waning (to diminish the effects of arthritis) and you've got to make up an oil for Mr Jones to rub on his shoulder, make a space in your social calendar and unplug the 'phone.

"And if you suggest to a solitary Witch that you'd like to come round and do some meditation with her, and a little drumming, she'll probably look at you sideways and suggest 'Get a life!"

Chapter 6
Western Ritual Magic - *To The Edge of Dream*

Ritual magic, according to *Man, Myth & Magic,* is the attempt to control powerful 'otherworld' forces through the use of impressive ceremonial, as distinct from comparatively minor and unceremonious acts of magic such as a healing spell, the concocting of a love potion or the wearing of a lucky charm. Unfortunately, to the uninformed, this would also be their definition of darker practises, since ritual magic is mainly concerned with the exploration of the more shadowy aspects of the inner and outer planes. This belief is compounded by the necessity of summoning up a power of some kind - a god, a spirit, a demon, a cosmic force, or whatever the Magus chooses to label it.

European magical textbooks, or grimoires contain all manner of processes and ceremonies, which vary considerably in detail but the common denominator is usually the summoning of 'spirit power'. In the preceding chapters the author had attempted to keep Witchcraft and Western Ritual Magic as separate Paths when, in fact, many coven workings lean more towards ritual magic than Craft tradition. Nevertheless, many Craft practitioners cannot accept that invoking the God/dess is no different to the Magus summoning up the energy-force of some long-forgotten primitive deity who appears in Gettings, de Plancy or the *Goetia* as a demon. The main difference between the two systems is that while the Magus seeks to order the forces, spirits or even deities to do his Will, Witches work with the deities following a mutual Path.

Anyone wishing to study Western Ritual Magic needs to

familiarise themselves with the concept of the macrocosm (from the Greek *makros kosmos* = great world) and the microcosm *(mikros kosmos* = little world). This theory is a 'spectacular development of anthropomorphism' which, in simple terms reveals the universal tendency of man to picture god(s), and the whole world around him, in his own image. The universe is regarded as a human organism on a gigantic scale and man as a miniature copy. Although occult philosophers of the Renaissance adopted the theory it was much older, having been well-known in medieval Europe, which in turn had inherited it from the late classical world, where again the universe was believed to be a living and divine organism.

No longer regarded as having any scientific value, the theory has retained its value for present-day occultists, satisfying two powerful opposite feelings that man has about himself and his place in the universal scheme of things. These ideas are also reflected in the Qabalah which was one of the fundamental pillars of alchemy and forms the basis of traditional astrology, reflecting the relationship between man and the universe while encouraging the construction of correspondences between different factors or forces in the universe and their equivalents in man.

The contemporary form of Western Ritual Magic is now a pot-pourri of theories and philosophies from great names of the past such as Agrippa, Paracelsus, John Dee and Eliphas Levi to the more erudite teachings of Aleister Crowley and Dion Fortune. Added to this, is a liberal mixture of Middle Eastern and Oriental influences from the Qabalah, yoga, tarot, Old Testament, Torah, tantra and Pyramid Texts to gnosticism and astrology. To muddy the waters even further, there is the added spice of elaborate ceremonial, obscure language and the identification with some strange or unfamiliar deity dredged up from the depths of some archaic culture.

"Ritual magic, sometimes referred to as 'high magic', is often the main alternative to Wicca for some students of magic," explained Graham. "Its adherents gave it this lofty title as they needed to feel important whilst they strutted about wielding expensive equipment in lavish robes and performing complicated rituals. This approach to magic is highly structured; the student needs to be aware of a wide range of magical symbolism (which cannot be questioned if part of an established 'Temple'), and an understanding of the way this symbolism fits into a set of magical correspondences.

"Ritual Magic is also extremely precise; it could perhaps be called scientific magic, in that if the precise steps of a particular ritual are followed each time that ritual is performed in exactly the same way, then the results should be duplicated. The big disadvantage is that those rituals are highly complicated. They can require a wide variety of magical implements, and they can be extremely time-consuming. To do it properly, a simple Golden Dawn ritual can take three or four hours of intense magical concentration. I know of some idiots who have followed high magic in a disciplined manner all their lives, and still haven't got it to work!"

On a compatible note, E. M. Butler wrote in *Ritual Magic* "The almost incredible complications and elaborations of these initial rites and ceremonies ... read like the worst sort of obstacle-race. They are certainly calculated to deal the deathblow to any notions harboured by intending practitioners that magic is a short-cut to their desires.

"On the contrary it appears here in the light of a severe discipline both on the mystical and the practical side ... Would-be sorcerers might well pause before embarking on the path traced out for them by 'Solomon'; but could comfort themselves that the results would be in proportion to the effort expended ... They could try and try again until they died of senile decay without losing hope ... but both the God-fearing and the graceless must have been in a state of great nervous tension and fatigue when they came at last to the actual rite of conjuration."

"Unfortunately both are accurate portraits of a large number of very strange people who style themselves ritual magicians," admitted Mélusine . "Another giveaway is their total disregard of 'keeping silence' and the dictatorial manner adopted when informing you that your methods of working must be inadequate or inferior to their own 'proper teaching'. This pathway of correct guidance usually costs a lot of money if you're daft enough to fall for it and I personally doubt there's much to be gained from them in the long run. One chap even had the effrontery to inform me that my own occult book-dealer of many years standing, the Sorcerer's Apprentice, wasn't authorised by their Secret Chiefs to supply particular magical works and therefore I should deal only with his trusted source. Yes - there are a lot of 'em about and most of them barking!"

Over many hundreds, if not thousands of years, true Adepts have worked on certain mental, spiritual and magical attitudes governed by the maxim 'To Know, To Will, To Dare and to keep Silence'. By qualification, the study of magic means that the Knowledge being sought is going to be difficult to find but from that Knowledge comes Will and the conscious ability to choose and pursue a certain course of action. Unless the Adept is prepared to convert his magical Knowledge into action, to Dare becomes obsolete. The reason for keeping Silence is twofold. Firstly self-protection and secondly secrecy can also help to concentrate magical power.

But what exactly is this 'knowledge'? Does it really exist, or is it yet another elitist whim to separate the microcosmic sheep from the macrocosmic goats? Whatever it is, global legend is pretty sure that millions of people have died because of it. The Great Flood or Deluge is part of our universal consciousness and all indigenous creation legends include a mass genocide inflicted by the gods on an (un)deserving human race.

According to the various interpretations humans were eradicated because a) they gained too much knowledge and used it unwisely (i.e. Atlantis/ Mu/Central and South America) or b) the populace went their own giddy way with a total disregard for the gods (i.e. Mediterranean/ Euphrates region). Whatever the cause, the results were death by drowning apart for the select/elect few. Geological and archaeological discoveries prove beyond a measure of doubt that the Deluge happened, while anthropological studies indicate that there are more than 500 Deluge legends known around the world, on every continent - the majority entirely independent of the Mesopotamian and Hebrew accounts.

According to the *'Popol Vuh'*, sacred book of the ancient Quiche Maya of Mexico and accepted by scholars as being 'a great reservoir of uncontaminated' pre-Colombian tradition, these early Central American's ancestors were endowed with superior intelligence.

"They succeeded in knowing all that there is in the world ... Great was their wisdom ... In truth they were admirable men ... They were able to know all, and they examined the four corners, the four points of the arch of the sky, and the round face of the earth." So, for some reason - abuse of power or arrogance - the gods decided that 'such a state of affairs could not be allowed to continue (*Finger-prints Of The Gods*)'. "Then the Heart of Heaven blew mist into their eyes which clouded their sight ... Their eyes were covered and they could only see what was close, only that which was clear to them ... In this way the wisdom and all the knowledge of the First Men were destroyed."

This is the knowledge that the great magicians of history have tried to regain: knowledge that was once the province of the masses was now something to be sought after. Myth and legend are full of men and women who possessed a degree of this arcane knowledge but nearer to our own time we still find those who were willing to brave the wrath of the Church, State and Inquisition in pursuit of Knowledge, Wisdom and Understanding in these esoteric matters. Great men of learning, these scholars of occult wisdom left an actual written legacy for those who came after, despite still being branded as frauds and charlatans by the less enlightened.

Cornelius Agrippa or Heirich Cornelius Agrippa von Nettesheim (1486-1535) - to give him his assumed title - was widely known for his books on magic and occultism in the courts and universities of western Europe. Described as 'undisciplined, unstable and erratically brilliant', Agrippa established a formidable reputation in his own time as a sorcerer but for the modern student, the real legacy was the publication of his book *Occult Philosophy*, 'in which he defended magic as the supreme path to the understanding of the world and God' (*Man, Myth & Magic*).

Like most of the magicians who followed him, little of Agrippa's work is original thought and he mercilessly plagiarised the writings of ancient and modern esoteric sources. Nevertheless, he produced a magical system which indicates a tremendous degree of learning and grasp of occult lore which he compiled into authoritative volumes of esoteric philosophy.

A flamboyant and eccentric personality (a characteristic which appears to distinguish occultists of every era), Agrippa was often forced to live by guile. At varying times in his life he mixed with royalty; at others he was imprisoned for debt. Having played the part of occult scholar and alchemist, he also took on the role of faith healer, demonologist, astrologer, theologian, lawyer and doctor. His highly developed intellect helped develop an analytical faculty which eventually led him to speak out against the whole unscientific basis on which the Witchcraft hunts were carried out.

He also turned his hand to historian, town orator, financial adviser and secret political agent - working for both Pope and Emperor - in addition to forming secret magical societies which exploited their own members. Finally, having offended the Inquisition (probably over his view on the Witch-trials) he was forced to keep on moving around Europe until he was imprisoned and tortured at Grenoble in 1535, dying a few weeks after his release.

Although he was detested by orthodox physicians of his time, **Paracelsus** (1493-1541) has since been recognised as 'the first modern medical scientist'; he was also a mystic whose writings and personality have fascinated generations of occultists. A skilled physician and a son of a doctor, his full name was Phillipus Aureolus Theophrastus Bombastus von Hohenheim. He wrote incessantly, although few of his works were published in his lifetime, and considered medicine as an art-form based on four important foundations. Firstly, a philosophical approach; astronomy or medical astrology; alchemy which he considered a servant of medicine rather than a system of transmuting base metal into gold; and the personal and moral purity of the physician himself.

His non-medical works, *De Occulta Philosophia* and *Archidoxis Magica* are hermetic writings reflecting his theory that Nature heals and man can only assist the course of Nature. In some occult circles practitioners believe there is still a place for 'Paracelsian' medicine, which takes the form of 'certain homoeopathic concoctions which probably owe little or nothing to Paracelsus' quotes Ellis Howe in *Man, Myth & Magic*. Paracelsus died in 1541.

Even by many of his contemporaries **John Dee** (1527-1608) was considered to be a charlatan, imposter and dabbler in black magic. On the plus side, however, his 'erudite works, his projects and treatises, reveal him as one of the most remarkable scholars' of his time. He was an authority on mathematics, navigation, astronomy and optics, as well as being Astrologer Royal to Elizabeth I but it was the dividing line between science and the occult which Dee found fascinating.

Although he spent some time in prison during the reign of Queen Mary, he was remarkably unhindered despite the fact that his 'assistants' were of extremely dubious character. Like all occultists of superior intellect Dee showed a disarming naivety when it came to dealing with his fellow man. During his travels across Europe he collected an assortment of manuscripts and many of his own manuscripts are preserved in The British Museum. It is still not known to what extent Dee was a secret agent (intelligence gathering was still in its infancy), nor how far his dabbling in magic was a cover for espionage. Nevertheless he retained the favour of Elizabeth, retiring to Mortlake in 1605 where he died.

Count Alessandro Cagliostro (born Giuseppe Balsamo in 1743) was a member of a noble but impoverished Sicilian family. At the age of 23 he travelled to Malta to meet with the Grand Master of the Order of The Knights of Malta, who was skilled in alchemy and a Rosicrucian and introduced Cagliostro to occultism. Ten years later he journeyed to London where he continued his studies in alchemy and theosophical theories which he attempted to introduce into the Freemasons' lodges. Following 'several disreputable incidents engineered by his detractors' he travelled from one European lodge to another, under the sponsorship of the Grand Lodge of England.

According to the entry in *Man, Myth & Magic,* Cagliostro's chief aim at this time was to combine the identity of Freemasonry, magic and religion, by going back to Qabalistic sources and the Templar tradition. Having been brought up a Catholic, he maintained that the Bible was full of magic and felt that there was an affinity between all three. "The motives of this extraordinary man have often been maligned through misunderstanding - a confusion increased perhaps by his showmanship, his love of mystery and his curious habit of travelling under assumed names," was an apt description that would fit Aleister Crowley a hundred years later.

Becoming a wealthy man in his own right, Cagliostro was a genuine philanthropist who believed that a man's first duty was to work for the good of others. In 1779 he visited Mittau, a centre of occultism and magic where he began carrying out magical experiments using methods discovered in an Egyptian papyrus which became known as the 'Egyptian Rite'. He introduced these ceremonies to numerous lodges and his reputation as a magician increased. Considered by his contemporaries as a natural and genuine magician, Cagliostro nevertheless attracted jealousy, hostility and slander, finally arousing the antagonism of the clergy who saw him undermining the authority of the Church. As a result, in 1789, he was arrested and following a lengthy trial was sentenced to death. This was commuted by the Pope to life-imprisonment and legend has it that he was strangled by his jailer on 6th August 1795 in the fortress of San Leo, near Urbino.

In any study of magic, one name crops up repeatedly, that of the 19th century French occultist the Abbé Louis Constant, or as he is better known: **Eliphas Levi**. Born in 1810 and educated in Paris, he was later ordained as a deacon but never did become a priest. He developed an interest in occultism around 1844 and some ten years later visited London where his reputation as a magus preceded him. He returned to Paris and attracted pupils who studied the Qabalah under his tuition and published his best-known books, *Transcendental Magic, The History of Magic* and *The Key of the Mysteries* which can still be obtained in English translation.

Unlike other magi, Levi's life was relatively untroubled, his name well-known in occult circles in France, Great Britain and Germany despite the fact that he had condemned magical ceremonies as 'dangerous on moral and health grounds'. Despite spending some 26 years studying the symbolism of the tarot, he never published a complete manual even though he believed the Major Arcana to incorporate a complete system of esoteric wisdom.

Sanctum Regnum, a system of ceremonial magic based on Levi's writings, was a "highly personalised commentary, loosely based upon the divinatory major cards of the tarot pack, in a form which lends itself to ceremonial magic, replete with diagrams, lists of angels, Qabalistic readings and symbolic interpretations which have nothing to do with the original tarot itself." (*Dictionary of Demons*). The text was highly regarded by the founding members of the Hermetic Order of the Golden Dawn but Gettings opines that it gained a 'notoriety and respect it scarcely deserves'. He died in Paris in 1875.

Dion Fortune was born Violet Mary Firth in 1891 and from an early age showed signs of extreme sensitivity to people and places; it soon became evident that she possessed strongly developed psychic faculties. Brought up in a Christian Science household she studied analytical psychology and subsequently occultism. "The power of the imagination plays a great part in occultism, and in later years she learnt to make use of reverie, properly controlled and directed, in the kind of occultism she was to teach and practice (*Priestess*)."

She became a member of The Hermetic Order of the Golden Dawn, applying herself systematically to the study and practice of magic, and emerged a fully fledged occultist. She produced numerous books on magic and much of her material complemented Crowley's researches in the sphere of magical correspondences and magical affinities. Like many occultists, she used fiction as a vehicle for her ideas, well aware that she could disseminate truths otherwise incommunicable to uninitiated minds. Her best known works in this genre, *The Sea Priestess, Moon Magic* and *The Goat-Foot God* communicate an accessible approach to understanding the Western esoteric Tradition. She died in 1946 of leukaemia.

The myth of **Aleister Crowley's** perverted life-style was fostered partly by Victorian attitudes prevalent in early 20th century society; by sensational newspaper reporting and partly by himself. In latter years, biographies were written by professional journalists - one a sports writer, another a radio commentator - whose principle interest in Crowley was financial gain, rather than an opportunity to present an objective view of the man. As a result, these negative commentaries have discouraged many students of the occult from studying his works. Neither is it uncommon for occultists themselves to promulgate the misconceptions surrounding him - such as the proprietor of the occult bookshop who, whilst professing to be an Adept, kept rare Crowley works under the counter because (he said) the very contents of the pamphlets themselves 'radiated evil'.

It would have given the media a great deal of satisfaction if Crowley had been finally carted off, barking mad to the lunatic asylum but he declined to oblige. Although a shadow of his former self, with a daily intake of heroin, originally prescribed to relieve his acute bronchial asthma but sufficient to kill a roomful of people, he lived to the ripe age of 72. Finally outraging Brighton Council by arranging for his own *Hymn to Pan* to be read aloud at his cremation.

Modern Magical Teaching:

Aleister Crowley is probably the most prolific of all occult writers and to make a formal study of his works is both expensive, frustrating and time-consuming. It just isn't possible to sit down and 'study' Crowley since his magical writings are deliberately obtuse and similarly, the famous Crowley motto "Do what thou wilt shall be the whole of the Law" is probably the most mis-translated and misunderstood maxims in the whole of his magical writings. For Crowley, despite its apparent license, this maxim refers to *self*-regulation. "Every healthy living organism relates its own activity on a haemostatic basis without reference to arbitrary man-made laws or codes. It rules itself, regulates itself, and does its own will. Every man and woman is thus autonomous," he wrote. It does not mean licence to indulge in every impulse and the majority of magicians are seriously aware of the consequences of infringing magical law.

Nevertheless, even Fred Gettings, well-known esoteric and occult historian, erroneously expressed concern in his *Dictionary of Demons* over his own interpretation of Thelemic theorem as: "Every man has a right to fulfil his own will without being afraid that it may interfere with that of others; for if he is in his proper place, it is the fault of others if they interfere with him."

Mélusine, however, does not agree with Getting's view. "Once the student learns how to cut through the waffle, you have at your finger-tips the most comprehensible magical system available, although I wouldn't recommend it for novices. There *isn't* a quick guide to magical working since we all have a different set of keys. For anyone with a serious intent to study Western Ritual Magic from scratch, I would suggest they first read the Dion Fortune novels and Crowley's *Moonchild.* It may appear rather strange under the circumstances to first be advised to read fiction but it's truly amazing just how much factual information is contained in those stories. The books give a tangible guideline to the morality of magical philosophy - if you can't accept this code of ethics then ritual magic is certainly not for you.

"Secondly, steer clear of the biographies written by those who either ridicule - as in the case of John Symonds writing about Crowley in *The Great Beast*, or sanitises them in the well-meaning manner of Alan Richardson in his biography of Dion Fortune, *Priestess.* Both Fortune and Crowley were prolific writers on the subject of magic, both fiction and non-fiction, and the serious student doesn't need the input of outside influences when there is such a wealth of material which stands on its own merit."

Crowley's own Thelemic philosophy offers to supply a new and scientifically sound basis for ethics and his books do cover every aspect of his teaching. He believed that self-sacrifice was romantic folly and that death did not end life since it was merely a temporary phase as night and winter are of terrestrial activity. Many other conceptions were implied by the term 'Thelema'. In particular, each individual is conceived as the centre of his or her own universe, their essential nature determining relations with similar beings and a proper course of action. Magick being the practical side of spiritual progress, Crowley ultimately found that his Magick proved more far-reaching in importance than his mysticism.

"Our spiritual consciousness acts through the Will and its instruments upon material objects, in order to produce changes which will result in the establishment of the new conditions of consciousness which we wish. That is the definition of Magick," he wrote. "The obvious example of such an operation in its most symbolic and ceremonial form is the Mass. The will of the priest transmutes a wafer in such wise that it becomes charged with the divine substance in so active a form that its physical injection gives spiritual nourishment to the communicant."

David Conway, writing about Crowley in his *Magic - An Occult Primer* was also quick to point out that behind all the posturing there was an almost 'encyclopedic knowledge of hermetic lore' which fortunately for posterity, found its way into his writings. "Even so, none of these are suitable for beginners, for they demand a certain basic knowledge if one is to extract anything of value from them. It is therefore wise to wait until you find an experienced guide to accompany you before you embark on Crowley's work. The consequences of following some of his ritual instructions could be disastrous."

Robert Anton Wilson referring to the approach of Israel Regardie to the highly complex and numerous works, wrote less reservedly. "Dr Regardie not only writes about mystical consciousness with unparalleled precision, but he has even succeeded in explaining the unique life and works of Aleister Crowley - the most difficult, perverse, enigmatic and generally gregarious individual in the whole history of occultism ... The reader can turn from this book [*The Eye In The Triangle*] to any of Crowley's works without being hopelessly baffled by Aleister's paradoxes, his brain-teasing riddles, his (seemingly!) childish jokes and the endless dialectic between the serious things Crowley had to say and the playful way he said them."

Although Conway was obviously uncomfortable with Crowley, he nevertheless unsympathetically described Dion Fortune as the 'darling of contemporary occultists' although readily admitting that despite her many faults, her 'lucid prose is compulsory reading' for any would-be magician. Fortune's magical writings lack the panache and flamboyance of her contemporaries and tend to be less bogged down with gobbledy-gook but they will provide a clear grounding in the initial stages of exploring the Western Ritual Magical Tradition.

Magic, Magik or Magick?

By rule of thumb anything written by or about Crowley in connection with his Thelemic teachings uses his own distinctive spelling - magick. Anything or anyone else using the term is pure affectation. The spelling used in ritual magic or Craft is - magic. For the record the rendering in Latin is - *magicus*; and in Greek - *magikos*.

But how does the seeker gain entry to this elitist world of - magic. Putting everything in perspective in his Introduction to *The Eye In The Triangle,* Dr Wilson endorsed Hemingway's belief that the only requirement a writer needed was a 'built-in, cast-iron, shock-proof bullshit-detector'. "A writer may have seen and felt a great deal; with extreme good luck, he may even have understood what he saw and felt; but without the tool Hemingway recommended, we will never communicate efficiently. This is especially true of writers on mysticism, who have produced more bad writing than any other single group on this planet, except for politicians."

And if Witches often appear 'strange', ritual magicians more often than not, fall into the category described by Alexander Rae's *Bluffer's Guide:* "For a start 90 per cent of the 'experts' on the subject spend the whole of their lives bluffing. The other 10 per cent are loonies and best kept clear of." Ritual magic is the perfect sink-hole for pseud and charlatan alike because of the lack of communication in this particular area of occultism.

The antecedents of a new Witch in the area can be checked out within hours if the pedigree is authentic but the heady background of ritual magic presents a far more difficult prospect. Because of this, it is advisable to never, ***never*** accept an offer to join any group or tutor which hasn't been endorsed by an experienced practitioner; the occult powers are *probably* non-existent but it could still lead to some extremely unpleasant experiences.

By qualification, most individuals drawn to Western Ritual Magic are egocentric, extrovert and flamboyant people before they start. They love ceremony and opulence although this might be difficult to accept when your new magical acquaintance operates out of a bedsit in Peckham, where the odours of yesterday's curry are inadequately masked by stale incense. Here, touch is the only reliable sense in this realm of blackness, since light has been banished by thick fabric tacked across the window, so do be wary of poking about under the cushions! Often succour comes in the form of second-hand paperbacks and makeshift regalia; but once on their contacts, their drab 9-5 existence with the local Planning Authority is forgotten as they transform themselves into masters of the universe!

At risk of further offence to genuine Adepts, Bob Clay-Egerton added his own contribution. "I tell the truth as I see it - plainly and without diplomacy - for which I am well known. I once had the occasion to refuse a young man entry to our Coven on the grounds that he would be a disruptive influence. I arranged to meet him privately on a number of occasions and although I did not think that Witchcraft was right for him, I drew his attention to other Paths. Over a period of several months I borrowed out-of-print magical books for him from the extensive library of the O.T.O.

"He is now developing a system based on the Draconian system of the O.T.O (though they hate it being called that). We are still occasionally in touch when he wishes to discuss some practical aspect of his research - though I am by no means an expert on the subject of Thelema. He agrees that he was not suitable for any Path of Witchcraft, though he could not see this when he first applied to join our coven.

"Another young man was refused entry on the grounds that he was conceited, self-opinionated and selfish. It was the look on his face that reminded me that people do not like hearing honest opinions of themselves. Then I pointed out that although many modern Witches were possessed of these qualities, they were not acceptable in *our* Coven. They were perfect, I told him, for the kind of Ritual Magician who was in the early stages of learning - as long as he was prepared to learn self-discipline and control. I put him in touch with someone who could help him on this Path and as a result he is now an extremely self-controlled person and an excellent Ritual Magician, well able to use his 'negative' qualities for a 'positive' end."

"One could be offended by all this, I suppose," admitted Mélusine, "but the fact of the matter is that it *is* a pretty accurate caricature of many ritual magicians you tend to come across. There isn't the same networking facility that you get with Craft so it's extremely difficult to keep tabs on those who set themselves up as Adepts. There are responsible teaching organisations with serious study courses but more often than not, it's the inadequately experienced who draw the most attention to themselves. Fortunately they have little power or real understanding of what magic is all about but they can still cause a lot of damage."

In addition to the poor quality of writing on the subject, another problem stems from the fact that it is often difficult to identify the authors of magical reference books. Most write under a magical name and the authenticity of the claim on the book jacket is usually impossible to verify since no one has a clue who they are. As a result, students would be best advised to collect books by *bona fide* magicians such as Crowley, Dion Fortune, Regardie, Kenneth Grant, etc., rather than sensational pot-boilers by anonymous writers. With this level of introduction under your belt, you do stand a better chance of recognising the 'bull-shitters' without too much difficulty.

As one of the leading authorities on occultism, Chris Bray gave what he considers to be a contemporary definition of Magick, explaining that there is a big difference between superstition and the supernatural, which tends to cloud a lot of today's thinking. "Superstition relies on the slavish belief and implicit trust in unexplained forces. It cultivates fear and promotes a reliance on exterior authority, ultimately perpetuating ignorance. Superstition is used by all suppressive forces, cults and religions to paper over the inconsistencies of their beliefs/philosophies in order to manipulate their congregations.

"The supernatural is completely different; this is what genuine occultism is really all about. There are forces which impinge upon humans which are supernatural - these forces exist in many forms, creating changes, mysteries and wonders which science has yet to come to terms with. Testing, invoking, challenging, experiencing and gaining skills to control, direct and benefit from these supernatural forces is Magick and it involves a constant task of self-refinement and the development of self-knowledge."

This is, of course, what Crowley meant when he called magick both a Science and an Art, in that all forms of creativity have to be controlled and directed in order for changes to occur. To understand what he meant, a definition of magick and occultism would be helpful but unfortunately, two of the most influential occultists of this century lay claim to the most often quoted definition of magick.

Aleister Crowley wrote: *"Magic is the Science and the Art of causing changes to occur in conformity with the will,"*

but according to W. E. Butler in *Magic - Its Ritual Power & Purpose*, it was Dion Fortune who coined the phrase first using: *"Magick is the art of causing changes in consciousness in conformity with the will."*

A subtle but tremendously importance difference as Chris Bray points out. "Whilst it is clear from his introduction to *The Goetia* that Crowley knew the purpose of theurgy [prayer] was to evoke aspects of self and control subjective consciousness (and therefore reality in that way), his own definition does not limit magic simply to subjective changes in consciousness; whereas Fortune's definition does. To add to the confusion, it is not uncommon for the definitions to be wrongly attributed and Crowley is often credited with Fortune's phrase. This has led many modern magicians to believe that magic works solely on the subjective consciousness, leaving objective reality unaltered.

"This approach demeans genuine magic and rationalises it into a kind of transpersonal-psychology, dependent upon altered states of consciousness. It has also allowed many non-initiated occultists to assume they understand the portent of magic and begin to teach others without any real knowledge of how occultism affects reality."

Even the serious student has problems in obtaining reliable guidance into the correct procedures governing ritual magical working, being hampered by the (often deliberately) veiled, cloaked and masked theses on the subject. Take the gigantic volume *The Complete Golden Dawn System of Magic* which is aimed at a full Temple working, complete with supporting cast: it sheds little light on the adaptation of rituals for the solo practitioner.

Graham was quick to pounce. "Also because of the precise nature, both of the rituals themselves and the magical preparations which must be undertaken before those rituals can commence, there are a great many things which can go wrong and condemn the ritual to failure. You could almost imagine that this form of magic is designed to fail!

"Ritual is in itself, of course, not undesirable. Most Wiccan rites and spells are performed within a ritualised framework. You do not have to do away with ritual, you just have to do away with the idea that a ritual must be fixed and unchangeable. Also understand that if things do not go according to plan, it doesn't automatically mean that your magic has failed. Use ritual as a framework and it will be flexible enough to allow alterations, to cope with unforeseen occurrences - or to take advantage of unexpected magical happenings."

Both magicians and Witches use a magic circle for their workings - again with subtle differences. In Craft workings the Witch casts the circle to draw power down *into* the circle to concentrate magical energies. In ritual magic the Magi uses the circle as a protective barrier to keep the supernatural power under his control on the *outside*. This, of course, can cause a problem when groups use the mix-and-match method and the poor entity doesn't know whether it's supposed to be inside trying to get out, or outside trying to get in!

Experienced occultist, Britomartis took the explanation a step further. "In ritual magic we are left in no doubt that the magic circle is a defence for the Magus, indeed in *The Key of Solomon the King* we read "... the Circle, whyerein whosoever entereth he shall be at safety as within a fortified Castle, and nothing shall be able to harm him'. The Magus performs his conjurations within the Circle, safe in the knowledge that all spirits, demons, etc., will appear outside the Circle and be unable to enter that area. In Witchcraft, however, this is not always the case. Witches use the Circle as a container for magical energies; building and concentrating the power inside the Circle until at a critical moment it is released to achieve whatever magical effect is required.

"So although both methods use a circle, the reason for its use is very different. This difference is an illustration also of the differing attitudes between Witches and ritual magicians when dealing with spirit entities. This is because the ritual magician is often from a Christian background and the majority of magical texts, i.e. the *grimoires,* were mostly written by clerics; therefore in Western Ritual Magic there are only two kinds of spirit beings - angels and demons. Angels are prayed to and entreated for help while demons are threatened, ordered around and generally bossed about.

"Witches, on the other hand, see all spirits as individuals, each with their own character. Some of the characteristics of a particular spirit may be helpful and friendly, other aspects may be distinctly antisocial, but all the characteristics are taken into consideration when asking for magical aid. This is very important to a Witch, because in many cases the spirit or deity will be invited into the circle to lend their power to the spell working."

Here we return to the question addressed in the last chapter concerning the breaking (or understanding) of magical rules. So which is the 'rule' here? Version 1 where all entities should be prevented from entering the circle or Version 2 when all entities are invited into the circle?

"Actually both rules are equally correct," responded Britomartis, "its how YOU work YOUR magic that's the critical factor.

"If you are being taught ritual magic, you MUST make sure your circle is safe from all intrusions. You must not cross over the boundary once the circle has been built and the entity invoked - whether you can see or feel that the conjured entity has heeded your call is irrelevant. You must behave at all times as if the entity is there, because it is and to behave in any other way is extremely dangerous. If you are learning Witch-magic, however, to prevent the entry of helpful spirits into your circle will be at best counter-productive, and can result in a permanent crippling of your magical effectiveness."

Spirits are conjured by using various texts taken from 16th century '*grimoires*' such as the *Key of Solomon, the Lemegeton* and the *Grimoire of Honorius* or a mixture of anything claiming to be of ancient origin. The rituals vary from one text book to another but there are no clearly defined rules on how to proceed because magic is an extremely personalised affair. *The Complete Golden Dawn System of Magic* compiled by Israel Regardie and Crowley's own *Magick* reflect an era of upper middle-class individuals whose intellectual and financial resources enabled them to indulge in flamboyant magical ceremonies unfettered by small houses and low incomes.

Whilst today's magician may settle for less salubrious surroundings, the correct preparations are still an integral part of the ritual. These may take several days of mental concentration and the ritual itself take a month to complete depending on the method of working. What all rituals must begin with are the consecration and purification of the magician and his/her working area; the preparation of equipment and the wearing of special robes to create the right atmosphere. The balance of prayer and command needs an authoritative stance since spirits are recognised as recalcitrant beings and need to be brought under the magician's control.

Better The Devil You Know

Despite the reports circulating about him in the 1920s, the claims that Crowley was a practitioner of black magic or devil worship are completely without foundation. The media, for want of any expert testimony, dreamt up whatever labels they saw fit to caption Crowley's scandalous behaviour. As Regardie wrote: "I never cease to marvel over the basic simplicity of this strange man. He experimented and adventured in these psychological and spiritual areas with a kind of indomitability that most of us have never had ... This is one of the reasons for my great irritation when I read of criticisms from people who have no concept of what Crowley did, or was attempting to do. They could have absolutely no understanding of the values by which this man operated and functioned in his everyday life."

For magicians, magic is *morally neutral* since it is the true goal of all magi to find and identify himself with an ultimate unity, underlying and pervading all things. It should also be understood that magicians invoke divinity not the devil, and that the intelligences invoked are servants to do the magician's bidding.

Before proceeding further, it is essential that the student knows exactly what is meant by references to these spirits/ demons. For example if we take the infamous 'Dweller in the Abyss'- Chroronzon; he is not a *real* entity. The Abyss is a void filled with all possible forms, each equally devoid of sense or matter, each therefore evil in the only true sense of the word - that is, meaningless but malignant, in so far that it craves to become real. It is the magician himself who gives it form and substance.

Demons can also be thought of in other different ways. Firstly, to the ancient Greeks, everyone had a personal demon, rather like a guardian spirit but it was much more than the guardian angel concept we have today. This personal demon was a guardian, a spirit guide, and even a source of mystical inspiration. Secondly, the conventional Western view of demons as evil spirits, fallen angels who owe their allegiance to hell and ready to cause mental, spiritual or physical harm to anyone foolhardy enough to have any dealings with them. Thirdly, the Pagan view that demons are simply the deities of the old religions which have been diminished and demeaned by the newer religions that superseded them.

"I look on demons as being mere extensions of the *human* condition," said Mélusine, "the ugly, grasping side of human nature. If you examine the characteristics of those in *The Goetia,* each one represents exaggerated aspects of the things most people strive for under normal circumstances: knowledge, money, ambition or a loving partner. If you distort those ambitions to the point of obsession, the thirst for them becomes a corruptive and insatiable desire for magical understanding, fabulous wealth, unlimited power and that old chestnut - licentious sex."

The demons or spirits of *The Goetia* are thereby recognised as portions of the human brain; the correspondences are methods of stimulating or regulating these particular areas. Using the example given for invoking the Spirit Cimieries, we can best understand the demon itself. Cimieries is the spirit governing logic, grammar and rhetoric and therefore refers to the portion of the brain which 'subserves the logical facility'. *The Invocation of Cimieries* can reasonably be used to stimulate and develop these attributes in an individual to enhance his career; over-stimulation could result in megalomania especially as he is depicted as a valiant warrior riding on a black horse.

The Goetia is based on the *Lemegeton* and the *Key of Solomon*; the two books in most common usage are those by A. W .Waite, *The Book of Black Magic & Pacts*, and Crowley's own *Goetia* which, for once, is more user-friendly and relatively simple to follow. The latter explains that there is no effect which is 'truly and necessarily miraculous' since all it offers is the ability to (1) obtain information; (2) destroy our enemies; (3) understand the voices of nature; (4) obtain treasure or (5) heal disease.

In the first instance, the gaining of information or knowledge brings up facts from the realms of the subconscious which the magician can utilise to improve his lot. Using privileged information for deception, treason or fraud is the demonised, i.e destructive, aspect.

The destruction of enemies, so often quoted in anti-occult propaganda as an illustration of the dark side of magical practice merely recognises the destructive forces within ourselves and enables the magician to banish them. The enemies are our own personal 'demons' and there is nothing morally wrong in destroying what is, in fact, capable of destroying you if it gets out of control, i.e. paranoia, alcohol or drug dependency, or sexual obsession.

The ability to hear the voices of nature belongs to our primitive past but there is much to be learned by tapping into this particular power-source as previously explained in the chapter on Earth Mysteries. This is the spiritual side to man's nature but if we allow ourselves to become corrupted or overwhelmed by these extremely powerful primordial urges then mayhem will ensue.

Obtaining treasure and riches means the opportunity to stimulate the commercial portion of the brain to increase income, generate business, cash-flow, to provide for family, employees, etc. If the businessman uses this acumen to ruthlessly destroy other companies, indulge in asset stripping and put people out of work, then the demon of greed and power has taken over.

Holistic healing acknowledges that many disorders of the body stem from the brain and therefore abnormal conditions may be corrected 'in obedience to currents started from the brain'. If the unscrupulous use this power to deplete the physical energies of another individual or rival then, again, the demon has triumphed.

Written down in this simplified manner obviously reduces magic to a mundane level which will no doubt disappoint many a reader, but to those who seriously develop these abilities, magical workings are only mundane in that they become part of everyday life. The great rituals are a necessary part of the psycho-drama *needed* for some aspects of magic but it can also be used spontaneously as Crowley often demonstrated in his *Confessions*.

This explanation shows why Crowley was so scathing about Waite's *Book of Black Magic & Pacts*, since the latter perpetuates the myth that demons are actual entities waiting in the depths of the Abyss merely to cause chaos whenever invited to do so. It also explains why it is necessary for magicians to 'order' demons to do their bidding; by imposing the magician's Will on the force being summoned, control is maintained. The magician remains within his circle protected from the temptation of excess while the demon secured in its 'triangle of conjuration' can only provide what it required of it - no more or less. The 'blackness' of the individual involved governs the outcome of the ritual not the essence of the ritual itself. It also illustrates why, put in its proper perspectives, ritual magic cannot be classed as devil-worship since the magician would be worshipping a portion of himself.

Gerald Suster writing in *Hitler - Black Magician,* made a similar observation. "Whether the magic is white or black depends not on whether sex or drugs are employed as adjuncts, but on how this energy is used. Its proper use is to induce a state of being called variously super-consciousness, the knowledge and conversation of the holy guardian angel, enlightenment, or liberation: black magic consists of using this energy for material gain, or, above all, for the pursuit of power."

There should, however, be some clarification of what is meant by material gain and power since nothing of a magical nature is cut and dried. Nearly all Witches and magicians will, at some stage in their lives, cast spells for personal advancement - a small cash advance or success in a job application, for example, and there is nothing wrong in using supernatural power in this manner. It is the *magnitude* of the demands that awake the 'demon' of lust for material wealth and power and once unleashed, it becomes extremely difficult to control. It also explains why magical writing should never be taken literally - the meaning may actually be the opposite!

Necromancy has long been considered the province of the ritual magician. It is an outdated practice which no longer serves any useful purpose within today's magical society but it is the accusation levelled at this particular aspect of occultism that more often than not finds its way into the tabloids in the form of graveyard desecrations. Whatever brand of vandalism occurs in the churchyard, it seems strange that the vicar is happier pronouncing it an act of diabolical black magic or devil worship than accepting the fact that these are the actions of moronic social inadequates at large in the community.

The ancient practice of necromancy was the province of sorcerers, but as Eric Maple points out in *Man, Myth & Magic*, it is not possible to understand the mysteries surrounding the operation without some 'knowledge of an attitude towards the souls of the dead which prevailed until comparatively recent times'. Western belief in an afterlife was somewhat blinkered until Eastern forms of philosophy began to grow in popularity - until then it had been taken for granted that the dead did not return, except under exceptional circumstances. It was also assumed that a spirit who was on its way to Life Eternal would be pretty angry to find itself dragged back to answer questions of a trivial or fatuous nature, and so there were lengthy and elaborate precautions needed to protect the enquirer from retaliation.

Today the vast majority of occultists accept the theory of reincarnation and therefore the disturbance or removal of a corpse (or parts of it) would have little use for genuine magical purpose since all that would remain would be a dried physical husk of the former owner. The nearest we can get to the ancient practice of necromancy is spiritism - since the motives for anyone wishing to disturb the 'mighty dead' for trivial reasons are usually of a mercenary/selfish, non-magical nature.

Despite the vast majority of demons being man-made, there are still strange occurrences of what the clergy like to identify as cases of possession. Bob Clay-Egerton has often been called upon to carry out an exorcism only to find that he merely needs to get rid of what he terms 'occult invaders'.

"These are entities or intelligences which have invaded the mind of a human being or another species of animal; they also invade non-living sites such as houses, or particular locations or objects. They may be said to be the original space invaders, as some come from the macrocosm, some from the microcosm; the outer planes of consciousness or the inner ones. Occult invaders may travel from the outer planes to invade the inner planes and *vice versa*, as in the case of thought forms which originate in the inner planes of a person's mind, and are then projected into the Outer plane of the dimension we inhabit physically. They may then, depending on their purpose, invade the inner plane of a person's subconscious mind.

"A bacterium or virus which enters the body, whether or not it is dealt with by the *polymorphonuclear leucocytes*, or any other aspect of the body's defence system, is an invader of the body. But this is a physical invader; the occult invader invades the non-physical body. The physical invader may cause death or permanent damage to the physical body; the occult invader may have the same ultimate results. Often the occult invader can lie dormant (like malaria) and the victim may appear to recover completely although often suffering from intermittent and less severe attacks unless the problem is dealt with.

"There is a need for the occult practitioner to take care because your psychic defences are daily dealing with some form of occult attack and sometimes the invaders may get past your auric defences. Occult invaders, whether from the inner or outer planes, are best opposed with the assistance of the deities in your armoury. Your own god/dess can be approached to help, like spiritual specialists with stores of psychic penicillin or streptomycin.

The First Steps

A sensible grounding for Western Ritual Magic is, in reality, an understanding of correspondences; a working knowledge of the Qabalistic 'Tree of Life'; uses of the tarot and development of chakra control and meditation. If this appears like a lot of hard work and study - it is, but you can't even begin to understand ritual magic without mastering a few of the very basic primers.

Correspondences

"It must not be supposed that I am obscure on purpose," wrote Crowley. "I have thought in the language of correspondences continuously, and it never occurs to me that other people have not at their fingers' ends the whole rosary of symbols."

Before leaving for Ceylon in 1899, Allan Bennett gave Crowley most of his magical notebooks, one of which contained the beginnings of a Qabalistic dictionary. Crowley expanded on this idea and the resulting book was published in The *Equinox vol I. no. VIII*. At the time it was the only dictionary of the Qabalah in existence that could claim any degree of completeness. Later combined with his *Gematria* and his own table of correspondences, *Liber* 777 became an essential reference tool for the study of ritual magic.

According to esoteric writer Francis King: "The next great principle of Western magic is the belief that the properly trained human Will is, quite literally, capable of anything. The motivating power, then, in all magical operations, is the trained Will of the magician. All the adjuncts of ceremonial magic - lights, colours, circles, triangles, perfumes - are merely aids to concentrating the will of the magician into a blazing stream of pure energy."

As discussed in some detail in Chapter One, correct correspondences are essential to the rite and symbolism of all effective magic. *Liber* 777 covers all manner of permutations from the very basic to the sublime, at the same time leaving a certain amount of leeway for the Adept to experiment with his or her own methods, since there are many (deliberate) contradictions and inconsistencies in the tables.

Qabalah:

Upon first introduction, the Qabalah appears to baffle the student with a blanket of pseudo-magical science and non-sensical imagery. Indeed there are dozens of incomprehensible tomes on the subject that do little to shed light on this ancient philosophy. Modern occultists have been influenced by the power of the Qabalah, although strictly speaking it is a system of Hebrew mystical thought which originated in southern France and Spain in the 12-13th centuries; there are Rabbinic references to much earlier influences, probably Chaldean. The word means 'receiving' or 'that which is received' and by 2-3AD, it had been re-interpreted as a tradition - especially of a tradition handed down by word of mouth.

The fundamental idea of the Qabalah is that the universe may be regarded as an elaboration of the numbers from 0-10, arranged in a certain geometric design and connected by 22 'paths'. Qabalistic study claims to reduce all possible ideas to combinations of comparatively few originals, the ten numbers, in fact; these ten numbers being of course interrelated. The problem for the novice is the acquisition of perfect comprehension as to the essential nature of these numbers.

The entry in *Man, Myth & Magic* states that the backbone of the Qabalistic system is its doctrine of deity, which distinguishes between the inaccessible and the unknowable, *deus absconditus* (the hidden god) on the one hand, and the self-revealing dynamic God of religious experience on the other. Of the former not even existence can be predicted. This is the paradoxical fullness of the great divine Nothing.

In simplistic terms the Tree of Life comprises of three columns which are positive, negative and neutral; its ten sephiroth (spheres) which correspond to a planet and are seen as a diagram of the way in which the universe came into existence. Each sephiroth is attributed with certain key-symbols and qualities but the student quickly learns to make his own associations 'until eventually he will relate to every aspect of his existence, every happening within him and without, with the interrelated symbolism of the spheres upon the Tree ." (*Priestess*)

Conversely, it is also seen as a diagram of the way in which man can unite himself with, or become the One by rising through the spheres - spiritually climbing the ladder of the ten sephiroth to reach God. The twenty-two major arcana of the Tarot pack symbolise the twenty-two Paths which link the ten sephiroth together, and provide mystical pathways along which the magician travels.

Perhaps the most accessible work on the subject is *The Mystical Qabalah* by Dion Fortune which focuses on the correspondences, which in turn are based on the *otz chaim,* or Tree of Life. This simple system has been described as 'the mighty all-embracing glyph of the Universe and the soul of man' capable of infinite interpretations on an infinite number of levels. Alan Richardson, writing on Fortune's approach to the subject in *Priestess,* added: "Once planted within the psyche it grows and grows, almost impossible to uproot. It links heaven and hades and leads mankind up or down, only to find that one is the same as the other. We can make it grow exactly how we want, give it any slant and make it bear any fruit."

It's also given Mélusine the confidence to explore the reverse side of the Tree of Life, the realm of the 'hidden god' which Kenneth Grant writes about quite extensively in his books, *Aleister Crowley & The Hidden God, Cults of the Shadows* and *Nightside of Eden.* "This draws on the primordial raw energy of the 'saturnic' [sic] path and far from being Darkness, burns with a brilliant fire. Crowley maintained that every student should construct their own Tree of Life, devising a system of their own so that it becomes a living source of power. A simple photocopy makes a start but beware those authors who shy away from mentioning Daath - the eleventh or 'hidden sphere' - as the writing will be hollow and insincere. Creating your own Tree does make study a lot easier, especially if you use symbols and images to fit your own particular Path and correspondences."

Tarot:
The tarot has already been discussed as one of the most popular methods of divination but the ritual magician is more likely to use the pack as a focus for magical and/or mystical workings. The 22 cards of the major arcana correspond to the twenty-two paths on the Qabalistic Tree of Life but as Dion Fortune points out in *The Mystical Qabalah,* there is little use going into a shop and buying a pack of tarot cards for magical purposes unless there is the basic knowledge available on which to build up the astral correspondences to each card.

Once that knowledge is there, however, the Adept can take the "cards into his hands with a considerable degree of confidence that his subconscious mind, whatever that may be, will all unwittingly deal the cards that refer to the matter in question. Exactly how the shuffle and deal is affected we do not know, but one thing is certain, when the Great Angel of the Tarot has been contacted, the cards are remarkably revealing." (*The Mystical Qabalah*)

There are dozens of designs now available for tarot decks but all consist of seventy-eight cards. There are four suits, as in modern playing cards but there are four Court cards instead of three; there are twenty-two 'trump' cards each of which offering a symbolic picture with a title to itself. "At first sight one would suppose this arrangement to be arbitrary but it is not," wrote Crowley in his introduction to *The Book of Thoth.* "It is necessitated by the structure of the universe, and in particular of the Solar System, as symbolized by the Holy Qabalah."

The tarot was an intrinsic part of Golden Dawn's course of ritual, mediation and study, offering as it did, an extremely 'lucid and systematic approach' to the Western mystery tradition'. Members of the Order undertook the most solemn oath of secrecy concerning details of the Order's own deck, which remained unknown until a facsimile was painted under the direction of Israel Regardie in 1978. Both Crowley and Fortune used the system extensively, Crowley later pouring the 'entire content of his magical mind into his tarot', incorporating the 'latest discoveries in science, mathematics, philosophy and anthropology' (*Atus of Tahuti* - The Thoth Tarot).

Much of modern tarot symbolism is the product of the 'scientifically-designed pack' created by Eliphas Levi; the *Atus of Tahuti* or Thoth Tarot, takes Levi's work a step by further incorporating the beautiful designs painted by artist Lady Frieda Harris for Crowley from 1938 to 1943. It really doesn't matter which pack the Adept uses because, as Chris Sempers explained in Chapter One, there is no one true way to read the tarot. Each set of cards will 'communicate' with its reader in their own special way which is a million miles away from the standard readings given by professional fortune-tellers. The tarot becomes one more magical tool in the magician's (or Witch's) armoury which can be used when requiring 'supernatural' guidance from other planes.

Chakras:

Although primarily an Oriental tantric technique, learning how to control the chakras teaches the magician how to control the flow of energy through his or her own body for a variety of beneficial reasons - both magical and physical. In Chapter Five it was shown how by using the flow of energy on a very superficial level could produce a feeling of well-being and relaxation.

The chakra is a centre within the body at which there is a concentration of psychic energy. Used correctly, this energy can be directed outwards from any, or all, of these centres to achieve specific magical goals. Originating from classical Indian tradition, the seven major centres are located at the perineum (between the sex and excretory organs), below the navel, the solar plexus, heart, throat, brow and crown of the head. These centres are opened up during meditation and can be used when performing magic, or simply as an exercise to calm and prepare the mind.

Author Benjamin Walker (*Hindu World*) described the chakras as psychic dynamos or centres of super-physical energy. "They have no physiological existence because, although the corresponding points of their contact with the physical body are known to occultists (such as the point next to the solar plexus), an examination of that area in the physical body will not disclose its presence ... The chakras cannot be laid out on a dissecting table like pieces of tissue; they can only be known through meditative experience."

The Base Chakra (*Muladhara*) is the location of the *kundalini* (the fire snake or life force) and the centre used as concentration during sex magic. If the chakras are to be opened in their correct order, the *kundalini* can be visualised as a coiled red serpent at the base of the spine, or more correctly between the anus and genitals. [According to Kenneth Grant (*Aleister Crowley & the Hidden God*) the process for this form of magic is easier for the female to accomplish because the 'serpent power' can be more readily imagined in phallic form - see Chapter 7.] This chakra is visualised as a red bud of the lotus, opening into a four petalled flower.

This is the centre of elemental earth and acts as a stabilising point for all magical and mystical practises but since it is also the centre ruling all instinctive passions, (i.e. fear, hate and lust), there needs to be a strong control over the psychic energies emanating from this point. If the kundalini remains 'unawakened' is can lead to anxiety and insecurity; on the reverse side of the coin, people who have all their energies concentrated at this level can become lethargic, ultra-conservative, stubborn and bigoted.

The Navel Chakra (*Swadhishathana*) is located just below the navel. This is the centre of elemental water and governs the ability of a person to move with the currents of magical energy. And, according to Chris Sempers, it is also usually at this centre that the majority of our emotional connections are made with people, objects and places, i.e. the 'gut reaction'. This lotus is orange coloured with ten petals.

The Solar Plexus Chakra (*Manipura*) can be located in the hollow just below the rib cage and is associated with self-healing; the ability to bring about balance within the bodily system and assimilates spiritual or magical knowledge for physical well-being. This is a six petalled, yellow lotus.

The Heart Chakra (*Anahata*) is the centre of creativity and renewal. Associated with elemental air it is the centre from which love and compassion spring. As with the Base Chakra, the correct balance is needed here because extremes of these emotions can cause imbalance on a psychological level. This lotus opens to reveal twelve green petals.

The Throat Chakra (*Vishuddha*) is the centre of self-expression and communication. "Opening this chakra," explains Chris, "can allow your true feelings and desires to surface, perhaps for the first time in your life, and this can be difficult for others to handle, if they have got used to your particular pattern of behaviour." This is visualised as a violet, eighteen petalled flower.

The Brow Chakra (*Ajna*) is the centre of clairvoyance and often referred to as 'the third eye'. Located between the eye-brows, just above the bridge of the nose, it is the centre of command of all faculties, physical, mystical and magical. With this chakra open the adept is given clear sight for anything not normally available to the physical eye. This is a blue, two petalled lotus.

The Crown Chakra (*Sahasrara*) is the centre of the highest spirituality and it is through this centre that we are linked to the universe. But as Chris points out, "This is usually used for the highest spiritual aspirations - which usually have limited applications to magical practice." This is the thousand petalled lotus that opens in the full brilliance of silver, gold and pure white.

Ritual magic is not a Path suitable for everyone to follow, although this may, at first, appear to sound like an elitist response. As we have seen, it remains at once an independent Path, while being flexible enough to dovetail quite comfortably into other magical systems. Much of today's ritual magic has its roots in 15-17th century *grimoires*, which were the product of scholarly minds; Craft practice was generally the province of the uneducated. As education became available to the populace at large, so the magical systems were found to be compatible to such a degree that many of today's practitioners are unable to separate ritual magic from traditional Craft working. Some Craft members are astounded to discover that a much-loved and well-publicised traditional Witch chant may well have been plagarised from Aleister himself.

"I O EVOHE, Blesséd Be!"

"I have come across the same invocation in many Wiccan Traditions and books produced by well respected Wiccan writers, used as a repetitive chant to build power for spell work," said Britomartis. "It is usually said to be a special Wiccan chant passed down through generations, and I suppose as people have moved from group to group, or exchanged chants and rituals between themselves, this chant and its use have become very widespread. I have even been told that it is extremely ancient; others have implied that it originated with the Basque Witches.

"I, however, have far more reason to believe that this is a 'Crowley joke'. There is little dispute that when Gerald Gardner was compiling his *Book of Shadows* (manual of Wiccan rituals) he used input from a variety of sources (many nothing to do with our native British Witchcraft) to 'flesh out' the fragmented remains he had been given. Doreen Valiente helped with much of it, but there are also significant lines and passages written by Aleister Crowley.

"Now to come to 'I O EVOHE'. While studying the *Goetia,* 'rendered into ye magical or angel-like language by our illustrious and ever-glorious frater, ye wise Perdurabo', I kept coming across the name 'Iehevohe' or 'Iehovohe'.

"In either case, this was the special magical name of the

Jewish god IHVH, translated into English as Jehovah. So now it was obvious that IOEVOHE was another version of IHVH (I-O-EVO-HE). 'I O Evohe, Blesséd Be!' will still work wonder- fully well as a power raising chant, but it can be seen that not by the wildest stretch of the imagination can it be linked with native British indigenous beliefs. It is a Jewish chant, taken over by Christian ritual magicians, and only lately introduced to Witchcraft."

Although the rituals can be moved about freely between ritual magic and Craft, and while some Crafters are drawn to the more elaborate aspects of ritual magic, it is rare for magicians to move into Craft. "My background was Rosicrusian and a bit of Qabalah, generally in the style of what some would erroneously label 'white Magick'," explained Frater Glendower. "The reason why I considered myself is this way was because I was naively unaware of anything else. I could never attempt a lot of practical work or major projects since I was in the army where it was 'not on' to acknowledge an interest in such things.

"It wasn't until I left the army that I could look at any sort of development. I'd always been connected with the soil and I now had time to stop and listen, though I didn't relate to the energy-shift side of things that I'd picked up during my magickal studies because there were certain other priorities - such as finding a job and getting on with my life. I very quickly became aware that one of my new colleagues was slightly different to the rest and following a series of lengthy discussions she introduced me to a Witch of her acquaintance.

"What I discovered was the similarity between what I'd been doing shut away in cellars and wandering around in the countryside - and what was happening there. There was a sudden blurring of the line of what I thought I really wanted to do and what I was possibly going to be *able* to do. I felt that there was more to what I'd been playing at than could ever meet the eye. The little schooling I'd had in the 'formal arts' started to expand rapidly into: 'That was one side of it - here's another - you don't have to choose, but what you have to do is take it all in because it's all valid.'"

Since that day, Frater Glendower has re-evaluated both options and found that they are both sides of the same coin. "In fact, I think they are sides of the same triangle or die. So when you have the die, you have definitely got the basis of Craft, of Qabalistic teachings, Rosicrucian, Odinist - every part of the slightly more esoteric, non-mainstream are represented on this die. But then, if you expand the shape you can represent all the mainstream religions. Therefore it's all valid. What you want to do with it, how you wish to work with it, how you wish to worship or portray it, is where the individual differences come in. But at the end of the day, whether you're standing in a pentagram of salt and sand calling on something that is quite hairy and nasty, or whether you're touching a tree, you're still using the same 'muscles'.

"People are beginning to realise that the 'muscle' works, and that once it has been activated it takes a lot to deactivate it. So, if I were asked about why I changed, I would say, availability - because anyone whose muscle has been activated should look elsewhere, even for just an exercise in comparison. I was given a comparison and felt happy about it.

"If it had been a Masonic-type thing instead, you'd probably find that I'd have been captured in the first instance by it (I need to be captured), but it's not until some way down the path that you actually realise that all options are open, all options are valid and quite often there are more options than you think. I'd say it doesn't matter where people start - and it doesn't matter how long it takes people to get where they're going - as long as the first thing that happens is that muscle is activated."

Frater Glendower's experiences echoes the sentiments of Alan Richardson (*Priestess*) who maintained that Adepts have the ability to recognise, during everyday contact, those who have already forged links with the same inner sources as themselves and know this beyond any doubt.

"They recognise a kindred spirit - in more than one sense - a fellow initiate of a peculiar and entirely compatible sort;

another member of their magical tribe, in fact, even though a complete stranger."

This 'knowing' manifests itself as psychic impressions or just a gut reaction. "Whatever it is, it enables an Adept to detect a 'fellow flame-bearer' from out of a crowd, including those who have potential and as yet no conscious interest."

We are not alone.

Chapter 7
The Beast & the Scarlet Woman - Marginalia

Bob Clay-Egerton's no-nonsense approach to occultism is probably the best way of introducing the inevitable subject of sex to the practice of magic. "I may often appear to be a little harsh towards some of my fellow Witches and Magicians," he wrote. "It is perhaps that I am getting grouchy in my old age but to be honest one can get a little tired of the rubbish being passed off nowadays as arcane knowledge by posturing poltroons who imagine that to have read a few books on Witchcraft and Magic makes them 'Masters' of the occult.

"No doubt the prissy-minded, the undefiled intelligensia of the Pagan world, the plastic Pagans, the sham shamans, the wishy-washy-Witches and the maudlin Magicians will wring their hands at the mere suggestion that some aspects of occultism have sexual overtones. The cry will arise that this is bad for the Pagan image and will provide ammunition for our enemies.

"From the Craft's point of view it is popularly hailed as a ancient fertility religion but although fertility is based on sex, modern Witches appear to be ruled by the sexual-moral bias of the religion which persecutes them! They have difficulty in getting off the bandwagon of early childhood brain-washing by parents, teachers and clergy by maintaining that the sex act should only be performed with one's partner. It is, they say, a 'sacred act'. *It can be*, in the right circumstances and with the correct intention. Otherwise it is a very *natural* act.

"The primary purpose of all sexual enactment in tantric and some of the other magical techniques is the raising of power by the manipulation of various wavelengths and energies through the physical and mental stages to affect the spiritual. The soft, the prissy-minded, the whiter than white do-gooder, the occult play-actor/ess, the dainty dabbler have no part to play in such searching. They may criticise - but that is what they are good at. Outsiders criticise without actual personal knowledge of what they are criticising and warning against; the occult equivalent (usually with less than three decades of study or experience, and that in one Path only) will be just as swift in their condemnation from a purely theoretical point of view."

There is no coincidence in the fact that the words 'venerate' and 'venereal' are etymologically connected to the name of the Roman goddess, Venus. From ancient time sacred sex has played an important vital role in the various religious and magical aspects of occultism. This train of thought goes back to the original creation myths which hold that the world, and indeed the whole universe itself, as being a product of divine sexual activity.

From an historical point of view, sacred sex has often been viewed as an integral part of religious worship. The Greek writer, Herodotus, recorded a Babylonian temple with a sumptuous apartment reserved for the woman who had been chosen by the god himself; he also recorded a similar practice in Egypt. This passage refers to the "voluntary self-dedication of women, who surrendered themselves in the sexual act to a representative of the god, either the king in his sacral function or a priest. (*Man, Myth & Magic*)". This represented a dedication of the procreative powers in the community; the king ritually joined with a specially dedicated woman who became the mother goddess, and "on that account held priestly office".

At the other end of the scale there was also ritual prostitution where ordinary, respectable women would make themselves available for sexual intercourse, not with the deity or dedicated representatives of the gods, but with the worshippers. This practice was known from Mesopotamia and Canaan and mostly connected with the goddess Ishtar/Astarte. The fact that this form of ritual prostitution was open to abuse goes without saying, and eventually degenerated into unlicensed promiscuity which spread throughout the Mediterranean. Notably this happened in the cult of Aphrodite in Cyprus; in that of Cybele, the Great Goddess of Asia Minor which was introduced into Rome during the Punic Wars; in the cult of Isis during its development as a Mystery religion in Ptolemaic Egypt and later in Rome, where it was introduced at the end of 3BC. In the East, sacred prostitution was common in India up until the end of the 19th century.

Despite the graphic claims of the tabloid press and anti-occult campaigners, gratuitous sex and magic *don't* mix. Orgiastic group gatherings, lewd assaults on infants and sacrificial virgins are the product of over-active imaginations and the pressing need for tabloid sales. In reality, an unwilling or terrified partner only generates negative energy which is detrimental to any positive magical working and will only result in failure. The experience related by Emma in an earlier chapter demonstrates how pointless an exercise, reluctant sex can be when introduced into a magical ritual.

Nevertheless, sex and sacrifice has been one of the most consistent charges levelled against occult practises - often perverted, always excessive. But no book on magic would be complete without references to both - and what it implies to *occultists*. As Chris Bray explains "Detractors always use the term 'sacrifice' so that they can turn historical records to their devious and wicked ends. Every mention of the word is immediately interpreted by these sectarians as the ritual killing of a human.

"In reality the word sacrifice comes from the Latin *sacrificium* whose root is *sacre* (sacred) and *facio* (to make). Sacrifice, therefore, simply means to make an offering to one's gods and that offering was usually, almost inevitably, a gift of food or incense. There is no evidence anywhere that the word sacrifice should be taken to even include human sacrifice, let alone exclusive to it. Pagans do not involve themselves in any form of human or animal sacrifice, but they do offer food, libations and incenses to their gods, as is traditional."

Blood sacrifice played an important role in the religious observances of the ancients, particularly the Aztecs, although it is ridiculous (and unwise) to judge those actions by 20th century standards. The slaughtered animals and captives were offered up in homage to their gods, not out of cruelty or a blood-lust but in thanks for the victory or deliverance over their enemies. Ancient man believed if the gods were not appeased or honoured, then drastic consequences would be inflicted on his tribe, clan or country. Blood is the 'life-force', therefore blood is the supreme sacrifice - even Christians refer to 'the blood of the Lamb', (i.e. Jesus) washing away the sins of the world.

In today's esoteric teachings we are no longer hampered by such superstitions and fully understand that such gruesome activities would serve no magical purpose, although evangelical fundamentalists still tout the accusations around as part of their Witches' 'gospel'. Clinical psychology has a name for those whose sexual excitement is stimulated by blood-letting and/or killing but these are *medical* conditions and not occult-oriented. It is pure superstition and enduring medieval politics that have clouded the issue but as Bob Clay-Egerton as found, a surprisingly large number of Pagans still consider sex/sacrificial magic to be 'dark practice'.

Public attitudes, of course, are willing to believe such actions are carried out as was illustrated by the prosecution in the Ruth Neave case, who claimed that her son's body "spread-eagled in a posture identical to Leonardo da Vinci's drawing of Vitruvian Man" suggested it was offered up as a sacrifice. The reason behind the claims? Ms Neave was alleged to have a "fascination with the occult and black magic, and performed tarot readings for neighbours. She owned a book entitled *Magic* (sic) by the mystic Aleister Crowley which gave details of sacrifice." (quoted from *The Daily Telegraph* court report).

Any Adept of ritual magic worth his salt knows *exactly* to

which extract the prosecution was referring. The most publicised of Crowley's rituals is the candid admittance that he had carried out a bloody sacrifice 150 times in a single year! According to Regardie and a senior British occultist, he was merely stating that he had 'spilled seed' 150 times that year, a fact corroborated by his diary. The sacrifice here refers to the spent semen, i.e. ritual masturbation - but it has been fixed firmly in the public mind that Crowley had indeed murdered 150 children! It is expected that the tabloid press should use misleading quotations such as this but for it to appear in a British court of law is untenable. [Ms Neave was later found innocent of her son's murder but imprisoned for neglect.]

In words of one syllable then: sacrifice is something consecrated to a deity, either with a view to bringing about a certain result; as a gift; an act of atonement; or as an act of communion. A great deal, of course, depends on the Adept's image of the deity and 'on the degree to which the god is thought to be accessible to human approach'. Primitive peoples indulged in blood (human or animal) sacrifices for a variety of reasons but mostly to appeal to deities who controlled the cycles of the year, fertility and re-growth, i.e. earth or sun-gods. The higher, or more remote deities would be contacted fire, i.e. smoke, which acts as a mediator between the worlds.

"I shall never forget the look on a neophyte's face when I casually mentioned that I'd once sacrificed a horse to Epona," said Aeron. "When I acquired the mare, I vowed that she would never be ridden by anyone, including myself. *My* sacrifice was to forego the pleasure of riding her and to pay for her keep - which I did until she died naturally many years later."

Mélusine quickly discovered that a new wand she wanted to use for mystical rites had a primitive streak to its nature. "Every time I picked it up I was 'bitten' - in the finish, instinct told me to consecrate it by using a smear of blood from a pinprick on the finger. From the moment it 'tasted' blood, I've had no further trouble in using it for magical workings. Having said that, my tutor hates the thing and doesn't want it anywhere near her."

All ancient cultures recognised blood as representing the life-force and any ceremony requiring the shedding of blood was considered to be and extremely serious and sacred affair. Oaths taken using blood are known as blood Covenants; blood-brotherhood creates an 'artificial kinship' between individuals who were not related. Witches were said (erroneously) to sign their pacts with the devil in their own blood. Blood washes away dishonour and the old belief that blood cried out for vengeance persisted long in folklore and literature according to *Man, Myth & Magic*.

Sacred blood, of course, doesn't always refer to that shed in honour of the god. There is still a deep-rooted fear or revulsion in the mind of both primitive and modern man for menstrual blood; contact could be highly dangerous and precautionary measures involved their females being isolated or even caged during menstruation. From ancient times, however, it was recognised that women generated sex-magical power during menstruation. According to Frater U D (*Secrets of the German Sex Magicians*) this is precisely how the social taboos concerning menstruation came into being, since these natural phenomena were rarely handled in a controlled manner and patriarchal societies were simply not capable of handling such 'bundles of power'.

"Experience of Western sex magic shows that menstruating women are an immense source of power in a ritual," he wrote. "Male sex magicians should rejoice in the opportunity to work with a menstruating female magician, because this can multiply many times the efficacy of sex-magical operations."

There is, however, another side to this sex-magic coin as Mishlen Linden explains in her *Typhonian Teratomas: The Shadows of the Abyss* and that is the fact that for the most part the little that has been written on the subject has been written by men. Most magical texts claim that a woman's power-time occurs during menstruation - and this is correct from the *male* point of view. During this time the power becomes available to those outside the woman, i.e. her magical partner.

"In actuality, it is during the days prior to her period in which the power builds. This is the time of empowerment for women. The three days prior to her period can be considered her most powerful, and all the days between the moon-time can be seen as leading up to these three days."

Linden maintains that the imbalances caused by the suppression of this magical energy results in PMT - pre-menstrual tension - as the body builds up excess power like an old-fashioned pressure-cooker. "... the body, buffeted by its increased power, tries desperately to equalize the force growing within it. This generally results in more imbalances which are the root causes of PMT."

In tantric practises the menstruating woman is put in a special category since during this time her female energy is said to be at its highest and intercourse with her is considered invigorating and healthy. According to Benjamin Walker, an acknowledged authority on tantrism, "Any woman in menses is the goddess incarnate and should be engaged in sexual rites in the appropriate manner. As the menstrual blood and semen represent the body-fluids of Shakti and Shiva this mixture is considered to be the true alchemic 'Elixir of Life'."

"Bring on Another Virgin, Sejanus"

Good old *Man, Myth & Magic* upheld the magical view of sex as a way of apprehending and achieving unity, not only in human beings but in the world at large. This is, of course, not confined to practising magicians. An increasing number of people consider sexual activity to be good, not just because it is pleasurable, but because it will somehow, magically and mystically promote general peace and harmony. This merely brings up-to-date the old principle that by imitative magic, human sexual acts promote the beneficent activities of the gods.

It also provides the basis for what have become reputable therapeutic exercises made popular by writings such as Margo Anand in her books *The Art of Sexual Ecstasy* and the rather misleading title *The Art of Sexual Magic.* Anand quite rightly believes that sexual energy can be used to transform a person's life-style. She also observes that there is 'nothing more powerful and attractive than a harmonious couple who co-create their success through sexual alchemy'. Cut through the publisher's waffle and it is easy to see how a psychologist has stripped away the magical elements of ritual and tantric practicses to use them for her own ends; imagine how much more potent they would be if properly realigned with magic.

Since the beginning of recorded time we have evidence of the sexual overtones of the religious practices of different civilisations but, like many other aspects of Christian doctrine, absorption of Rabbinic lore and myths from other classical sources led early scholars to interpret old beliefs in a completely different and sometimes, contradictory light. The first 'religious' sexual difficulties originated with Lilith, a Hebrew deity, whose antecedents can be traced back to 3,000 BC in Sumeria. She is possibly the first identifiable 'creation' goddess but with the spread of the mono-Semite culture she, like many of her kind, were erroneously forced into the ranks of demons.

Whilst Adam was made from clay, Lilith (his first wife) was immortal, created out of the primordial slime - from which came all living things. Legend has it that the couple had a difference of opinion because Lilith considered herself equal to her spouse and objected to lying supine during their conjugal couplings. When Adam tried to enforce his masculine superiority, she decamped from the marital lair and went off on a jaunt with Asmodeus who was more proficient in the bedroom stakes.

A disgruntled Adam complained to God, who sent three celestial 'heavies' to bring her back but Lilith refused to return to the poor specimen the Hebrew Creator had furnished for her and so God was forced to create a more compliant Eve, by way of compromise and to shut Adam up. Lilith, it would appear, had the last laugh on her unsatisfactory spouse for his unimaginative sexual qualities. One of her emblems is the serpent, and it was in this guise she tempted Eve into taking the apple which resulted in the eviction from Eden.

Hebrew tradition developed the myth to claim that Lilith attacked men who were sleeping alone, seducing them in their dreams and drinking their blood; it is this aspect of Lilith which is most prominent in legend. She became identified as mother of the incubi and succubi (*lilin* or *liliot*), and originator of the vampire myth, in that both entities are charged with drawing the life-force ,(i.e. semen and blood) from their human victims. Her medieval French counterpart, *Le Succubé*, is always searching for reckless and amorous young adventurers who become her lovers and victims. As in Keats' poem, *La Belle Dame Sans Merci,* the kiss of *Le Succubé* was sweet, but it drained the life strength from mortal men.

From the beginning of the existence of the vampire in ancient times to its 'recreation' in Victorian Gothic literature, we have the barely suppressed sexual undertones that have persisted in vampire/demonic stories to the present day. The fiend, whether based on *Dracula* or *Carmilla,* is a charismatic creature, capable of drawing willing victims like moths to a flame despite the exhortations of their mortal family and friends. Incubus or vampire, the lure is irresistible and very much a sexual response although this was unsuccessfully suppressed by a craving for blood in Victorian fiction. Etchings of the period always depict the succubus on top during the sex act, i.e. the reversal of what the church considered normal.

Although the church was determined to stamp out fornication, medieval scholars (usually clerics) were obsessed with sexual activities and rather than blame themselves, were more than willing to find a suitable demon to blame for their nocturnal emissions. The incubus, like the vampire is a creature of the ancient world. Unlike the vampire, however, who has been relegated to the realms of literature, folklore and superstition, the existence of the incubus was given credence by the early Church to explain away the illicit sexual activities (nocturnal or otherwise) of cloistered monks and nuns.

"The Fiend that goeth a-night
Women full oft to guile,
Incubus is named by right;
And guileth other men while,
Succubus is that wight."

'The Description of Wales' -
Caxton's 'Chronicle'.

Incubi (male) and succubi (female) were emissaries of the Devil according to the Church, and innumerable discussions took place during the early Middle Ages about the 'corporeal manifestation' of such demonic entities which haunted the night-dreams of God-fearing Christian men and women. The original concept, as we have seen, was taken from Rabbinic lore and classical mythology, absorbed into Christian doctrine and by the 13th century the learned men of Rome conceded that such creatures did, in fact, exist!

Church scholars came up with the theory that succubi seduced males in order to procure their semen and then turned themselves into incubi to impregnate their female victims. According to Dr Rossell Hope Robbins (*The Encyclopedia of Witchcraft & Demonology*), incubi went to extreme pains to acquire the best quality semen. He cites Dominican sources - always known for their pre-occupation with the sexual habits of demons - for the following account:

"What incubi introduce into the womb is not any ordinary human semen in normal quantity, but abundant, very thick, very warm, rich in spirits and free from serosity. This, moreover, is an easy thing for them, since they merely have to choose ardent, robust men, whose semen is naturally very copious, and with whom the succubus has relations; and then the incubus copulates with women of a like constitution, taking care that both shall enjoy a more than normal orgasm, for the greater the venereal excitement the more abundant is the semen."

What the early Church amassed, in fact, was one of the greatest collections of legal pornography allegedly supporting the charges of heresy, Witchcraft and consorting with demons. Since members of the clergy, high and low, spent a considerable amount of time discussing, debating, cross-examining, writing, reading, copying, dictating and learning about such highly charged sexual manifestations amongst their flocks, it is hardly surprising that their nights were spent in a state of lascivious excitement. "The myth of the incubus remains one of the most ugly manifestations in all history of man's frequent attempts to cripple and pervert his own sexuality in the name of religion," wrote Douglas Hill in *Man, Myth & Magic.*

Medieval sources abound with deliciously ribald Chaucerian tales of nuns granting sexual favours to bishops who appeared to them in the guise of an incubus - the convent accepting the bishop's explanation that some demon had assumed his appearance for the purpose of the seduction. They were not so charitable to the widow of one Jerome Auguste de Montleon, however, who claimed to have borne her husband a child some years after his death. The lady claimed she'd been impregnated by him in a dream but the law courts weren't having any of it and the son was declared not to be the lawful heir to his father's estate.

Nuns, it would appear from ecclesiastical sources, were especially susceptible to the lecherous advances of incubi and according to one Thomas of Cantimpre, the confession box was a favourite place of solicitation. Alphonsus de Spina related how nuns would engage in nocturnal frolics with incubi, waking to find themselves 'polluted just as if they had commingled with a man [*si cum viris miscerentur*]'.

Sinistrari tells of a nun who, having been spied upon by another sister, confessed under the threat of torture that she had regularly been 'indecently intimate with a comely youth'. A sight the observer took great care to let the other sisters enjoy through the spy hole before reporting the matter to the abbess.

Since women were judged to be more licentious than men, according to the clerical experts of the time, incubi tend to appear more frequently in works on demonology - it was even supposed that incubi outnumbered succubi by nine to one. The *Malleus Malificarum* maintained that Witches by qualification were 'tainted with this sort of diabolical filthiness' and devoted a considerable number of pages to the subject of human copulation with demons. The first accounts of succubi made them much more desirable than a mortal woman and Pico della Mirandola told of a man who had slept with a succubus for 40 years and would rather die in prison than give her up!

Most of the early saints encountered the succubus as part of their nightly trials and tribulations; they resisted, of course, but one hermit is recorded as having 'so given himself to lechery that he died within a month'. Stories of succubi recur throughout medieval times and although the charge appears in Inquisitorial records from about 1430, it was not until the 16th and 17th centuries that intercourse with demons featured prominently.

During the Middle Ages all manner of symptoms due to the menopause, genital over-stimulation, the missing of periods, or other psycho-pathological states were said to be caused by having sexual intercourse with incubi. It was not until 1725, when the personal physician of Louis XV suggested that the incubus was the result of an over-stimulated imagination and/or an excuse for illicit relations, that the phenomena was put into perspective.

Nevertheless, the sexual/blood obsession continues to the present day in the accusations levelled at occultists and Witches by anti-occult campaigners. This gigantic historical sexual obsession is extremely difficult to put aside but it is worth a moment's speculation over what might have happened to mankind/society if Adam had thrown his fig-leaf over the Euphrates and kept Lilith as his wife, instead of preferring to take the biddable Eve as a mate. Western civilisation would not have been forced into almost two thousand years of sexual repression and intolerance.

Tantra & Reality

Tantra is term banded about by many but understood by few. Tantric practice is deeply rooted in Eastern religious history and involves the interplay of two basic forces encapsulated in Shiva and Shakti - the male and female principles that underlies the entire universe. Although this yogic belief and practice is becoming more widespread in the West, its existence was more evident in India, where sexual symbols and activities are depicted in temple statues of the God and the Goddess.

Authority on all tantric methods and approaches, Benjamin Walker manages to explain in simple terms how, of this divine pair, Shiva is the subordinate one, for it is the *Female Principle* that ultimately underlies all manifestation; everything, including Shiva himself is contained within the Female Principle. Women are treated on terms of complete equality with men, and in many of the tantric rites are assigned a superior status, as living embodiments of Shakti, the mother goddess herself.

The main subjects dealt within tantric philosophy are the creation and final destruction of the world (as Kali, the personification of the elements of terror and dread in Shakti); the identification and correspondences of the appropriate pantheon; physical, mental and spiritual discipline; and the 'rites by which magical powers can be acquired to enable one to control oneself, control others, the forces of Nature and, on the highest plane, even the gods themselves'. Not surprisingly the magical/sexual emphasis clouds the true principles of tantra and it remains, unfairly, tainted with the label of 'black magic'.

As Walker points out, however, there is hardly an occult procedure that is not dealt with in tantrism since some of the rituals are strangely reminiscent of ceremonial magic described in Western grimoires. Candles, incense, bells, wands, spells, circles, postures, gestures, symbols, and words of power are as much part of tantric paraphernalia as of any Western magic.

"Much of the ritualism has in fact been embodied into their own traditions by Western magicians who have been largely influenced, especially in the rites of sex mysticism and sex magic, by what they have found in tantric manuals or learned from tantric teachers."

An important distinction should be made between Western Sex Magic and Eastern Tantrism, in that while both methods employ similar stimuli, sex magic can be devoid of love, merely seeking the creative twin powers as a means to an end, while tantrism assumes a worshipful attitude full of love and adoration for the beloved. Like all higher levels of occult practice, however, the secret door will not open to the uninitiated. This is not along the same lines as the elitism described in the previous chapter, the misuse of sexual energies for magical purposes can be downright dangerous.

Walker goes so far as to add his own warning that the dangers of this discipline can be very real unless one has been trained to deal with the fire-force released by the waking of the *kundalini,* or sleeping snake at the base of the spine. Its arousal is the goal of an elaborate technique usually taking many years to master, since the chakras are compared to centres of occult fire. This flickering ember has its 'incendiary' point in the *Muladhara,* or base chakra; by the mastery of tantric discipline this fire can be made to blaze and ignite the one above, carrying on in a 'stream of flame going from chakra to chakra' until it reaches the crown.

In *Tantrism,* however, there is the admission that the concept of the *kundalini,* which is so essential to the practice of Western Sexual Magic, may be entirely illusory. In fact a 5th century tantric, Patanjali called it 'imaginary', while a present-day authority, Agehananda Bharati bluntly states that '*kundalini* is a lot of claptrap'. Many modern tantrics tend to view the whole chakra mythos as illusory despite them having undergone 'unbiased scientific study and thought by some to correspond to certain parts of the physiological system. It is important to realise that the 'present seven-chakra system' is a very recent concept and, according to Walker's researches, cannot be found in any of the early authoritative texts.

Although generally, women are held in high esteem in tantric philosophy, they are nevertheless still regarded as dangerous within certain ascetic areas. Echoing early Christian and Rabbinic teaching, women were believed to be natural psychic vampires, able to devour male energies without effort. Tantric experts maintain that 'the wrong kind of *dakini* initiatrix' can permanently deplete the young or inexperienced male of his sexual vitality. On the other hand, older tantrics can make use of young women purely for the purposes of rejuvenation since during orgasm, the woman generates a current of 'gynergy' - a powerful female energy which the tantric can learn to absorb.

Esoteric traditions teach that many of the Adepts of the 15-17th centuries (namely Rosenkreutz, Paracelsus, Saint-Germain and Cagliostro) travelled in the East although there is little to support the claims. Serious studies of Eastern philosophies and methods began in the 18th century, according to Walker, when the 'great British, French and German orientalists embarked on their pioneering work of translation and commentary, often at second-hand'. Nevertheless, most of the Western occult Orders claim some form of ancient antecedents based on the tantric mysteries and it is now in this bastardised form that tantra is often served up in magical groups in the West.

It would be unwise, therefore, to confuse sex magic with tantra, for they do follow different aims. Tantric practice is always oriented towards worship and mysticism, combining the powers of Shiva and Shakti in order to transcend them. Sex magic, as defined by Frater U D is oriented more towards the earth element. "For the sex magician the sexual power is first of all a neutral energy, to be directed magically for whatever purpose. Experience shows that it is very suitable for 'success magic' - i.e the achievement of professional, material and psychological advantages."

Western Sexual Magic

Not all sex magic, of course, hails from the East. Within genuine traditional Craft circles instruction is given on the subject, but the teacher realises that sex magic isn't for everyone and so the Adept chosen to receive this knowledge will have been very carefully schooled before any further steps along this particular Path are taken. It is also necessary to reiterate that here we are not referring to the smut-pedlars who perform sexual athletics during their rituals as some form of carnal gratification.

The Great Rite is, in truth, a sex-magical practice although the vast majority of High Priestesses would have a fit of the vapours if this were alleged in their presence. Nevertheless, it is part of the ritual of 'third-degree Wicca' and practised at the highest level by other Craft groups who do not operate a grade system. The ritual usually involves the whole group in building up the necessary energies but the priest and priestess are usually left alone to 'perform the act in undisturbed togetherness'. There is also a more popular variant where the Great Rite is performed symbolically by the priest plunging his athame into the chalice held by the priestess.

Jörg Wichmann's *Wicca - Die magische Kunst der Hexen* (*Wicca - The Magical Art of Witches*) describes it thus: "The Great Rite is the union of god and goddess, of heaven and earth, the fusion of polarities. The Horned One and the Earth unite in ecstasy and rapture. The Great Rite is performed by priest and priestess who have identified with the deities. It may be performed physically or symbolically."

The one ritual in Witchcraft which gets the most media attention is that known as 'The Great Rite', simply because it may involve sexual intercourse between the Priest and Priestess involved explained Chris. "The Great Rite is one of the greatest 'mysteries' of Witchcraft and is both the symbolic and actual joining of the male and female energies. In certain Wiccan traditions, The Great Rite is the ritual which celebrates the participants' spiritual development to the highest human levels and, as such, can sometimes be found as the ritual of initiation into the third or highest degree of the priesthood. Because of this, the ritual is never undertaken lightly, and certainly not for the mere sexual gratification of the participants.

"The Great Rite should be a celebration of spiritual and physical love, a mystical symbol of the reuniting of male and female energies. The participants should feel empowered, and filled with joy and love by the experience. If these sensations are absent in any of the build up to the ritual, then the physical sexual ritual should be abandoned and performed symbolically instead."

Sexual instinct and energy is inherent in everyone. Driven by the laws of attraction and repulsion, we are all sexual beings unless damaged by injury (mental, emotional or physical) or illness (when libido may be impaired or removed). Or when the individual chooses to be celibate - pouring their sexual energy into other areas under a condition known as sublimation, the ability to exchange the original sexual aim (physical gratification, orgasm and reproduction) for another. Aeron Medbh-Mara explained her teaching approach to sex magic in the following terms:

"Sex magic is usually governed by the Occult Laws of (1) Equalities - where two energies meet and one gives way to the other, which will rise in status/power as a result (unless the two are melded to present one stronger force to be used jointly and (2) Law of Abundance - the attraction of like for like ... True sex magic is the conscious use of sexual energies to achieve a specific end result. It tends to be broken down into three main parts - gender potential, sexual expression or sublimation. It's a wise Witch who knows the difference between the 'sex-magics' and 'gender magics', understands them and uses them. It's a foolish Witch who only sees the genitals.

"I find it interesting to say the least, that many Witches, neo-Pagans and occultists who place so much emphasis on symbolism, analogy and syllogy can't (or won't) raise their level of awareness when it comes to working with sexual energy. Despite their reassurances of having trained their mental faculties, visualisations and imaginations, I am despairing of those individuals who avoid the same facilities when it comes to sex magic."

Chris went on to explain in some painstaking detail that in Witch rituals, sex magic takes two forms. "Pure sex magic is the use of sexual intercourse to raise the spiritual levels of the participants. In Witchcraft, and particularly in this form of sex magic, the couple involved will be (usually) already married, or involved in a long-standing sexual relationship. This is nothing to do with social morality, it is simply because an established couple know each other so well that any foibles of shyness, titillation or general embarrassment will be out of the way and the couple can then get on with their serious magical work.

"The other form of sex magic simply uses the arousal of sex as a power-raising exercise, and the release of orgasm as the release of that energy to fulfil the desires of the Witch. In this case, the Witch can have sex with a partner who may not even be aware that this is anything more than normal sex - only the active Witch needs to keep her/his mind on the job! Although both forms of sex magic may well include orgasm, the aim of the ritual isn't sexual gratification. Arousal and orgasm are simply the mechanics by which the magical and spiritual powers are awakened, raised and released.

"Sex magic can be a solitary experience, but again one must at all times concentrate on the desired outcome of the magic, not get caught by the sensations of sex into focusing on the sex itself. Using sex is a very easy way to gain access to your own magical powers, and can lead to the most fulfilling orgasms you will ever experience, but because it's so wonderful, that can encourage you to forget about your planned magic at the critical moment. To stay focused through a sex magic ritual, requires practice and dedication - and great strength of purpose."

Operative Craft, according to Aeron, is all about potential and its use: fertility, life, death and rebirth. "It's all about changing and transforming the inner and outer realities according to Will, yet there is a puritanical 'sterilise everything into a corner' attitude prevalent in Craft today. No longer are people being objective and using their minds - they merely see sex magic as some sort of vicarious thrill-seek, or rush to blindfold themselves (and others). Do they faint when they see animals mate and, like the Victorians, metaphorically cover the legs of their chairs in case they see something 'inflammatory or impure'?

"When it comes to squeamishness on this subject, I always ask if they realise that they are being voyeuristic when they refer so heavily, and at the drop of the (pointy) hat, to the (presumed) sex life of the God and Goddess!"

Despite the fact that sex-magic is used for more material purposes in Western practises, we should overlook the fact that the borders between sex-magic and sex-mysticism are far from being clearly defined. Frater U D is adamant that the magician should not fall to the opposite extreme and completely deny the mystical, transcendental aspects achievable by the Adept.

"This is precisely what is so great about sex magic: namely that it represents a system which knows how to balance its material and transcendental aspects. Mysticism does not strive one-sidely to heighten spirit at the expense of matter. On the contrary, mysticism, and sex mysticism in particular, strives to transcend the opposites and seeks to lead us into the realms of the transcendental, of the divine beyond Good and Evil."

All those occultists asked to discuss sex magic are adamant that there is a great difference between sex for sex's sake and sex for magic's sake. "If you are thinking of using sex magic as an excuse for 'getting your leg over', that isn't magic and it certainly isn't sex magic," said Graham.

"Because the use of sex in magic is so misunderstood, it is open to abuse by the unscrupulous, or by the sensation seekers. We have heard of cases where, in order for one to become a 'proper' Witch, one must submit to sex with another Witch - Let me state loudly and clearly, having sex with someone does not make you a Witch, and being coerced into sex for whatever purpose is rape!"

A Question of Personal Morality

An individual's attitude towards sexual matters can possibly be best summed up by that old *Penthouse* cartoon of the voluptuous damsel draped over the neck of a rather magnificent dragon, retorting to a bemused knight: "OK, it's kinky St George, but who's it hurting?".

Whether we like to admit it or not, attitudes are formed by strong ethnic conditioning to such a degree that fears and prejudices are almost genetic. Since the liberating 60s, the West has been obsessed by sexual imagery but to be considered respectable it is not allowed to wander very far from the code of opposite sex coupling with a regular partner, no matter how liberally society views on other matters.

Dion Fortune's novels, particularly *The Sea Priestess* and *Moon Magic* (the latter published posthumously in 1957), are fictional attempts to restore Paganism to a world that has lost touch with the elemental forces that make life truly dynamic, according to the biographical extract from *Man, Myth & Magic*. Again we can use fictional insights to gain an, albeit second-hand experience, of a force which is not 'simple unregenerate Nature, or primal emotional and sensual pleasure, but the power of the primordial and elemental essence of Woman, embodied in the Black Isis in her power aspect'.

During the closing stages of her life, Dion Fortune committed to fiction the realisation of inherent divinity; a power capable of effecting profound transformations in human consciousness when mated to its complement in the male. Denuded of the 'accretions of civilisation', this aspect of the Black Isis embodies the shakti elemental power that destroys all that is detrimental to spiritual development. "The basis of Fortune's work involves the bringing through into manifestation of this shakti, by the magically controlled interplay of sexual polarity. This is embodied in the priest, or consecrated male, and the specially chosen female. Together they enact the immemorial Rite and form a vortex in the ether, down which the tremendous energies of Black Isis rush into manifestation."

Crowley considered that the sexual characteristics of the individual to be symbolic indications of its sexual nature, and when these are 'abnormal', we may suspect that the self is divided against itself in some way. "Experience teaches the Adepts that when any complex (duality) in the self is resolved (unity), the initiate becomes whole. The morbid sexual symptoms (which are merely the complaints of a sick animal) disappear, while the moral and mental consciousness is relieved from its civil war of doubt and self-obsession. The complete man, harmonized, flows freely towards his natural goal."

Regardie noted that Crowley accepted the one simple fact that sex - sex in any shape or form, the emergence of the instinctual, that is, divine tendencies - is not to be thwarted or warped. "So long as no one is hurt or injured, it is a private matter between any two people as to what form or practice of sexuality they wish to indulge in. His interpretation of sex is then clear. You have the right, the divine right in his opinion, to express sexuality in your own particular way. As he faithfully recorded in Part I of the *Book of the Law* dedicated to the goddess Nuit: "Take thy fill of love where, when, and with whom thou wilt - but always in the love of Me!"

Contrary to popular belief, many members of the Hermetic Orders of occultism were extremely conformist, believing that an Adept should not drink, fornicate, have fun and raise hell. All of which young Crowley did with some enthusiasm; laying the foundation for the scandalous reputation which would remain with him for the rest of his life and beyond. Political shenanigans within the Golden Dawn produced the lasting accusations that Crowley was "a show-off, a charlatan, and perhaps a black magician."

A point which Regardie strongly repudiates, in that at this stage, since Crowley was only in the throes of learning basic magic, he could hardly be accused of debasing what little practical knowledge he had acquired! "It was customary," Regardie continued. "amongst the sanctimonious blue- stockings of that time to call anyone a 'black magician' who had rational attitudes about sex ..."

The Grand Master of the Magical-Sexual technique, Crowley himself paid dearly for his ritual excesses but as David Conway is forced to admit, it would be foolish to conclude that this was the inevitable result of using sex in magic. "In Crowley's case it was due to his deliberate flouting of all the rules conducive to good health. Anyone, magical or not, who indulges almost continuously over several years in hashish, fasting, self-mutilation and pan-sexuality is bound at the very least to end up with bags under his eyes. But to imply, as some writers do, that the same effects are caused by occasional ritual sex is not unlike warning adolescent boys that masturbation leads to blindness."

Compatible 'morality' will therefore play an important role in the choice or selection of a magical partner. As Chris has explained, a couple who live together are better placed if their relationship is correctly attuned but magic does not exclude a different partner if the circumstances call for it. This does, of course, bring us into conflict with the social and religious teachings of the society in which we live and the age-old bugbear of morality creeps in to cloud the issue. An 'exclusive fixation on monogamy' can produce a barrier to practical sex magic as can other social or sexual taboos and if your lover disapproves of anything magical, let alone sex magic there are some important decisions to be made over the practicality of continuing your study.

In reality, the practice of sex-magic doesn't usually start with 'partner-workings' but rather with auto-erotic techniques and exercises which enable the magician to avoid any possible conflict with an unwilling partner. As Frater U D points out "Many sex magicians work exclusively on an auto-erotic level ... Nothing can be said against this as long as it does not strengthen a pre-existing lack of balance or inability and so exclude other practises."

Aeron Medbh-Mara defines the various approaches and practises of sex magic as follows:

Consensual Gender Magic

The interaction of (usually) male-female participants.

1) Usage does NOT imply automatic physical attraction.
2) Emphasises on the differences between the two and is used to charge the Cup of Life, during the consecration of the ale and bread. The woman offers the symbol of 'all-female' to the 'all-male' thereby creating 'all-potential'. She works with the male gender and takes his (freely offered) different but complementary energies, moulding it into the required shape and either returns it or channels it to its designated goal/purpose.
3) Relies upon the attraction between the sexes to form a new energy from the newly combined energies. Focuses mainly on the fertility aspects of projecting mental energy into a receptive mental place to be formed into a new life/form.
4) Need not necessarily involve physical contact.
5) In same sex circumstances it is the combining of the two 'like' energies. (On the physical plane opposite energies attract, on the spiritual, similar energies attract).

Consensual Sex Magic

Whereby sexual energy and power is raised through the physical sex act and released (either at orgasm or the physical completion of the task perhaps in the form of a 'psychic orgasm').

1) Usage does NOT automatically imply physical attraction.
2) Where a known and identified sexual object (phallus/lubricant, etc) is used to signify sex or create sex as a projective force or utilised to symbolise the sex act. (i.e. female masturbation by use of an artificial phallus containing amulets/talismans/other charms).
3) Need not be cross-gender.
4) Can be performed solo by masturbation.
5) Need not necessarily involve physical contact as some Adepts can, by using strong visualisation, heighten their sexual awareness and raise enough energy to be released in the form of magical power during the rite, at the point of, or instead of, physical orgasm.

6) Or use the sexual electricity as a form of the 'intercourse of magic' instead of physical - in the way it used to be said of ballroom dancing that it was "vertical expression of horizontal intention".

(6a and 7) Celibacy and sublimation. Either as a combination of 5 & 6

or simply analogous to the cloistered situation.

When discussing sexual magic as defined in Craft workings, Aeron would estimate that Witches tend to use the former (consensual gender magic) 80% of the time and the latter (consensual sex magic) 20% for a wide variety of differing reasons. Like anything in life, however, there are always the pros and cons to be considered before embarking on any form of experimental practice and sex magic is no different.

Cross-Gender Potential

Advantages

1) It's cheap monetarily, but not cheapened.
2) There is a high level of return.

Disadvantages

1) If Partners can get the wrong idea and project a relationship problem.
2) Some people go on to 'mythic overlay' where they can only satisfactorily see/relate to their partner as the God/dess.

Same-Sex Gender Potential

Advantages

1&2) As above

Disadvantages

1) In 'immature' individuals may lead to sexual crisis in the areas of preferences and expression, i.e. the inability to separate the act and reality, or come to question validity if homosexual (male and female).

Sexual Expression

Advantages

1) It's cheap monetarily but not cheapened.
2) There is a high level of return.

Disadvantages

1) Moral confusion if taken out of a monogamous situation.
2) Partners can get the wrong idea and confuse the magical act with the 'act of love'.

Celibacy/Sublimation

Advantages

1) It's cheap monetarily but not cheapened.
2) There is a high level of return.
3) Virtually no chance of catching a disease! (In female cloistered orders the incidence of cervical cancer is almost eliminated).

Disadvantages

1) For some it is too difficult to achieve.
2) Over a long period of time it can adversely affect the 'normal' libido - sometimes permanently.
3) In some cases can damage relationships if the partner requires sexual gratification and cannot/will not accept the other's 'withholding' of their own body (even if masturbation is offered they may see this as a personal slight/ offense).

Harnessing the Power of Sex

Using cross-gender sexual energy for magical purposes requires two people who can work together in an harmonious atmosphere of 'perfect love and perfect trust'. Like all other aspects of magic, sexual rites need a great deal of preparation and practice. There is little point in deciding the night before an extremely important interview that you might as well try a little bit of erotic fine-tuning in order to achieve success.

To achieve a working knowledge of sexual-magical techniques requires many years of practice and study - so start simply and progress slowly.

In the Chapter One we discovered how aromatherapy was considered to be another method of magical healing. It also helps those who are afraid of touching and being touched. When working with a sexual partner on a magical level, it obviously requires a high degree of intimacy and the necessity of being at ease with one another. Prior to the magical working (or as an integral part of it) the couple can use sensual massage to stimulate or to relieve tension. In *Fragrant Sensuality,* Valerie Ann Worwood demonstrates the possibility of using massage and essential oils to encourage sensuality and confidence and as a trigger for low sexual response. Used in conjunction with Margo Anand's psychology in *The Art of Sexual Magic* and the couple should find that inhibition is something that can be overcome before going onto a serious study of sex-magic.

It may be surprising to learn that sex magic can also be used for more down to earth purposes. The principle is that, by concentrating his will on the object of the operation, the magician can bring powerful physical and psychological energy which he conjures up in himself through sex magic to bear on people and events around him. In magical theory a sexual working has no hope of success if the magician allows himself to be swept away in the thundering surf of desire and orgasm. Unless he remains the master of the force he has aroused, he cannot direct it at his objective. In general in religious and magical sexual rites the element of pleasure is secondary. It is the means to the goal not the goal itself.

"The use of sex in magic is simply using the energy of sexual arousal, and transmuting it into magical energy for the fulfilment of a particular goal - this could be anything you want or need; more money, healing for a friend, to obtain a job, you name it," said Graham. "Whatever the object of the ritual when using sex, sex is not the goal. To use sex in magic, whether for mystical enlightenment, or to gain a physical effect in the material world, requires very strong and resolute mind-control. One must remain aware at all times, of the ultimate reason for the ritual, of its aim, and of its desired outcome - despite the delicious allure of the physical sensations one may be experiencing."

Sexual magic calls on the more primitive god-forms and as fanciful as it may at first appear, the cult of Lilith has not passed entirely into folklore. Experienced magical practitioners maintain that by invoking the goddess they can transmit their likeness in the form of a succubus/incubus to engage in a little astral fornication with the person they desire - a subject often depicted in late Victorian pornography and by the occult artist Austin Osman Spare. Once seduced by a succubus, legend tells us, man can never again be satisfied with mortal woman, and so the modern magician binds a lover magically in the form of erotic night-dreams.

Putting Inquisitorial and literary material aside, magicians identify incubi and succubi as sexual manifestations which are used for astral intercourse. In Frater U D's experience, the practice is 'strenuous to the point of being exhausting' and can lead to obsessive sexual behaviour if the magician does not maintain control and allows the sex-demons to take over. The inherent danger lies in the lack of a clear definition of personal space rather than a threat from the energy forms themselves. Since the practice requires a considerable amount of occult knowledge and magical self control, it is not an exercise for the inexperienced.

Evidence that Lilith was still being invoked right into the 20th century is borne out by Aleister Crowley's magical writings in which he summons the ancient goddess in the form of 'Babalon' or the Scarlet Woman. Frater U D records his own *Hymn to Hecate* in which he invokes Lilith as the shadowy side of the female principle. He warns against misunderstanding the gloomy undertones of the Hecate/Lilith principle since it has 'surprising orgiastic potential' and following the invocation, the sexual act should usually be performed with the man lying down and being ridden by his partner - but this should not be a rigid (no pun intended) rule, he adds.

In his book *Cults of the Shadow,* Kenneth Grant examines the universal failure to understand the proper function of left-hand Path workings which has led to its total denigration - even amongst experienced occultists. The principal reason Grant believes, is on account of its unconventional practises which involve the use of sexual energies as a means of "awakening the Serpent Power or Fire Snake, the key to Cosmic consciousness, and also of controlling and directing the occult forces of the subconscious mind, the reservoir of infinite knowledge".

The 'shadow' refers to a 'genetic, primordial knowledge' which is buried deep within the subconscious and the roots of successful sex-magic can only be found in the primordial reaches of cultural origins. Whether the Adept turns to Walker, Frater U D, Fortune, Crowley or Grant for elucidation, the answer will always be the same. True magic is not to be found in the here-and-now, quick-fix sound-bites of modern Wicca and Paganism, as it careers closer and closer to a peculiar blend of neo-Pagan-Christianity. Primordial magic is linked to those powerful creator/destroyer forces embodied in deities such as Kali, Lilith, Tefnut/Sekhmet and Tiamat but the modern Magus does have an advantage over those who worshipped in ancient times. Today's Magus understands the necessity of stripping away the superstitions, taboos and tribal rules that surrounded what Frater U D describes as the 'dubious myth of the noble savage who lives in perfect harmony with his environment'.

This magical power is a natural part of human mental and spiritual development although for the past 2,000 years both Witches and magicians have always been accused of 'unnatural' practises. In *Secrets of the German Sex Magicians* we find an extremely valid comment from its author which forces the would-be seeker to face up to the suppressive doctrines of the West. "One really obscene aspect to Western history is the way that a religion which has raped nature at every opportunity, with its hatred for the flesh and its exploitive mentality, could have the impunity to accuse magic of being unnatural!"

Frater U D goes on to state that shamanic practicses must have appeared inexplicable and strange to the medicine man's people because of the manner in which he handled these specialist skills and knowledge. They accepted that this god-given knowledge was not accessible to everyone but never, at any time, did they consider him to be unnatural.

As we have said before magic is, by qualification, morally neutral; it is neither good nor bad, black nor white. To successfully explore the veiled realms of universal subconsciousness, it is first necessary to liberate the conscious from the restrictions indoctrinated by established monotheistic religious order. This is, of course, not always as easy as it sounds but the seeker should always begin the first step with the question: Why? Never accept a book as 'gospel' or a tutor as a guru; conduct your own research and never stop asking questions; have faith, but not blind faith and lastly observe the most important occult credo:

> ***"The Good that ye do shall be returned to thee Three times over - and the Evil also that ye do shall be returned to thee, Three times over."***

To understand the full implications of magic in general and sex-magic in particular it is necessary to remove all preconceived ideas that have been formulated from badly written occult books, repeated dénouement by the clergy and tabloid exposés. The secret key to occultism, esoteria and arcane wisdom lies in the willingness to delve into the depths of ancient history and culture to find where the Path will lead, irrespective of the seeker's colour, race or creed. Occult Paths have the unpleasant habit of twisting and turning in unexpected directions and the true seeker needs all the strength his or her faith can offer to navigate the precipices, dead-ends and bolder-strewn byways. The one thing that is consistent in all of those who have contributed their views and experiences throughout the book - none of them would want it any other way.

In conclusion, however, Frater U D makes an extremely valid observation when he advises those who practice sex-magic to keep quiet about it on the grounds that, even in our liberated age, most people still fear sexuality and magic. As he rightly warns, although magic is widely scoffed at in public, magical practitioners are enjoying a boom - as is the fear of them! "Anyone who thinks this is an enlightened world shaped by cosmopolitan, worldly tolerance should take a look at the reports in the gutter press. Turn a deaf ear to this advice and you will find out the hard way!"

Mélusine agrees wholeheartedly with Frater U D's warning but admits it is extremely difficult at times to keep silence, especially when confronted by foolish utterances. "Although I never suffer fools gladly, I do keep very quiet about my own occult interests. Trust none and keep silence are two of the most important lessons any serious Witch or Magus can learn. If you want to draw attention to yourself by openly discussing ritual magic, then you must be prepared to face the consequences.

"I recently attended a dinner party where one of the other guests, a doctor, started pontificating on what a fraud Crowley was. How having read all of his books, there was nothing there but an inflated sense of his own importance and bluff. Without revealing my own personal interests, I asked if he practised or had any hands-on experience of magical practises. 'Good God, no!' came the vehement reply. Although strongly tempted to correct his ignorance I sincerely believe that in discussing magical matters with outsiders, discretion is definitely the better part of valour."

This is a classic example of how easily magical works are dismissed by learned men and women who do not find it within themselves to admit that they cannot understand esoteric writing. The written legacy left by Crowley is phenomenal. In the entire history of magic no other single person has managed to produce such a wealth of material for others to follow. Without some basic experience of occultism, however, the seeker-after-truth's attempt to understand Crowley's work is akin to reaching for the moon. He never intended his teachings for the idly curious or the magically inept.

Even so, as Frater U D continued in his warning, by declaring an interest in Thelemic practises - "You might just as well publicly declare an interest in sadism or sodomy. You will be asked - in a manner half shocked and half fascinated - for details and in no time you will find yourself labelled a 'satanist' or 'devil-worshipper', and the spectrum of defamation may even extend to 'pervert' and 'sex fiend'."

There is still a time to keep silence.

Timepiece:

While putting the finishing touches to *What You Call Time,* Aeron voiced her doubts over the wisdom of publishing books such as this which explain the intricacies of magical practises in some detail. There was, she explained, a dichotomy of thought at the moment within various Pagan movements regarding the dissemination of information. Her reservations stemmed from the fact that magical information is not always easily reconciled with other religious belief and could, if not addressed properly (in the minds of some), be a source of problems for years to come since it involves both the amount and type of occult information released into the public arena for wider examination.

Although there are those who believe that once all information is in the public domain, the demonstrations of intolerance, prejudice and 'pagan-bashing' will disappear. "There is, however, an underlying hidden agenda or, as one Roman Catholic priest put it, 'We don't need to put you on the rack nowadays. If we show you a little kindness, a little bit of interest, then you are more than happy to tell us everything we want to know'."

Aeron continued to air her misgivings. "We are now finding certain groups and individuals are again beginning to take themselves and their practises underground for fear of misrepresentation and future reprisals - the prospect of being hoist on their own petard being particularly unpalatable."

As recent anti-occult campaigns have shown, the church

itself is adept at picking out the bits and pieces to misrepresent, as Crowley was quick to demonstrate back in the 1920s: "It is illogical to pick out of the gospels the texts which happen to suit one's own prejudices and then claim Christ as the supreme teacher ... his claims to pre-eminence are barred by the fact that all the passages which are not fiendish superstition find parallels in the writings of earlier masters. The works of Lao Tzu, the Buddhist canon, the Upanishads, the Bhagavad-Gita, the Talmud and the philosophy of many of the early Greeks, to say nothing of the sacred books of Egypt, contain the whole of the metaphysics, theology and ethics to which modern enlightenment can assent."

Aeron's fears are not ill-founded. So what does the occult author do? Pander to current market forces in the belief that almost 2000 years of repression and fear can be wiped out by education. Rehash old material in the same time-honoured way or point out that not everything may be said in a way that will be instantly understood. Reveal everything, or conceal the information within the text - or simply go about their business of writing whatever comes into her head. "As an author, each time I put pen to paper I ask myself 'How could this be used against me and mine, now or in the future, should the desire arise to do so? Do I honour knowledge or wisdom in this act?'"

Bigotry is impervious to facts - and facts can always be twisted to fit any hypothesis as Crowley knew to his cost. "Test the average man by asking him to listen to a simple sentence which contains one word with associations to excite his prejudices, fears or passions - he will fail to understand what you have said and reply by expressing his emotional reaction to the critical word."

Magic can be liken to mountaineering. Only a fool would attempt to scale even the most modest of peaks with inadequate training and without proper equipment. But as news events have shown during the past couple of years, even the most experienced of climbers have met their deaths whilst indulging in their chosen occupation. Mountains can be dangerous and unpredictable. So can Magic. With the proper training and the correct approach, mountaineering can be an exhilarating and exciting experience. So, too, can Magic. As one leading British occultist remarked to me during an interview. "Dangerous, of course it's dangerous. It wouldn't be worth doing otherwise!"

There are, of course, armchair kill-joys who never venture from their firesides who would ban mountaineering every time a climber perishes on the icy slopes. But climbers will continue to climb. There are those of religious bias who would outlaw Magic because fools choose to ignore the rules and warning signs. But they will never stop those who seriously want to scale the dizzy heights of knowledge, wisdom and understanding.

The underlying, recurring theme that runs through *What You Call Time* is the unavoidable message that book learning, i.e. knowledge, is not enough. Magic, whether it be that of Witch or Magus, must be actively practised if the Adept is to fully comprehend the magical universe which lies spread out before him. The wisdom comes from experience and exploration - and you can't get that out of a book.

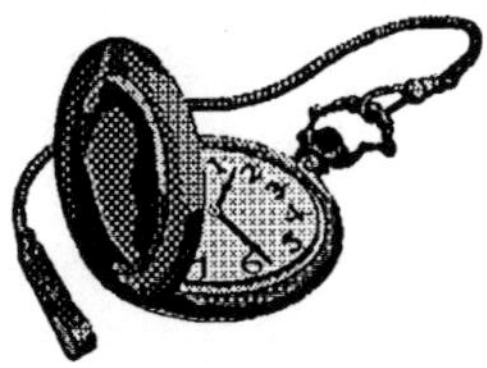

Glossary:

Abyss: The gulf between the real and the unreal. Crossing the Abyss is the most critical step taken on the spiritual path.

Acolyte: From the classical Greek/Roman meaning follower. In occult terms an attendant or lower ranking member of the Temple or Coven.

Adept: One completely versed in a particular occult Tradition or Path. In classic occult tradition, one who was supposed to have obtained the elixir of life and the philosopher's stone.

Alexandrian: A modern Wiccan Tradition named after its founder Alex Sanders.

Athame: Traditional Witches' knife which is often described as being black handled and decorated in mystic symbols. In reality, all types of knives are used according to personal preference.

Aura: Can refer to either the visual or physical psychic 'coating' which surround all living things. Often described in rainbow colours which reveal the mental/physical/emotional state of an individual.

Astral Projection: The ability to voluntarily leave the physical body and travel to other planes/dimensions.

Candle Magic: Spell casting or divination by the use of different coloured candles.

Celtic: In occult terms, Celtic Tradition is a form of traditional magico-religious system based on the history and deities of the ancient Celts.

Ceremonial Magic: Usually refers to the more flamboyant ritual magic practised by a large group who prefer strict adherence to set forms, i.e. the rituals of the Hermetic Order of the Golden Dawn.

Circle: Both magicians and Witches cast a circle for protection and to concentrate magical energies within a confined sacred area.

Chakras: In tantra, the seven points in the body used to focus and generate energy, concentrating occult energies that work through the glands of the endocrine system.

Chaos Magic: "The primal substance that is, paradoxically, in nowise substantial, out of which the illusion of Matter appears to rise." It is the Gnostic matrix of manifestation according to Kenneth Grant (*Aleister Crowley & the Hidden God* and *The Magical Revival*).

Cord Magic: Spell casting by the use of different coloured cords.

Correspondences: A system of co-relating colours, incenses, gemstones, etc., with deities representing the qualities or magical energies of which the practitioner wishes to make use.

Coven or **Covenstead:** The name for a formal grouping of Witches. Traditionally this should number 13 but many groups work with many more, or even as few as three or four members.

Craft: The in-term for Witchcraft *per se.*

Dakini: The chief female hierophants among the tantrics who were often old crones of revolting ugliness.

Demonology: The classic academic study of demons and their habits.

Dianic: Covens or groups that have come to be all-female and devoted solely to the goddess.

Divination: Predicting the future by a wide variety of different methods.

Dowsing: The method used to search for hidden objects, underground springs, sacred sites, etc. using dowsing sticks or rods.

Draconian: The Cult of Set whose symbol is the Dog-Star, Sothis. With his mother, represented by the seven stars of Ursa Major, Set was the eighth, and the first male deity ever to be worshipped.

Earth Mysteries: Harnessing and utilising the earth's natural energy forces and channelling them through magical working.

Egyptian Tradition: A modern adaptation of the ancient magical/ mystical tradition based on the religion and magic of Egypt.

Elements: The components of the magical universe - earth (north), air (east), fire (south) and water (west) ascribed to the four cardinal points of the compass for the purpose of magical working.

Evocation: To call or summon forth, i.e command, as opposed to invocation which is couched in the form of a prayer or request.

Faerie: Manifestations of nature spirits; also refers to the world of Faerie which runs parallel to this one.

Gaia: A popular term to refer to the Earth as an idealistic form for the Great Mother; taken from the *Gaia Hypothesis* presented by Dr James Lovelock and Dr Sidney Epton (1975) in *New Scientist.*

Gardnerian: A branch of modern Wicca named after its founder Gerald Gardner.

Goetia: A form of magic involving the 'penetration of subconscious strata', i.e. the abode of spirits and demons dissociated from the human life-wave. (*The Goetia* - Aleister Crowley)

Geomancy: Divination by interpreting the patterns and shapes of objects or events found in nature.

Golden Dawn, Hermetic Order of the: A magical Order founded by Samuel Liddell MacGregor-Mathers in 1888 which boasts Crowley and Dion Fortune as members.

Great Rite: The joining of the male/female or god/goddess principles as part of the higher grades in various different Craft traditions.

Great Work, The: An alchemical term denoting the bringing of substance or energy to the fullest possible degree of perfection. Also designates the nature of the next stage in the evolution of humanity/consciousness = the union of the microcosm and the macrocosm.

Grimoire: A magical text-book containing instructions for magical workings. Wiccan version: *The Book of Shadows.*

Handfasting: A general Wiccan term for marriage, i.e. being bound at the hand.

Hedge-Witch: A newly coined term to describe a solitary Witch, especially one working in a rural area with natural products and ingredients.

Hereditary: Craft knowledge which is passed down within a closely confined grouping of a family line. Usually very private covens with a very strict code of practice.

High Priesthood: Western Ritual Magic is overloaded with high-ranking titles and High Priest/ess is usually a term used in modern Wicca. Hereditary and Tradition covens more often than not use 'Master' and 'Lady' for those responsible for the group. Dion Fortune chose to call herself 'Priestess' rather than anything of a grander nature.

Incubus: A male night demon intent on sexual gratification. Can be a natural phenomena or deliberately manifested by a magician. see **Succubus.**

Initiation: The rite of initiation marks the rite of passage from neophyte to acolyte and the beginning of the spiritual journey on a chosen Path.

Invocation: To address a deity in the form of prayer or supplication, i.e by magical means, to solicit earnestly for assistance and/or protection.

Kundalini: The Fire Snake coiled at the base of the spine which is dormant in the spiritually unawakened individual.

Left-Hand Path: The lunar-female-goddess aspect of magical/mystical working.

Ley Lines: Direct lines of natural electro-magnetic energy which criss-cross the landscape (*The Old Straight Track* - Alfred Watkins).

Light Bearers: see **Watchers.**

Magick: This distinctive spelling denotes anything written by or about Aleister Crowley's magical philosophy of Thelema. He used it to distinguish his magick of the New Aeon which is (according to Kenneth Grant - *The Magical Revival*) of a directly electro-chemical nature, from the ceremonial techniques of the previous Aeon.

Magus: Originally an exalted title of the highest rank in magical Orders; now used to describe anyone who practicses Western Ritual Magic.

Mantra: The vibration of subtle sound in the form of a word(s) constantly reverberated to transform consciousness.

Meditation: The mental transition from the mundane to the spiritual level or plane. Common to nearly all forms of religious worship.

Monotheism: The doctrine that there is only one god.

Mystery Paths: A modern adaptation of the classic Mystery Schools of Elesius, Mithra, Kybel, etc. A mystical initiation mirroring the experience of death, descent into the Otherworld and rebirth.

Necromancy: Divination by summoning the spirits of the dead to interpret omens and predict the future.

Neophyte: A beginner or novice; one who is newly entered (i.e. converted) into a magical, religious or mystical order.

Northern Tradition: A magical Tradition based on the old Scandinavian deities.

Numerology: A divination system that uses the application of numbers to the letters of the alphabet.

Old Ways: Any Pagan Path which is followed by worshipping the gods of that particular Tradition.

O.T.O: The Order of the Temple of the East (*Ordo Templi Orientis*) - the East being the place of ascending solar-phallic power.

Path: In occult terminology all Paths lead to a single destination; the chosen Path can be any form of religious or magical application.

Pathworking: A form of guided meditation, the subject being held by story-telling into a situation or mystical encounter, during which they begin to interact independently.

Pantheism: The worship of all gods and the doctrine that god and the universe are identical.

Pantheon: The famous domed temple in Rome which was dedicated to all the gods. The collective term for all the divinities of a nation.

Pentagram or **Pentacle:** The five-point star representing the four elements and spirit; used as a protective symbol by nearly all occult Paths or Traditions.

Power Objects: Personal items which have magical properties.

Qabalah: Literally meaning 'received tradition'. Knowledge of the mysteries of creation and cosmic consciousness illustrated by the pattern of the Tree of Life.

Reincarnation: The belief that the human soul or consciousness continues to be reborn through a series of lifetimes.

Rites of Passage: The transition from one state to another; a way of entrance or exit either spiritual (initiation or advancement) or temporal (birth, death, marriage, etc).

Ritual: A prescribed manner of performing divine rites or ceremonies especially in an elaborate or excessive way.

Ritual Magic: Magical operations following a prescribed method using regalia/correspondences chosen especially for the purpose.

Rosicrucian: A mystical Order based on the legendary teachings of Christian Rosencreuz.

Sabbats: The sacred days in the Witches' calendar. There are four Great Sabbats at Imbolc, Beltane, Lughnasad and Samhain and four Lesser Sabbats at the solstices and equinoxes.

Sacrifice: The gifts or offerings made to the gods during a ritual in the form of food, libation and/or incense.

Sacred Area: Places that have been dedicated to a particular god, or group of gods.

Scrying: Divination by meditation using the play of light on a shiny surface or object.

Sephiroth: The ten spheres or emanations of cosmic consciousness located on the Tree of Life.

Sex Magic: The conscious use of sexual energies, with or without physical contact, to achieve a specific end result

Shamanism: In the strict anthropological sense, shamanism is best represented among Siberian and South/Central America native tribes whose shaman is a magician or healer who contacts the deities and spirits sacred to his people.

Sky-clad: The modern Wiccan term meaning to work naked.

Solitary: The generic term for Witches who work alone or with a selected partner rather than in a group or coven.

Succubus: Female night demon - see **Incubus**.

Superstition: Detrimental to true occult working since it relies on blind faith in something as opposed to a questioning/enquiring creed, or a degenerated magical teaching relegated to folk memory.

Supernatural: The unexplained or hidden world which the genuine occultist must seek to explore in order to gain knowledge.

Tantra: The term applies particularly to certain oriental *grimoires* or manuals of ritual technique

Tarot: The wheel or cycle of life in a series of symbols consisting of cards making up 22 Major Arcana and 56 Minor Arcana. The correct assignment of the symbols corresponds to the 22 paths of the Tree of Life.

Thelema: The word means Will and discovery by each man and woman of the True Will, his or her true purpose, is the central theme of Thelemic doctrine (Kenneth Grant - *Aleister Crowley & the Hidden God*).

Tradition: A magical/mystical Path following pre-ordained antecedents or traditions.

Triangle of Conjuration: Area for containing demons during ritual magical operations; the demon is confined to the triangle and forced to do the magician's bidding.

Varma Marg: Sanskrit for left/woman and path which denotes the worshipping of the female principal in the form of erotic ritual.

Wand: The most important tool in magical regalia. There are numerous instructions concerning the correct material to be used but this does depend on the specific Tradition or Path being followed.

Watchers: Ancient concept that the Watchers or Light-bearers are semi-divine humans who remained behind after the collapse of the Golden Age to watch over mankind's progress and prevent another Deluge/Destruction.

Western Ritual Magic: see **Ritual Magic**

Wicca: A generic term for Witchcraft when not referring specifically to Traditional or Hereditary Craft. In America all Witchcraft is referred to as Wicca, while in Britain it is usually used in connection with the Alexandrian and Gardnerian Traditions.

Wildwood: The dark, untamed part of natural woodland.

Will: In occult terms, the mental power or faculty by which one initiates or controls one's activities, as opposed to external causation, impulse or instinct. The exercise of this power is an act of authoritative purpose.

Appendix I

Magical Tutorials

Those providing the important insights into Craft and Ritual Magic for *What You Call Time,* appreciate that the book will provoke more questions than it answers. Whereas the publisher cannot guarantee an answer for every letter, attempts will be made to forward enquiries to someone qualified to respond.

Write direct to Comhairli Cairde, c/o BCM-Writer, 27 Old Gloucester Street, London WC1N 3XX enclosing 2x1st class stamps and the publisher will forward any correspondence to those willing to answer any queries or provide details of recommended magazines, magical suppliers, specialist book shops, tutorials, etc.

Or visit the Comhairli Cairde web site:

http://.vigin.net/ignotus.press/docs2/comhair.html

for details of *Comhairle* magazine and other related services.

e-mail: ignotus.press@vigin.net

Acknowledgements:

Angela, Frater Asmodeus, John Billingsley, Chris Bray, Brighdhe, Britomartis, Alastair (Bob) Clay-Egerton, Dr Meriem Clay-Egerton, Emma and Simon, Mélusine Draco, Hazel, Philip Heselton, Frater Glendower, Marget Inglis, Evan John Jones, Bernard King, Maeve, Magpie, Frater Marabas, Aeron Medbh-Mara, Janval Phagan, Graham Raven, Patrick and Cath Regan and Chris Sempers.

Appendix II

Recommended Reading:

Each chapter in the book deals with specific areas of Craft and Magic. To help further research the following books have been recommended by the contributors to provide a deeper insight into the subjects raised.

Chapter 1 - Forty Shades of Grey - *Twill By Twilight*
Book of Divining the Future - Eva Shaw (Wordsworth)
Guide to Stars & Plants - Patrick Moore (Philip's)
Liber 777 - Aleister Crowley (Weiser)
Magic: An Occult Primer - David Conway (Mayflower)
Malleus Satani: The Hammer of Satan
Suzanne Ruthven (ignotus)

Chapter 2 - The Passage of Time - *Far Calls, Coming, Far!*
A Book of Pagan Rituals - Herman Slater (Weiser)
Paganism Today
Graham Harvey & Charlotte Hadrian (Thorsons)
The Witch's Bible - Janet & Stewart Farrar (Phoenix)
Witchcraft - A Tradition Renewed - Evan John Jones (Hale)

Chapter 3 - Earth Mysteries - *I Hear The Water Dreaming*
Dagger & the Plough - Aeron Medbh-Mara (Feasac)
The Old Straight Track - Alfred Watkins (Abacus)
Secret Places of the Goddess - Philip Heselton (Capal Bann)

Chapter 4 - Coven Magic - *A String Around Autumn*
Life-Rites - Aeron Medbh-Mara (Thoth)
Witchcraft for Tomorrow - Doreen Valiente (Hale)
Witchcraft - A Tradition Renewed - Evan John Jones (Hale)

Chapter 5 - The Solitary Path - *A Way A Lone*

Good Magic - Marina Medice (Macmillan)
Hedgewitch - Rae Beth (Hale)
Magic: An Occult Primer - David Conway (Mayflower)
A Witch Alone - Marian Gren (Thorsens)

Chapter 6 - Western Ritual Magic - *To The Edge Of Dream*

The Book of Thoth - Aleister Crowley (Wieser)
The Confessions - Aleister Crowley (Arkana)
The Eye In The Triangle - Israel Regardie (Falcon Press)
Inner Traditions of Magic - W. G. Gray (Weiser)
Magical Revival - Kenneth Grant (Skoob)
Magical Ritual Methods - W. G. Gray (Weiser)
Magick Without Tears - Aleister Crowley (New Falcon)
The Mystical Qabalah - Dion Fortune (Aquarian)
Western Inner Workings - W. G. Gray (Weiser)

Chapter 7 - The Beast & the Scarlet Woman - *Marginalia*

The Art of Sexual Magic - Margo Anand (Piatkus)
Cults of the Shadows - Kenneth Grant (Skoob)
Fragrant Sensuality - Valerie Ann Worwood (Bantam)
Secrets of the German Sex Magicians - Frater U.D (Llewellyn)
Sexuality & Spirituality - John Moore (Element)

Fiction:

The following are novels written in the true occult tradition and provide valuable insights into the magical world. Most can be obtained from reputable booksellers.

The Goat-Foot God - Dion Fortune
Julian - Gore Vidal
Moon Child - Aleister Crowley
Moon Magic - Dion Fortune
The Sea Priestess - Dion Fortune
Whittlewood - Suzanne Ruthven

Appendix III

Planetary Correspondences

This listing is for guidance only. For a full listing of cross-cultural correspondences refer to Crowley's *Liber 777*.

SUN: For magic relating to health, confidence, prosperity the ritual should be worked on a Sunday, ideally three hours after sunset or during the hour of sunrise. The deities invoked are Apollo, Ra, Lugh or Mithras by using corresponding colours (gold, orange or yellow), gemstones (amber, diamonds or citrine), metal (gold) and herbs (ash, broom, frankincense, ginger). This planetary sign also corresponds to Tiphareth (sephiroth), Leo (zodiac) and The Sun (tarot).

MOON: For magic relating to psychic powers, divination and astral travel the ritual should be worked on a Monday, ideally three hours after sunset or during the hour of sunrise. The deities invoked are Isis, Cerridwen and Artemis by using corresponding colours (silver, white or midnight blue), gemstones (crystal, pearl or moonstone), metal (silver) and herbs (eucalyptus, gardenia, jasmine or vanilla). This planetary sign also corresponds to Yesod (sephiroth), Cancer (Zodiac) and The Moon, the Empress or the High Priestess (tarot).

MARS: For magic relating to courage, physical strength, passion and conflict the ritual should be worked on a Tuesday, ideally three hours after sunrise or during the first hour of sunrise. The deities invoked are Mars or Odin by using corresponding colours (strong, deep reds), gemstones (ruby, garnet or fire opal), metal (iron or steel) and herbs (musk, myrrh and wormwood). This planetary sign also corresponds to Geburah (sephiroth), Scorpio and Aries (zodiac) and The Chariot (tarot).

MERCURY: For magic relating to prediction, knowledge, writing or inspiration the ritual should be worked on a Wednesday, ideally three hours after sunset or during the first hour of sunrise. The deities invoked are Mercury, Thoth or Athene by using corresponding colours (yellow and heather mixtures), gemstones (pale yellow or cream coloured stones, or those with bandings), metal (quicksilver) and herbs (cinnamon, mint or violet). This planetary sign also corresponds to Hod (sephiroth), Gemini and Virgo (zodiac) and The Magician and The Fool (tarot).

JUPITER: For magic relating to trade, business, material growth or legal matters, the ritual should be worked on a Thursday, ideally three hours after sunset or during the first hour on sun rise. The deities invoked are Zeus, Thor, Hera or Demeter by using corresponding colours (purple or lilac), gemstones (amethyst or sapphire), metal (silver-gilt or tin) and herbs (lilac, clove or thistle). This planetary sign also corresponds to Chesed (sephiroth), Sagittarius and Pisces (zodiac) and The Tower, The Empress, The Emperor (tarot).

VENUS: For magic relating to love, partnerships, sexual matters and compassion, the ritual should be worked on a Friday, ideally three hours after sunset, or during the first hour of sunrise. The deities invoked are Aphrodite, Ishtar, Lilith or Eros by using corresponding colours (pink, light blues and greens), gemstones (rose quartz, jade or lapis lazuli), metal (copper) and herbs (foxglove, peach, sandalwood or rosemary). This planetary sign also corresponds to Netzach (sephiroth), Libra and Taurus (zodiac) and The Lovers (tarot).

SATURN: For magic relating to duty, responsibility, building, death and time, the ritual should be worked on a Saturday, ideally three hours after sunset, or during the first hour of sunrise. The deities invoked are Saturn, Sutekh, Persephone or Arianrhod by using corresponding colours (black, brown, dark grey or indigo), gemstones (jet, obsidian or smoky quartz), metal (lead or pewter) and herbs (belladonna, blackthorn, camphor or cypress). This planetary sign also corresponds to Binah (sephiroth), Capricorn and Aquarius (zodiac) and Death and The Hanged Man (tarot).

Appendix IV

The Mercian Tree and Lunar Calendar

This calendar should only be used as a general guide; there are dozens of similar ones available and each can differ quite considerably from another as both calendars and traditions can vary from county to county.

January is the Snow Moon because this is the time of the year when snow usually makes its appearance - represented by the Rowan.

February is the Death Moon. The long, cold days of winter would take their toll in times past and would also be when food-stocks were beginning to run low - represented by the Ash.

Imbolc (2nd February) is one of the major festivals of the Craft and represents the quickening of new life in the womb of the Earth Goddess and traditionally the start of the Celtic lambing season. This is the time of year when the first green buds, and the first spring plants are beginning to show. It is the feast day of the versatile Celtic goddess Bride who was seen as the triple moon and patron of the martial arts and warfare, as well as her more homely pursuits. This is also the time of the year for the lesser Eleusinian Mysteries and the Roman Lupercalia when Demeter/Ceres went searching the Underworld for Persephone. It would be a time for directing energies to new ideas or ventures which have only just been 'conceived' - i.e. in the planning stages.

March is the time for the Awakening Moon when spring sunshine and plants are beginning to appear - represented by the Alder.

Spring Equinox (21st March) is a minor festival which marks the move into summer as the nights begin to get shorter. The spring equinox does not appear to be a Celtic festival although pre-Celtic megalith builders, including those who constructed Stonehenge, certainly knew about the equinoxes as various stones and other features around the monument can be used to predict sunrise on those days. Also known as Eostra, after the Norse goddess of spring, which later gave name to the Christian festival of Easter - the only moveable feast in the Christian calendar which is sited according to the pagan Lunar cycle. The spring equinox is one of the festivals of Isis which celebrates the Egyptian harvest and included a vital magical ceremony which ensures the inundation of the Nile to secure the following year's harvest.

April is referred to as the Grass Moon when pasture lands are glowing green with fresh grazing - represented by the Willow.

Beltane (30th April) is one of the major festivals of the years, second only to Samhain in importance. It is held on May Eve or the 1st May - May Day and is the feast day of the fire god Bel and also associated with the Horned God, Herne/Cernunnos and the Greek/Roman deities Maia, Flora, Fauna and Kybele. Beltane was the start of the Celtic summer and the time of year when the fertility of the flocks, crops and humans had to be ensured. Time for celebrating as those new plans or ideas come to 'fruition' - i.e. ideas put into practice.

May is the time of the Planting Moon when seeds were scattered on the earth for harvesting in the autumn - represented by the White-thorn or Hawthorn.

June can be called the Rose, Flower or Honeymoon as a time for celebration - represented by the Oak symbol of the God in his guise as Oak King or the Green Man.

Summer Solstice (21st June) also referred to as Litha, which appears to be a Saxon name for the longest day of the Solar year. The name may well also mean 'the Festival of the Stones' because many ancient stone circles, or single standing stones were used as places of worship, particularly on the day of the summer solstice - hence the continued insistence that Druids be allowed to pay homage at Stonehenge. Around this time the festivals of many of the Great Mother/ Love Goddesses - Ishtar, Astarte, Aphrodite, Venus, Aine, Cerridwen - are celebrated. It was an almost universal practice for bonfires to be lit on the summits of special Beacon Hills, which can still be located on large scale Ordinance Survey maps. The earlier Egyptian New Year co-incided with the summer solstice, the inundation of the Nile and the rising of the Dog Star, Sirius.

July is known as the Lightning Moon because of the particular violence of summer storms - represented by the Birch.

Lughnasad (1st August) is literally the festival of the god Lugh and the fourth great Celtic Sabbat. The celebration is linked to the harvest - especially in former times when the festival dated by the Julian calendar was approximately a fortnight later in the year. This is a time for giving thanks and associated with the ancient god Crom Cruach; Demeter/Ceres was also worshipped along with Dionysus who presided over the harvesting of grapes for the wine. Offerings at this time give thanks for the 'rewards' from previous months and requests for the bounty to tide over during any lean times to come.

Following Lughnasad is the **August** Harvest Moon - although some Traditions use this name for the full moon following the Autumn Equinox - represented by the Hazel.

September brings the Hunter's Moon when meat stocks were set aside for the winter and cattle culled to conserve food and fodder - represented by the Apple.

Autumn Equinox (23rd September) known in Celtic as Modron which marks the start of the Dark Half of the year. This festival represents the closing down of the Earth's fertility, growth is slowing and the leaves are beginning to change. As the nights grow longer, so the powers of the Solar (male) deities lose their dominion and the emphasis turns to the Lunar (female). As the Sun is linked to the conscious mind, so the Moon is associated with the subconscious and with magic, often it is in the Dark Half of the year that much magical work in undertaken. In ancient Greece the autumn equinox was the time of the greater Eleusian Mysteries.

October is the Falling Leaf Moon which heralds the dying year of Samhain - represented by the Blackthorn.

Samhain (31st October) is for many, the most important festival of the year. It is a time when spirits of the living and the dead can mingle freely as the veil between the worlds is at its thinnest. Samhain or to give it its more popular name, Hallowe'en is still celebrated all over the world, especially in Latin American countries with their combination of strong Roman Catholic and African beliefs. A good time to work on the spiritual aspects of the chosen Tradition.

November is the Tree Moon when wood felled for winter is replaced by new saplings - represented by the Elder.

December - Yule time and the Long Night Moon represented by the Holly, symbol of the winter aspect of the God as the Holly King.

Winter Solstice/Yule (21st December) represented the 'wheel' or the turning of the year and the shortest day of the Solar year, i.e. the re-birth of the Sun. This symbolic rebirth explains why so many Sun gods have their natal festival at this time. In Egypt this was the festival of Isis and Horus, in Persia of Mithra, the Norse gods Balder and Frey, and the Greek/Roman Dionysus. The modern feast of Christmas is a mixture of relics from various Pagan traditions, including Norse, Saxon, Celtic and Roman - and not incorporated into the Christian calendar until the former pagan, the Roman Emperor Constantine changed the celebration of the unconquered sun (Mithra) into a birthday of the 'son of righteousness' (Jesus).

December-January - the time of the Ice Moon which only occurs every three years as the moon's progression changes - represented by the Yew as a symbol of mystical journeying between the worlds.

Bibliography & Sources:

Aleister Crowley & The Hidden God - Kenneth Grant (Skoob)
The Art of Sexual Magic - Margo Anand (Piatkus)
The Black Art - Rollo Ahmed (Senate)
Book of Diving the Future - Eva Shaw (Wordsworth)
The Book of Thoth - Aleister Crowley (Weiser)
The Confessions - Aleister Crowley (Arkana)
Cults of the Shadows - Kenneth Grant (Skoob)
Dagger & the Plough - Aeron Medbh-Mara (Feasac)
Encyclopedia Britannica
The Eye In The Triangle - Israel Regardie (Falcon Press)
Fingerprints Of The Gods - Graham Hancock (BCA)
The Goddess of the Stones - George Terence Meaden (Souvenir)
Hitler - Black Magician - Gerald Suster (Skoob)
Lamp of Thoth (Sorcerer's Apprentice Books)
Life Rites - Aeron Medbh-Mara (Thoth Publications)
Magic: An Occult Primer - David Conway (Mayflower)
Magick Without Tears (New Falcon) Aleister Crowley
Malleus Satani - Hammer of Satan - Suzanne Ruthven (ignotus)
Man, Myth & Magic - Marshall Cavendish
The Mystical Qabalah - Dion Fortune
The Necromancers - Peter Haining (Coronet)
Nightside of Eden - Kenneth Grant (Skoob)
The Old Straight Track - Alfred Watkins (Abacus)
*Phoenix Magazine (*House of Phoenix)
Priestess (Aquarian) Alan Richardson
Secret Places of the Goddess - Philip Heselton (Capall Bann)
Secrets of the German Sex Magicians - Frater U. D. (Llewellyn)
Sex & The Occult - Gordon Wellesley (Corgi)
Tantrism - Benjamin Walker (Aquarian)
Typhonian Teratomas: The Shadows of the Abyss (Black Moon) Mishlen Linden
Witchcraft for the Non-Witch - Brighdhe (Feasac)

Index

Malleus Satani - The Hammer of Satan

Suzanne Ruthven

This book destroys the myths the media has built up about two unrelated magico-religious systems, Witchcraft and Satanism. A frank and well-researched document, revealing the true practise, and genuine practitioners of Magic today, it is the real story behind the anti-occult campaign which many Pagans still believe to not have existed. ***Malleus Satani*** reveals the behind the scenes story which led to much of the current political in-fighting that has done untold damage to the Pagan community. It offers a startling insight which often surprises Pagan readers; an education for anyone who has shuddered at the words 'witch' or 'satanist'.

"It was very refreshing to read - for once! - a sympathetic study of the subject, and one which was, not only very well researched but also managed to avoid ever being dull or academic." ***Dr Terry Hale***
University of East Anglia

"I found this a thought provoking account which well illustrates the dangers inherent in any religion or social institution which maintains that its way is the only true one and all others are therefore to be condemned."
Bulletin of The Welsh Academy

ISBN: 0-9522689-0-6 : 194pp : paperback : £9.95

ISBN: 0-9522689-4-9 : 230pp : paperback : £9.95